Linkage and Retrieval
of Microeconomic
Data

A Strategy for Data Development and Use

Linkage and Retrieval of Microeconomic Data

A Strategy for Data Development and Use

A Report on the Wisconsin Assets and Incomes Archives

Martin H. David

William A. Gates

Roger F. Miller

University of Wisconsin–Madison

Lexington Books
D.C. Heath and Company
Lexington, Massachusetts
Toronto   London

Library of Congress Cataloging in Publication Data

David, Martin Heidenhain.
   Linkage and retrieval of micro-economic data.

   Bibliography: p.
   1. Information storage and retrieval systems—Social sciences—Case
studies. 2. Information storage and retrieval systems—Economics—Case
studies. I. Gates, William A., joint author. II. Miller, Roger F., joint
author. III. Title.
Z699.5.S65D36   029'.9'3   73–1003
ISBN 0–669–86850–7

Published simultaneously in Canada.

Printed in the United States of America.

International Standard Book Number: 0–669–86850–7

Library of Congress Catalog Card Number: 73–1003

To: Guy Orcutt whose vision made this work
a reality.

Table of Contents

List of Tables

List of Figures

Acknowledgments

Two of the authors are professors of economics who supervised the development of the data archive described in this monograph at the Social Systems Research Institute of the University of Wisconsin. William Gates became our indispensable teammate for matching the substantive interests in the project to the logical capabilities of the computer. Substantial financial support for this data development has come from the Brookings Institution, the National Bureau of Economic Research, the Social Security Administration, the National Science Foundation, the University of Wisconsin Graduate School Research Committee, the State of Wisconsin, and the Wisconsin Alumni Research Foundation.

We could hardly begin to list (much less fully acknowledge) the many other individuals who made personal contributions of time and effort to development of these data. On an organizational level, however, we wish to recognize the invaluable cooperation of the personnel of the Wisconsin Department of Taxation, the Social Systems Research Institute, and the Wisconsin Survey Research Laboratory.

We have a special debt of gratitude to the Survey Research Center of the University of Michigan and Carolynn Crandall for their efforts toward preparing this monograph for publication, to Julie Wosk for her excellent editorial help, and to Barbara Aldrich for her continuing assistance in retrieving important details of processing on the archive from our files.

1

Introduction*

1.1 The Nature of Economic Data

Insight into the economic behavior of individuals and households can be obtained from a wide variety of information. Much of what we know is gleaned from study of markets—sales information, prices, and inventories. A major task of economics has been to find conceptual frameworks within which that information can be organized to yield both estimates of the forces that impinge on economic decisions and models of the interaction among those forces.

One of the principal frameworks used to organize economic information has been based on the notion that the aggregate of inputs to the economy must equal the aggregate of outputs. From this schema economists have derived a complex system of accounting for the national product and predicated an associated effort aimed at creating models for the changes in components of the national product.

Another framework has been the concept of a labor force whose effort can be deployed, or wasted, depending upon the degree of unemployment. And large amounts of energy have been devoted to building models of worker behavior on the basis of aggregate statistics on manpower and the labor force.

What is lacking in these approaches is an ability to link specific kinds of behavior to the characteristics of particular individuals or families. To understand the impact of taxation on individuals, the relationship of economic to ethnic characteristics or age, or the relationship between economic well-being and family characteristics requires data of a different kind than can be assembled from aggregate indicators of activity in the marketplace. What is needed are accurate descriptions of family or individual characteristics in conjunction with data on economic activities of these persons. Detailed information on individual units is necessary to provide distributions and in order to study the joint distributions of demographic and economic characteristics and events.

1.2 Tools for Microeconomic Data Collection

In the past a variety of special-purpose tools have been developed to provide this kind of distributive information on families and individuals. Administrative records, censuses, and personal interview surveys have all been employed to

---

*Notes, indicated by numbers in [ ], begin on p. 281.

1

gain insight into the behavior of individuals (and in some cases business or corporate organizations). With a few notable exceptions, innovation and development of new measurement techniques have not figured prominently in continuing data collections, and innovative technique has been limited to special-purpose samples or data collected on a one-time basis (e.g., Ferber and Maynes, 1969; Lansing, et al., 1961).

The obvious shortcomings of this situation appear to call for the development of a set of research strategies that make it possible to link continuing data collections to a larger matrix that can be used for a wide variety of analytical purposes. Such strategy can produce time series of data on critical variables for individual decision units. At the same time, a richer collection of complementary data on those individuals can be obtained at particular times for particular analytic purposes.

Against this background it is not surprising that extensive discussion of data banks and data libraries has excited social scientists for a number of years (Rosander, 1970). Early discussions and grand schemes for instantaneous answers to difficult social problems have been disappointing (Dunn, 1967; Hoffman, 1969). Understandable caution over the problems of confidentiality and data security has been a barrier to the development of useful data banks. An even greater barrier has been the technical problem of amassing the resources to provide continuing data collection and adequate documentation of the data archive. Perhaps the most serious obstacle blocking the development of large integrated bodies of data, however, has been the lack of research-oriented data-processing techniques that are inexpensive, reliable, and operate efficiently within the computer environment of a large, scientific, computing establishment (Aron, 1969; Dodd, 1969).

Work that has been done on management information systems has been geared to routine and predictable reports. The management information system is economic only when applied to high-volume, standard throughputs. The means for dealing with unusual data inputs or complex data reduction for reports have not been generally achieved. Similarly, work that has been done on scientific statistical data processing has been oriented toward relatively small volumes of data for which efficient handling of information in the computer is not a high priority. The data archive requires systems analysis and special-purpose computing precisely because of these limitations. The systems design must be sufficiently flexible to accept new types of information; at the same time, powerful techniques must be available to extract information from the archive and subject it to standard statistical analysis. Coincidentally, solutions to the design of data archives and associated software will be enormously useful for management information systems that will truly provide sophisticated information for top-level management.

1.3 Purpose and Design of the Monograph

In this monograph we report on the history of a large-scale data collection project in sufficiently general terms so that our experiences with data linkage and data manipulation can be of use to others who attempt the assembly of large-scale data archives on limited budgets and without captive computer facilities. The manner in which we have handled the development of the data archive from disparate document systems, the techniques that we evolved for linking items of information collated from several sources, and the strategies that we have followed in extracting substantive findings from the archive will be of interest to others who embark on complex data handling activities.

The Wisconsin Assets and Incomes Studies (WAIS) archive includes data on individuals from a number of administrative sources. In addition, personal interviews were taken with a select group of persons in the sample. The type of data available includes income information and a number of demographic items. This sketch of material in the archive is incomplete. It is intended only to emphasize the availability of information that links economic variables to the personal characteristics of individuals.

The breadth of data related in the archive makes a wide variety of studies possible.

Since information on age, occupation, marital status, county of residence, and number of dependents are all available, it becomes possible to reconstruct the career history, the life cycle of earnings, and even the marital history of individuals. Perhaps the most ambitious and complex use of the data is to reconstruct the value of investment portfolios by combining information in the archive, the survey, and securities microdata (Miller, 1969). The wide variety of uses of such microdata and the techniques for handling them will be spelled out in later chapters.

To introduce ideas that will recur in later chapters, we first outline some basic principles that appear to be critical for the development of data structure. The matching or linking of materials from different data sources and measurement techniques poses special problems when the data are to be used for reliable social research.

A brief history of the data archive is given in Chapter 2 to provide a rough idea of the nature of the archive and the research resources that we have used. In Chapter 3 the principal substantive features of the archive are summarized for those who would like to make use of the data. This statement complements earlier documentation (Moyer, 1966a,b; Bauman, David, and Miller, 1967). Chapter 3 also provides illustrations of alternative analysis techniques. Chapter 4 discusses the process of linking the original tax record sample to records of the Social Security Administration and illustrates the need to conceptualize the data integration process. In Chapters 5 and 6 methodology of data processing used on the project is discussed, and the interdependencies of research technique and computer environment are analyzed. In Chapter 7 the housekeeping and controls that are required to maintain a library of machine-readable data and specialized programs are outlined. In Chapter 8 we discuss some analytical problems and the relationship of those problems to file structure, retrieval of information, and computational technique.

1.4 Archives and Confidentiality

At the outset, we should clarify the functions and limitations of an archive. Our view is that research archives require a data processing and documentation system distinct and separate from the administrative data system that directly enters the lives of individuals whose behavior is recorded in the archive. Secondly, the archive must be established in such a way as to protect the individual from disclosure of information that was not generated by official due process. The archives are intended to provide statistical generalizations about behavior, not reports on the idiosyncracies or malfeasance of individuals.

Because the establishment of a complex data archive such as WAIS requires identifying information to bring about the linkage of information that is so valuable, there is no possibility of accomplishing the desired result without trusting the persons responsible for the archive with identifiable information. (Indeed, one of the authors discovered himself in the WAIS archive.) We feel such trust can be appropriately institutionalized through legal agreements. The social benefits of building the archive far outweigh the risk that identifiable materials are improperly used.

In the WAIS archive we were fortunate enough to obtain the cooperation of the Wisconsin Tax Department who repeatedly asserted that the development of this research tool and subsequent findings warrant release of the basic records to state employees outside the Revenue Department.[1] In agreeing to release identifiable data, the Social Security Administration protected its responsibilities to nondisclosure by a legal contract. WAIS was required to keep records of the passage of data from SSA files into merged tapes and return the data when analytical studies using the data were complete.

At present there is little precedent for how microdata can be released to researchers for data archiving. We feel the trust and agreements secured in our particular case with the Social Security Administration, the Wisconsin Department of Revenue, and the respondents to our interviews represent a well-placed confidence in the importance of building complex data bodies. While the conditions that enabled us to secure the data described here may never be repeated, we feel it is certainly well worthwhile to explore a variety of means for releasing data from diverse sources and to be able to link them into archives in order to study individuals, businesses, and government behavior.

1.5 Some Principles for the Development of Data Archives

The development of data archives capable of producing sustained time series of information on particular individuals or families requires a set of research designs that are open-ended and sufficiently flexible to meet a number of specific research objectives, while at the same time providing continuity and integrating principles that make it possible to pursue a sustained analysis of individuals or groups.

Five dimensions appear to have been particularly important to the development of the data archive associated with the Wisconsin Assets and Income Studies (WAIS), and would appear to be particularly important for the development of archives generally:

Sample. The sample design for a data archive must be sufficiently flexible to remain representative in spite of sustained population growth, migration, and continuing change in the constituent units (i.e., families) that are being sampled. In addition, the sampling technique must be easily adapted to a wide variety of data collection techniques and sources—from the extraction of data from existing files to personal interview sample surveys. In WAIS this was achieved by selecting random clusters of surnames. Once included in the sample, an individual would remain in the sample permanently. Three exceptions should be mentioned: (1) individuals die, and no further records are generated; (2) individuals marry and change their surnames; and (3) individuals migrate out of the state, i.e., out of the jurisdiction in which our records were collected. At the same time, new individuals could enter the sample. The sampling frame could easily be applied to a wide variety of types of data.

Identifiers. A prerequisite to the reliable integration of data from several sources is the existence of a *unique* identifier containing sufficient redundancies to prevent mismatching of data about several units derived from different sources. In practice, this implies that more identifying information is required than an individual's name. The experience of the Social Security Administration has shown that birth data and mother's maiden name can be used together with surname to provide a unique identifier.[2] Given the near universality of Social Security account numbers today, they are the most natural identifiers in studies of individual behavior. It is extremely important to have redundancies in the identifier; that is, there should be at least two ways of identifying the same

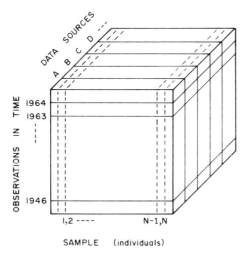

Figure 1-1. Data Linkages

individual. Errors in transcribing information are prevalent, and mismatching of data resulting from such errors greatly reduces the potentiality for discovering relationships involving more than one body of data. The presence of two identifiers, such as name and social security number, assures a ready way of checking for mismatches and correcting the resulting errors.

Data Linkage. A third element necessary in a data archive, which is implied by the foregoing, is that the archive provide a matrix within which information from a wide variety of sources can be integrated. Administrative records are unlikely to provide great breadth of information about the life history of individuals, but may supply important details that can not be obtained from other sources (e.g., medical histories). However, administrative records are likely to provide periodic measures of individual behavior; thus records can be chained together to give time series of information on a particular individual and provide a basis for generalization about behavior. In the case of WAIS, income tax records from 1946–1964 were chained in this fashion. Figure 1–1 illustrates the links that are formed.

Personal interviews, on the other hand, are likely to provide great breadth of information and detailed measurements of individual attitudes, but do not provide reliable histories; interviews are also likely to produce substantial response errors in certain areas of financial reporting.

Given the weaknesses of the various data sources, it is clearly desirable to be able to combine information about a particular individual from several sources into a single observation for research purposes. Redundancies in the information collected then give readings on the biases and reliability of different types of data collection instruments, and the entire data archive can be analyzed to give a far richer matrix of variances and covariances than would be possible on the basis of a single data body alone. Furthermore the data archive can yield panel data far more easily than a one-shot data collection effort, and in some cases at far less expense.

The WAIS archive contains information that is equivalent to a combination of 18 years of *Statistics of Income* samples supplemented by the Social Security Administration's Continuous Work History Sample and Beneficiary Sample and a personal interview survey comparable to the *Survey of Financial Characteristics* conducted by the Federal Reserve Board.

The complexity of the linkage is at least as great as the link established between social security data, the "Current Population Survey," and the U.S. income tax records for a single year (Steinberg, 1969).

Data Recycling. A feature of data archives that closely resembles business accounting applications is the data recycling that occurs when individual records of persons are verified, corrected, and augmented by the addition of new sources of information. To some extent, data recycling occurs in all well-conducted processes of transcribing data from written records into machine-readable form. Consistency checking and editing for illegal characters has long been a vital step in assuring the reliability of survey and census information and its compatibility with the requirements of computer software (Minton, 1969). The editing and consistency checking that is associated with a large data archive differs because the archive files are dynamic and can not be considered fixed relative to the original data collection instruments. For example, in the WAIS files social security numbers may not have been available for taxpayers at the time that income tax records were first collected for some individuals. However, Internal Revenue Service insistence on taxpayer identification numbers makes it highly unlikely that data collected since 1963 do not have some identifier on record with the Social Security Administration. As a consequence, data collected at an early point in time can be brought up to date by assimilating data from later years.

Over the period that WAIS has collected data, a substantial increase in correctly identified social security account numbers has also made it possible to obtain birth data for an increasing number of individuals in the sample. In some cases, however, dynamic changes in the file and differences in the reporting of an item via various techniques may not be so easily resolved. The items of information collected at earlier and later points in time may be inconsistent; for example, income data for a given year collected from both survey and income tax records are likely to disagree (Katona, 1961).

Numerous applications of consistency checking and augmenting data files on the WAIS project have made it clear that the logic of both operations is similar and calls for identical data handling capabilities. Systems analysis of the process has given considerable insight into techniques for making both processes more reliable without increases in costs. At the same time, the concepts embodied in "on-line" correction of data using a teletype installation make it clear that the construction of machine-readable records will proceed most accurately if the conventional technology of keypunching and sequential data processing is discarded altogether.

Unit Flexibility. A fifth important ingredient for a data archive is that it provide aggregation and disaggregation capabilities so that analyses can be conducted on appropriate analytical units while data may be gathered and edited on other kinds of units. For example, tax records in Wisconsin are filed by individuals. In many cases, analysis of economic behavior or welfare calls for study of the family or husband and wife as a decision-making unit. Aggregation of individual records is required (Morgan et al., 1962).

A second example comes from data on the sales of capital assets. Such data are embedded within the tax record. The unit record here is a transaction; however, analytical studies of investment behavior relate that transaction to an entire protfolio; therefore the data archive must provide sufficient data and appropriate linkages to reconstruct transactions in assets and asset-related income (Miller, 1969).

A third example comes from the social security beneficiary information that is part of the archive. The basic record for data collection again consisted of a transaction—in this case, an instruction to the U.S. Treasury to alter the amount of the beneficiary check. Integrating transactions over time produces a history of monthly benefit payments. Adding the monthly payments over the year then provides information comparable to other income data collected for the individual in the tax record.

The five concepts that have been briefly outlined above evolve from two roots. The mechanics of data management impose a discipline on anyone who undertakes to handle tens of thousands of records. Clearly, the other root of these concepts lies in the substantive information that is being assembled in the archive. The substantive information relates to a conceptual structure that dictates the role of the sample, the units of analysis, and the extent of the data being collected. The mechanics of data management dictate the need for identifiers, recycling capabilities, and the ability to manipulate a variety of different unit records. The interrelationships between the data management needs and the substantive information being collected will be illustrated by WAIS experience with Social Security Administration data in Chapter 3.

1.6 Summary

Several general concepts appear to be associated with the development of a large archive of data—on individuals—that can be used flexibly for research purposes:

a.   A universal sampling principle for obtaining data on identical units
b.   Identifiers with built-in redundancies to prevent mismatching of data
c.   Data linkage capabilities to provide more measurements per unit of observation
d.   Data recycling to permit error detection and file expansion
e.   Unit flexibility to permit analysis of several types of data and aggregation of data to the most appropriate unit for analysis

It is equally clear that such an archive will increasingly be required in order to develop quantitative analysis of the behavior of social systems and gain insight into the problems of making policy that affects those systems (Aron, 1969). The principles outlined here apply whether the data collected are for individuals, municipalities, businesses, or voluntary organizations. In this monograph, we attempt to relate experiences of the Wisconsin Assets and Income Studies (WAIS) project that may be useful to other individuals who wish to develop data archives consisting of complex bodies of interrelated information about related units of analysis.

2 A Brief History of the WAIS Data Archive

2.1 Motivation

Early in 1960 a number of interests converged at the University of Wisconsin to provide the impetus to create a major data archive on the incomes of Wisconsin residents. Guy Orcutt, who had just completed his path-breaking book, *Microanalysis of Socioeconomic Systems* (Orcutt et al., 1961), was extremely interested in developing the data base for much more extensive simulation studies of the economy. He also wished to exploit microeconomic data to obtain more reliable information on consumer behavior that would be useful for policy-making purposes.

About the same time, Joseph Pechman began a major set of benchmark studies in public finance, the 33 volumes of *Studies in Government Finance,* published by the Brookings Institution. He was particularly eager to have his former mentor, Harold Groves, continue work on problems related to income averaging for tax purposes—problems that continued to occupy Groves for a long period of his later life. Furthermore, both Groves and Pechman had collaborated in a major analysis of Wisconsin income data from tax records of the 1930s, so that both knew of the potentialities implicit in tax returns as well as the extremely cooperative attitudes of the Wisconsin Department of Revenue toward research on their administrative records (Hanna, Pechman, and Groves, 1949).

Finally, Roger Miller, through his connections with the National Bureau of Economic Research, had encouraged the Bureau to utilize the portfolio information available in tax return data in order to pursue studies of investment behavior, especially behavior motivated by the provisions of the federal capital gains tax. This work was a logical successor to the studies of investment holdings by Wisconsin taxpayers undertaken by Thomas Atkinson (1956), also a student of Groves.

The work of Groves, Miller, and Orcutt, which became the basis for the beginning of tax record collection in 1961, was underwritten by financial resources from the Brookings Institution and the National Bureau of Economic Research. The project would never have been initiated had the enormous cost of the operation, the length of time required for data integration and editing, and the difficulties of handling so large a data body on the available computers been adequately foreseen. Both the National Bureau and the Brookings Institution were frustrated in their desire to see important policy-oriented analyses develop within the time and financing of their initial grants. Support was subsequently requested and received for completion of the original data collection and addition of five more years of income tax record information. The National Science Foundation thus became a major source of funds from July 1965 to June 1970.

In 1962 David and Bridges joined Miller and Groves in working on the original tax record information. David had recently completed a major work on income distribution that excited researchers in the Social Security Administration (Morgan, et al., 1962). Through the cooperation of Mrs. Ida Merriam, and the Division of Research and Statistics of the Social Security Administration, Groves and David were able to establish a cooperative research grant with the Social Security Administration that made it possible to link the wage history (Form 805 earnings record) of individuals in the tax record sample to the data already at hand. In addition, the Social Security Administration encouraged the researchers to link beneficiary data to the tax record file in order to give insights into the extent to which beneficiary payments replace former earnings levels and the impact of social security regulations concerning the retirement test on labor-force participation.

The result of these combined interests was what may be termed a bad case of data indigestion (indeed, Miller did develop an ulcer). By 1970, many of the originally planned studies had been executed only in pilot or preliminary form. Nonetheless, the insight that has come from those limited studies clearly reveals the value of the archive and the validity of the original visions of Orcutt, Groves, and Miller. The publications to date indicate the wealth of material that can be obtained from the file (see Appendix A).

2.2 Concepts Underlying the Tax Record Sample

Three features of Wisconsin tax law and administration strongly influence the character of the sample of tax records that forms the keystone for the WAIS archive:

a. Tax liability is on the individual, so that individuals report income. Husband and wife may not file a joint return.[1] Unlike the federal tax return, the Wisconsin return clearly allocated income between the husband and wife, who are required to file separately. This fortunately yields data that relate to specific individuals, rather than to marital units; marital units may change their composition through marriage, death, divorce, and remarriage.

b. The filing requirement, i.e., the statutory rules determining which individuals must file a tax return, provides that persons with extremely small incomes, or extremely limited gross receipts (from a business), need not file a tax return.[2]

c. The actual measurement of income available from the tax return corresponds to the legal constructs of Wisconsin statutes and omits a variety of sources of income that constitute an important part of personal income. Further-more, the accuracy of the income measurement depends on compliance with and enforcement of the law. Some types of income are more easily concealed and some are more carelessly reported, so that the tax record is not an equally good measuring rod for all types of income.

We shall discuss these points in detail in the remainder of this section.

The Sample

The data collected from the archives of Wisconsin tax records were sampled from the universe by taking all returns filed by individuals whose surnames fell within certain alphabetic segments. Fifty groups of surnames were chosen in such a way that each group contained a minimum of 30 and no more than 100 individuals according to the Tax Department's Madison District tax roll in 1958 (Moyer, 1966a, pp. 57-64). Each group was defined by the names of the first and last persons in the group. Each year's tax returns were then sampled by finding all tax returns of persons whose names fell within the fifty name group clusters. Only taxpayers in the Madison District were studied to establish the sampling criteria, although the sample was actually drawn from all four state tax districts. Subsequent analysis of the sample in relation to state data on the amount of net taxable income reported in each county indicates that income from the Madison tax district is slightly overrepresented in the sample. However, the sample appears to be representative of income from the four major geo-graphic quadrants of the state and from areas of varying population density, so that bias involved in using the Madison District as the basis for sampling does not appear to be serious (Moyer, 1966a, pp. 70-88).[3]

Organization of the tax archives dictates additional sampling rules to apply to wives of males in the chosen name groups. Normally, both the tax return for the husband and for his wife are filed in the same folder (bearing both names) in any year of their marriage. Furthermore, the Tax Department attempts to integrate the folders of two separate persons at the time of the marriage; thus a large number of folders with the returns for single women are filed with the returns of the man whom they subsequently married. To maintain the representa-tiveness of the sample, such returns are included in the sample, although the maiden name of the single woman was not in the fifty name groups. By this procedure, women in years prior to their first marriage enter the sample either (1) from folders bearing their maiden name when their records prior to marriage were not integrated with those of their future husband or (2) from folders bearing their future husband's surname.

The success with which the Tax Department integrated folders of persons who marry does not affect the representativeness of the single women. However, the time series of data resulting from (2) is longer and gives insight into the

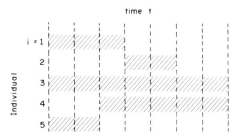

Figure 2-1. The Time Series of Tax Records Available for Analysis

impact of marriage on the earnings of husband and wife. The time series from
(1) terminates at marriage. Unfortunately, data of type (2) will be less representative than data for all single women since the Tax Department successfully
integrates folders only in some instances of marriage. Failure to report maiden
name at the time of marriage, marriage to a woman who previously lived in
another state, and defects in the state's filing system all limit the extent to which
the data linkage in (2) can be obtained.

The sample that results from these procedures contains a changing panel of
individuals. Persons enter the sample when they move into the state, when they
marry, or when they begin to earn income in excess of the filing requirement.
Persons leave the sample when they emigrate from the state, when they marry, or
when their incomes fall below the legal filing requirements. The resulting
collection of data includes information for various periods of time for different
individuals. Gaps appear during periods for which a person did not file a tax
return for any of the above reasons (see Figure 2-1).

The sample is representative as a cross-section of taxpayers for any one year.
However, the further selection of persons who file for a period of time clearly
subsamples those persons whose lack of mobility and income level require
them to report income in Wisconsin more frequently than average. Wives with
intermittent labor-force experience, persons who retire, and low-income families
will be represented in a panel of data for a given number of years by fewer
returns than males of working age whose income requires an annual report to
the Tax Department.

One of the chief limitations of the tax record information that was foreseen
at an early date was the lack of any information on the age or birth date of the
taxpayer. Since so many economic processes affecting the taxpayer are related to
his stage in the life cycle, his accumulation of assets, and other processes that
are related to age, it seemed extremely desirable to obtain data on age for the
sample of income tax records, if that were possible. Data on birth date were
obtained in several ways over an extended period. The primary source of birth
data was the Form 805 wage earnings record loaned to WAIS by the Social
Security Administration. In other cases birth data was supplied from motor

Table 2-1
Reconciliation of Wisconsin Income Reported for Tax Purposes and State Personal Income, 1963 (amounts in millions of dollars)

Source of Income	Number of Receivers (×1000)	Reported on Tax Returns		Personal Income[a]	(2) − (3)	Discrepancy	
		Wisconsin	Federal[a]			Amount (2)−(4)	(6) ÷ (4) (× 100)
	(1)	(2)	(3)	(4)	(5)	(6)	(7)
Wages and salaries	1482	$6302	$6309	$6457	$ −7.3	$−155	2%
Dividends	288	230	215	256	+14.0	−26	10
Interest	643	200	216	373	−16.5	−174	46
Rent	184	82	70	133	+12.2	−52	38
Business and professional	b	829	b	1187	b	−358	30
Total	1827	7643	b	8406	b	−763	9

Source: Communication from Billy Dee Cook, formerly at the Wisconsin Department of Revenue.
[a]Reconciled to Wisconsin income tax definitions.
[b]Not available.
[c]Including some items shown under rent, interest, and dividends.

vehicle license or death records. Ultimately age was included on the tax form in 1964. Thereafter age information is an integral part of the tax file.

The need for age data explains the need to sample other records for individuals located in the tax record sample. The details will be described in Chapter 4.

Validity and Meaning of Wisconsin Income Reported for Tax Purposes

Since large portions of the data available in the sample were collected from the State of Wisconsin tax returns, the income concepts used are those which can be derived from tax return data. Wisconsin's definition of adjusted gross income, which is the principal measure investigated in this paper, closely resembles the federal definition of adjusted gross income. The Wisconsin definition includes all capital gains, unemployment compensation, and interest on nonfederal government securities. Some income from pensions, real property outside Wisconsin, and federal government securities is excluded. Wisconsin income is generally more inclusive (Wisconsin Taxpayer's Alliance, 1964; Moyer, 1966) and state Tax Department tabulations hint that a number of income items are more faithfully reported on Wisconsin tax returns than on federal returns (Table 2-1).

Since our income data are collected from tax returns, they are subject to the same under-reporting and distortion that has already been observed in a variety of studies (Lansing et el., 1961; United States Senate, Committee on Finance, 1962). The discrepancies are substantial, as indicated by column 5 of Table 2-2. However, Murray (1964) indicates that Wisconsin has monitored its tax collections with exceptional care. The adoption of withholding in this state produced far less added revenue in relation to previous collections than the adoption of withholding elsewhere. Tax collection was enforced through extensive information returns and "doomage" assessments on persons who failed to file returns in successive years (Penniman and Heller, 1959).

Table 2-3 indicates that the Wisconsin population has less income than the national average when compared to federal tax data. The difference is largely due to the smaller number of tax units with extremely high incomes. In 1959, 2.4 percent of Wisconsin incomes reported on federal returns exceeded $50,000, while 4.2 percent of federal returns as a whole reported incomes in excess of $50,000.

2.3 The Basic Data Files

The machine-readable records resulting from the data collection activities of WAIS are organized into eight basic files. In addition, several general-purpose

Table 2-2

The Sources of Adjusted Gross Income: WAIS Sample Totals and Federal
Statistics of Income Totals for Wisconsin Adjusted to the State Definition, 1959

Source	WAIS Sample Aggregates		Ratio estimates of Wisconsin Aggre- gates, adjusted for Federal Definitions		Ratio of Sample to Adjusted Aggregates (X 100)
	Amount (X 1000)	Percent	Amount (X 10^6)	Percent	
	(1)	(2)	(3)	(4)	(5)
Wages and salaries	38,400	81.1	5,388	78.9	.71
Dividends received	1,040	2.2	197	2.9	.53
Interest received	740	1.6	92	1.3	.79
Rent income	430	0.9	76	1.1	.56
Self-employment income	5,140	10.9	736	10.8	.70
Capital gains net of losses	1,080	2.3	213	3.1	.51
Other sources	480	1.0	132	1.9	.36
Total state adjusted gross income	47,310	100.0	5,834	100.0	.69

Source: Moyer, 1966a, Table 28.

Note: Adjustments were made whenever possible to reconcile the amount of income taxable
under federal law to that taxable under state law. The low ratio of capital gains may reflect
an inadequate adjustment, as well as under-reporting.

Table 2-3

The Mean Adjusted Gross Income Per Federal Return: Wisconsin and the
United States, 1947-1959

Year	Wisconsin	United States	Ratio of Means*
1947	$2547.77	$2727.73	.933
1948	2958.73	3152.82	.938
1949	2811.97	3114.46	.902
1950	3201.25	3419.09	.936
1951	3566.33	3694.27	.965
1952	3732.34	3852.13	.968
1953	3815.65	4004.55	.952
1954	3780.83	4091.96	.953
1955	4041.96	4270.74	.957
1956	4332.17	4522.66	.956
1957	4479.23	4684.26	.950
1958	4522.72	4750.55	.960
1959	4863.44	5064.76	.952

Source: U.S. Government, Internal Revenue Service, *Statistics of Income*, 1959; pp. 109–
110; *Statistics of Income*, 1956 pp. 65–70.

*The mean is .955 with a standard error of .019.

files were generated for analysis purposes. The strategy and usefulness of those files will be discussed in Chapter 8.

The eight basic WAIS data files are: Master Tax Record File (MF); Property Income File (PF); Social Security Benefit File (B); Social Security Earnings Records File (ER); Personal Interview Survey File (IN); Household Assets Diary File (AD); Identification File (ID); and two extracts from the state's billing and refund files, referred to as the State Tax Roll (STR).[4] Descriptions of the contents of each basic file follow.

The Master Tax Record File (MF)

The Master Tax Record File contains summary data from tax records that were available in archives of the State of Wisconsin for a period from 1946 to 1964. The basic tax-year records were collected by taking a random alphabetic sample of names in fifty clusters as described in the preceding section. Clustering maximized the possibility that the name of a particular individual could be identified with a series of records supplied to the Tax Department over this period, so that we could collect the time series of data for each individual in the sample. (Misfiled returns were included automatically in the sample unless the misfiling resulted in a record being placed physically outside of the name clusters.) Also, the files were in twelve separate locations around the state (by person in each of three subsets of years, for four geographic subdivisions or "tax districts") and an individual could have had one return in each location. Cluster sampling made it possible to find them all.

The summary data included in the MF for every individual in the sample are of four types:

Coded demographic data, e.g., place of residence, occupation, marital status.

Summary income data, e.g., income by major source categories (wages interest, etc.), total income from all sources, adjusted gross income, net taxable income.

Summary deduction, tax computation, and tax data, e.g., standard deduction, deductible interest paid, personal exemption allowance, net normal tax.

Computed data, e.g., standard deduction (this had to be computed to find net taxable income for taxpayers who could use a tax table to calculate their tax), and discrepancy indicators (see Chapter 5 below).

For many individuals, then, the MF contains essentially a computerized image of their tax records. Detailed data covering certain sources of income that are not reported by all taxpayers is contained in the Property Income File which is described below.

The basic unit for the MF is a tax return for an individual for one year. Approximately 205,000 taxpayer-year records are included in the file. Of these, approximately 135,000 were collected in the first collection covering 1946–1960 and the remainder in a second collection covering the years 1959–1964. Only a partial sample for the years 1946 and 1960 was available in the first collection. The overlap between the two batches was intentional, and provides a virtually foolproof technique for identifying mismatches. It also provides a validity check on the change in coding demographic information between the first and second collections.

The Property Income File (PF)

The Property Income File, also containing tax return data for sample individuals, is composed of detailed flows of property or business income for a taxpayer. The file includes approximately 85,000 such records, for which the basic unit is an asset-taxpayer-year. Included in the file are separate entries for dividends on different stocks, for capital gains received from the sale of stocks or other properties, and for different items of rent, interest, or business income. The identity of the asset source of the property income (e.g., the name of the corporation paying dividends) was coded into the data for each source that could be identified. An ancillary file of firm identification codes to supplement existing firm identification systems in sources such as Compustat was developed to facilitate portfolio estimation at a later date. This file was also used to identify assets found in the Household Assets Diary.

The Social Security Benefit File (B)

The Social Security Benefit File was collected from benefit payment records at each of the Social Security Administration's benefit payment processing centers throughout the United States.[5] As noted earlier, this file and the Earnings Record File (ER) were loaned to specific senior WAIS analysts by the Social Security Administration under restrictions safeguarding confidentiality. Uses of these data were restricted to specific studies. The Benefit File contains data on the benefit status and monthly benefit payments to beneficiaries of the Social Security Accounts of taxpayers in the Master File sample. Some beneficiaries of these accounts (primarily wives and dependent children of taxpayers) do not appear in the MF because they did not file tax returns during the period 1946–1960. The monthly payment data has been aggregated for beneficiaries so we have beneficiary-year records as basic units which are comparable to units in the

MF. (The original data received from SSA only reports all *changes* in monthly payment amounts; in this form the data could not easily be integrated with annual tax record data.)

The Social Security Earnings Records File (ER)

Earnings Records, the second file obtained from the Social Security Administration (Farber, 1963), contain annual information on the amount of all earnings on which social security payroll taxes were paid since the year 1951; quarterly indicators of covered earnings in excess of $50; and age, race, and administrative data such as the number of quarters of covered earnings. The Earnings Records file contains data for every individual who correctly reported a social security account number on any of his tax records.

An ancillary file, the Supplementary Age and Death File (SAD), was created when we discovered that approximately 25 percent of the individuals in our MF did not provide valid social security account numbers. By cooperation with the Wisconsin Motor Vehicle Department (driver's license records) and the Wisconsin Board of Health (death records), we were able to supplement our data on ages and deaths for this group. More than half of the individuals without earnings records are included in the Supplementary Age and Death File.

Personal Interview Survey (IN) and Household Assets Diary (AD) Files

The Interview File contains coded data obtained from approximately 1300 personal interviews taken in 1964. Prior to the interviews a stratified subsample of the taxpayers in the MF was obtained. The subsample permitted more than a proportional number of interviews with high-income taxpayers, taxpayers with income from property, and taxpayers with a long filing experience in our sample. Each interview elicited data on occupational history, education, housing, and attitudes toward portfolio management.

At the time of the interview, an Assets Diary was left with certain members of the interview sample in order to obtain reports of their portfolio holdings and recent portfolio changes.[6] These data are recorded separately as the Household Assets Diary File. Attrition in the return of diaries resulted in an asset data file of 1100 diaries, approximately 200 less than the Personal Interview File.

Identification File (ID)

The Identification File is primarily for administrative convenience. It contains identification numbers associated with the tax-record sample and social security account data. It also contains a fixed-format coded version of the taxpayer's most recent address and his birth year. The file is used to merge tax records from different years, and to assure that appropriate social security data are merged with the tax record, even when multiple account numbers occur, etc.

The State Tax Roll (STR)

The WAIS State Tax Roll File is an extract of the WAIS name clusters from the 1962 Wisconsin Administrative Tax Rolls. It contains the name, address, and social security number of the taxpayer in addition to adjusted gross income, net taxable income, and other administrative information. This file provided an identification check with our fixed-format identification file and was also a source of social security numbers. A similar extract was made for the 1965 Administrative Tax Roll. In addition the entire universe of data on adjusted gross income and one or two other variables was obtained for the purpose of checking sample reliability and obtaining ratio estimators from the tax-record sample for counties and other small units.

2.4 Processing the Data

Process Steps

Translating the raw data into machine-readable form involves five easily recognized steps: (1) extraction of information from files or interviews; (2) coding; (3) translation of data into a form consistent with available hardware; (4) edit checks; and (5) error correction involving a return to step (1) for some portion of the data, from some (or all) of the records initially generated.

It is interesting to note that these steps are basic, whether the original data source is a paper document or in machine-readable form.[7] The Social Security earnings records, for example, were transmitted to us in the form of magnetic tapes plus paper records for persons with multiple social security account numbers. In order to generate these tapes, the Social Security Administration (SSA) used data we transmitted to them (steps 1 and 2). WAIS reports of social security account numbers for the individuals in the tax record sample were checked, edited and corrected by SSA. In this case step 3 amounted to extracting data from the SSA national administrative archive. Steps 4 and 5 consisted of integrating multiple account information under one taxpayer identification number in our files.

The order of the five basic steps can be varied. Editing and error correction can occur during the coding phase of the work (Minton, 1969). Card-punch verification is carried out immediately after step 3. The arrows in Figure 2-2

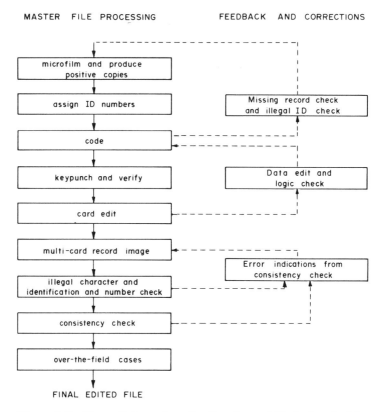

Figure 2-2. Flow of Operations for Creating and Updating the Master File, Years 1946–1960 (First Collection)

indicate that four separate error and correction loops were built into the processing of the first collection of MF data.

The order of the steps could also be varied by adapting the processes to create machine-readable records via direct "on-line" record construction. In the process, the computer can direct the clerk who is coding the data to check the location of entries and provide immediate feedback on inconsistencies or errors present in the data. If this approach is taken, the data processing shifts from a sequence of operations on a batch of records to a batch of operations applied to a sequence of records as they are constructed.[8]

To summarize, all data processing can be outlined as a sequence of the five steps above. The extent to which feedback and error correction occurs early in the processing, and the extent to which all error correction is deferred until a large record is assembled in the core of a computer, depends on the intricacy of the editing required, the elapsed time required for updating the file, and differences in the cost of error correction at various times during the process. It is thus simple to edit coded data so long as the staff originally trained to do the work are still available. If the correction process is deferred, however, those who originally coded the data may no longer be available and additional training costs may be incurred. On the other hand, premature error detection and correction may be of little value. The verification of keypunching on peripheral equipment, for example, appears to have little value when the archive is subjected to the exhaustive editing and consistency checking that we have been able to follow.

Job Lots

In addition to the phasing of the data processing entailed in the series of steps outlined above, the data processing can be characterized by the number of independent job lots that are being processed. In processing the first collection of records, all records were treated as one lot. The second collection of tax records (those covering 1960–1964), however, was processed in 51 lots based on the name-group identification. This division of the work into lots was intended as a device to increase the control over the raw data and permit the experimental development of the flow of operations sequentially, with work on some data preceding the volume processing on the remaining data.

Before the work on the second batch of tax records was completed, how-ever, the concept of a rigid lot based on the name-group identification gave way to a much more flexible division that we can characterize as "test lot-production run." In this latter system, five types of lots characterized the file organization: (1) A basic test lot of simple records was developed to check the most basic programming being developed. (2) A systematic sample of records known to create program complexities—the problem record lot—was developed and used. (3) Errors were introduced into test records—the mutant record lot—to identify program responses to pathological cases. (4) A preliminary sample of data—the sample production lot—was processed in order to provide information on the frequency of errors, contingencies that were to be handled manually, and the operating characteristics of the program in use. (5) The remaining data—the residual production lot—was processed after any necessary adjustments to conserve time and staff effort had been effected. (The relationship of the basic test lot to program development and testing is discussed in Chapters 6 and 7.)

Data Processing Technique

The reasons for development of the more complete data lots discussed in the previous section have a great deal to do with the changing computer environ-ment with which our work was associated during the period 1960–1970. Early work was programmed in machine assembly languages; later work relied on COBOL. For the first collection of tax records nearly all the work indicated in Figure 2-2 was executed in machine assembly language programming. Because it has proved impossible to make such programming independent of the programmer, most of the programs developed for the initial processing of the MF have since been scrapped.

Our experience has made it clear that programming for an archive in which much work is of a special-purpose nature can only be economic if languages more powerful than assembly languages are used in software. Only in this way can programs be generalized for different files by different programmers. In practice, using a higher-level language, such as ALGOL, involved a trade-off between efficiency in coding, documentation, and mobility of program segments and efficiency in the production of output. The higher-level languages permitted exchange of subroutines among programmers, piecewise development of systems of programs, and ready documentation of the underlying procedure. In practice, assembly language programming involved so many idiosyncratic devices by the programmers that the resulting programs were neither legible to anyone other than the author nor readily moved from one computer environment to another. In higher-level languages change in the computer environment is thoroughly specified within the compiler language. Change in the environment requires simple changes in parameters of the program.

Virtually all the data processing associated with the first collection of tax data was conducted on the IBM 1410.

The variable word size of the 1410 was particularly well-adapted for our data processing needs and tape handling was relatively easy. The machine also could deal easily with the alphabetic characters included in our files. These characteristics were in marked contrast to the CDC computers available to us for analysis purposes. The CDC computers had no facility for dealing with alphabetic characters within the framework of standard decoding programs then available. Tape handling proved unreliable; numerous aborted analysis runs due to system failures beyond our immediate control resulted. Given the time required for production of even simple tabulations from the first batch of tax records collected, aborted runs were extremely costly, not only in terms of real computer time wasted (because of the lack of procedures for reinstating jobs in the computer executive system), but also in terms of the tremendous amount of WAIS staff time that had to be spent on distinguishing system errors from our own programming errors.

Initially we resolved these problems by using the 1410 for data processing and changing from assembly languages to COBOL. Extracts were specially prepared for the CDC 1604 or 3600, and standard analysis programs developed by others were then used in conjunction with these extracts. Special-purpose programs to read the extracts were written in FORTRAN in order to interface existing analysis programs.

All procedures on both the IBM or CDC equipment were run in batches. Jobs were required to queue. Those that required long periods of elapsed time, a large number of tape drives, or multiple-reel files were given low priority. WAIS jobs generally combined all these delaying features. These chracteristics of the relationship between the computer, programmers, and the data archive proved to be cumbersome, expensive in both testing and data processing, and limited the control and quality checks that could be made by WAIS staff.

The computer environment changed radically in 1967 when it became possible to access a Burroughs 5500 computer via remote teletype. The advent of the B-5500 also brought a new programming language. FORTRAN was available on the CDC machines, COBOL on the 1410, and ALGOL became available on the B-5500.

Large amounts of permanent random-access disc storage added a third new dimension of computer processing available with the B-5500.

The interactive use of the computer was economical as multiprogramming permitted simultaneous access to the central processing unit by a number of users. Furthermore, the combination of multiprogramming and the size of the B-5500 (and the 1108 Univac that WAIS used beginning in 1971) permitted economical use of a part of the computer. The distinction between economical resources for data processing (IBM 1410) and high-speed large capacity required for data reduction (CDC 3600) was thereby eliminated.

The (a) remote, (b) interactive, (c) disc, and (d) ALGOL features of the B-5500 were to make a radical change in the nature and efficiency of our data processing operation. We learned that the use of interactive programming and data management hinges on the ability to describe interactive files in higher-level programming languages. Without that capability, the level of programmer sophistication required and the problems in using the interactive mechanisms efficiently are such that the archive-oriented programmer is unlikely to be able to secure an advantage from the hardware capabilities. Multiprogramming and the integration of file handling capabilities in a truly general manner into the higher-level languages made effective use of permanent random-access disc capacity.

Interactive use of the computer removed several of the hazards of earlier batch processing. Control over production runs can be maintained by using the teletype as a monitor of activity. Data on the handling of tapes can be double checked; and the intervention of an operator who is not versed in WAIS file handling is totally eliminated from runs involving only the use of disc or drum storage. These features plus interactive debugging of computer setups and programming eliminated many of the false starts and much of the waste of both human and computer resources entailed by the batch processing that character-ized the early days of WAIS.

Interactive processing also enhanced the security of data processing operations. The Burroughs 5500 hardware and operating system contained elaborate protections to assure that no file could be read or manipulated by persons other than the creator. At the same time use of the combination of the B-5500 system with a system of file inventories, programmer passwords, and program acronyms made it possible for the several programmers on WAIS to exchange programs and data files in a foolproof fashion (see Chapter 7). A specific individual was continuously responsible for each file, and transfers of responsibility meshed with the computer's system for recognizing new users. The result was far more reliable than earlier file accounting procedures in which tapes were occasionally mislaid (i.e., relocated from one file vault to another without appropriate updating of inventories), or transferred from one person to the next without double-entry bookkeeping of the transaction.

At present we stand on another divide in computer processing. CDC machines are no longer available and were replaced by a Univac 1108 whose interactive characteristics differ from the B-5500. At the same time, cost of long-distance telephone has dropped to such an extent that we can begin to think of remote access to computers located in other cities, providing that they have file handling facilities that meet our special needs. Our prior experience with alternative machines and operating systems makes us wary of the latter possibilities. "Once bit, twice shy." We have been bit more than once already.

2.5 Summary

This chapter introduces the collection of materials that constitute the WAIS archive. It also describes the archive in terms that can be generalized to other operations involving complex data files and complex analysis objectives. The problems of dealing with a file of information that contains inherent biases and sample limitations are anticipated.

The sampling frame that was used to extract the basic file of tax records clearly constitutes a powerful tool that can be generalized to many types of administrative records. The use of name clusters maximizes the probability of establishing familial relationships and locating records that are not in proper alphabetical sequence. The sampling frame also provides an easy way to maintain representativeness over a succession of years while maximizing the sequence of information on particular individuals. A sampling frame of this type can be used for collections of different types of information at the same time, or repeated observations of the same variables at different points in time, or both.

The data processing that is described is common to all information gathering activities. Discussion of the processes as they apply to the WAIS archive not only provides essential documentation that must be available for persons who wish to use the archive, but also points out how the development of computer technology and sophistication in data processing has increased the efficiency with which we have been able to deal with the file.

The substantive character of the WAIS archive is explored in the following chapter. A concrete explanation of the process by which social security data were linked to the files follows in Chapter 4. Concepts and developments in the strategy by which data were processed are then discussed in Chapters 5 and 6. The reader who is primarily interested in the development of data processing can omit reading Chapters 3 and 4. At the same time, these chapters provide some motivation for changes in data processing techniques and illustrate some of the peculiar difficulties that can arise in a complex archive.

3

The Substantive Character of the WAIS Archive

A glimpse of what can be done with the information in the WAIS archive will serve a double purpose: concrete illustrations will reinforce the general description of the archive given in the last chapter and at the same time will indicate the range of problems that must be solved in analyzing the data. The material in this chapter exposes the numerous populations, definitions of explanatory variables, and statistical models that can be applied to the archive. These illustrations gloss over the mechanical problems of preparing data for analysis and linking information from several sources. The specific problems raised by linking tax record to Social Security Administration data will be dealt with in Chapter 4; Chapter 8 discusses some more-general aspects of analytical work with the archives.

This chapter treats four problems in the analysis of a data archive. Section 3.1 discusses the universe to which the data apply. Section 3.2 indicates ways in which units of analysis and replications of observations can be organized to give statistical results. Section 3.3 discusses the problems of defining explanatory variables that may be considered exogenous or fixed, when the data apply to individual time series for a number of years. The fourth section of the chapter makes some elementary observations on multivariate analyses of longitudinal data on individuals.

3.1 The Universe

The sample of tax records is drawn from the universe of Wisconsin taxpayers. That universe overlaps both the adult population and persons with social security account numbers. Thus the tax-record sample therefore can be construed in relation to several universes. See Figure 3–1.

Taxpayers

The easiest way to regard the sample is as a clustered random sample of tax returns. The sample generalizes to a universe of Wisconsin taxpayers. Appropriate ratio estimators can be used to give information such as: (1) the distribution of legal constructs such as net taxable income under Wisconsin law; (2) the revenue loss associated with particular deductions; and (3) the revenue derived from

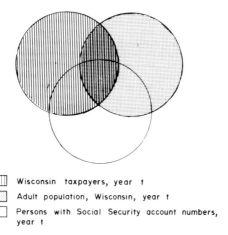

Wisconsin taxpayers, year t

Adult population, Wisconsin, year t

Persons with Social Security account numbers, year t

Figure 3-1. Relationship Between the Universes to Which the Tax Sample Relates

taxpayers with particular characteristics. When data are presented in this manner they appear analogous to information that can be drawn from the Internal Revenue Service *Statistics of Income* or the tax model that has been used by Pechman and others in a variety of simulation studies (Pechman and Okner, 1969, 1972). Table 3-1 presents information yielding the mean of net taxable income observed in the sample from 1947 to 1959; the proportion of taxpayers who report losses (that can be carried forward to other tax years) or file non-taxable returns is also shown.

Because the random sample of all taxpayers is also a random sample of tax-payers with any given specific characteristics, the data are representative of taxpayers with highly specialized financial situations—proprietors, investors with capital gains, or heads of households reporting alimony as income.

The Adult Population

Taxpayers are not a random sample of the population. Only a few minors are taxpayers; many young adults and retired persons have insufficient incomes to require the filing of a tax return. Even so, it is sometimes useful to visualize the tax-record sample as drawn from a larger universe than the population filing tax returns. The adult income-receiving population or the adult population generally are tractable universes to consider. The archive must then be supplemented by estimators for the income and other characteristics of individuals that have not been sampled.

The extent to which nonfiling of tax returns occurs in the adult population

Table 3-1
Mean Net Taxable Income, Mean Loss, Percent with Loss, and Percent with No Net Taxable Income, by Sex (Wisconsin Taxpayer Sample)

| | All Taxpayers | | | | Taxpayers with No Net Taxable Income | | Taxpayers with Negative Taxable Income | | | |
| | Number of Sample Tax Returns | | Mean Net Taxable Income* | | As a Percent of Total | | Mean Amount for Those with Loss | | As a Percent of Total | |
Year	Men	Women	Men	Women	Men	Women	Men	Women	Men	Women
1947	5496	1957	$2906	$1483	2.1%	2.0%	$-2618	$-1107	0.4%	0.2%
1948	5927	2158	3104	1581	2.0	1.6	-1562	-2472	0.4	0.3
1949	5910	2078	2993	1606	2.1	2.0	-2472	-356	0.5	0.5
1950	6264	2278	3143	1642	1.8	1.9	-2594	-859	0.5	0.3
1951	5670	2462	3571	1768	1.5	2.2	-1588	-657	0.5	0.3
1952	6728	2707	3649	1808	2.2	2.0	-1202	-2229	0.4	0.3
1953	7063	2669	3463	1598	7.7	12.2	-1585	-847	0.8	0.4
1954	7019	2677	3420	1604	7.8	11.9	-1378	-810	1.0	0.6
1955	7062	2853	3643	1710	6.3	9.6	-440	-661	0.8	0.5
1956	7357	3014	3823	1705	6.1	9.7	-1198	-1939	0.7	1.0
1957	7435	3420	4072	1916	1.7	2.0	-1536	-1008	0.9	0.6
1958	7469	3454	4117	1987	1.8	1.8	-1351	-897	0.8	0.9
1959	7607	3743	4393	2072	1.3	0.7	-1333	-1360	1.1	0.8

*Definitions relate to Wisconsin income tax law.

Table 3-2
Estimated Proportion of Males Filing Tax Returns by Year and Birth Cohort

Year	Retired 1875-1884	Retiring 1885-1894	Mid-Career 1905-1914	Entering Labor Force 1924-1929	1930-1934
1947	.44	.63	.77	.39	.02
1948	.44	.66	.83	.46	.08
1949	.39	.64	.81	.60	.15
1950	.36	.65	.85	.66	.25
1951	.36	.68	.88	.67	.34
1952	.36	.71	.91	.71	.40
1953	.37	.71	.92	.81	.47
1954	.36	.69	.93	.86	.50
1955	.35	.66	.93	.85	.61
1956	.35	.66	.94	.86	.61
1957	.34	.64	.94	.88	.75
1958	.34	.62	.94	.88	.76
1959	.34	.59	.94	.88	.78

varies by age, sex, and marital status. (David, 1971a) Changes in the real significance of filing requirements expressed in fixed dollars also affects filing.

Table 3-2 illustrates variation in filing rates for several male birth cohorts from 1947 to 1959. The impact of changes in real filing limits can be seen clearly for men in their prime working years, born 1905-1914. The impact of retirement can be seen in the oldest cohort, and the process of entering the labor force can be seen in the youngest cohort.[1] Comparable estimates of the rate of filing could be developed for married and single women.

Estimates of Adjusted Gross Income for the adult male *population* based on the tax sample and filing rates are shown in Figure 3-2 and will be discussed in detail in Section 3.2

Validating Source Material

The sample data in the archive serve as a basis for studying the quality and validity of information according to source and measuring technique. Age reported on tax returns can be compared with age according to Social Security records; income on personal interviews can be compared to that reported on tax forms; and security holdings reported in interviews can be studied in relation to dividends reported on tax returns. This mine of validating data has not yet been used for studies of response error and tax evasion, despite the conceptual value of such studies.

The only validating work on the archive has proceeded at a macro level. Estimates derived from the tax archive have been compared to statistics derived from other sources—the U.S. Census, Federal *Statistics of Income* for Wisconsin,

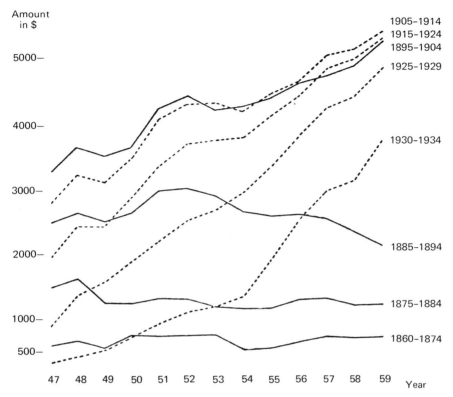

Figure 3-2. Mean Adjusted Gross Income (adjusted for nonfiling) within Birth-Year Group by Year (Wisconsin Males) *Source:* David and Miller (1970).

and records kept by the Wisconsin Department of Revenue. Moyer (1966) validates income estimates from the sample; and Bauman (pending) discusses biases in the reporting of occupation relative to Census data. Table 3-3 illustrates the comparison.

3.2 Alternative Structures for Information in the Archive

The WAIS archive contains a complex of repeated observations and some one-of-a-kind benchmark measurements. The data can be assembled in a wide variety of ways, depending on the analytical question to be answered. The very richness of the data is also the source of complexities in developing an optimal plan for statistical analysis.

The discussion in this section begins with the simplest types of presentations

Table 3-3
Comparisons of Occupation Reported in Census and WAIS (Wisconsin Males Only)

| Occupation | 1950 Employed | | 1959 Employed WAIS | 1960 | |
	WAIS	Census		Employed Census	Extended* Census
Professional	4.8%	4.1%	6.4%	5.8%	5.4%
Semiprofessional	2.0	2.3	2.3	3.5	3.4
Managerial	6.5	4.9	7.4	5.9	5.6
Self-employed business	7.9	4.9	7.7	3.6	3.4
Self-employed farm	11.9	15.6	11.6	10.7	10.1
Clerical	5.0	5.7	4.4	6.1	6.0
Sales	5.8	5.8	5.2	6.5	6.4
Service	4.8	5.1	4.8	5.2	5.6
Skilled	16.8	18.9	16.2	20.2	20.0
Semi- and unskilled	34.4	32.6	34.1	32.5	34.1
Total	100.0	100.0	100.0	100.0	100.0
Number of observations	5946	954,937	6893	964,344	1,078,769

*"Experienced civilian labor force" plus "not in the labor force/worked during 1959-1960."

that are possible, and progresses to illustrations of some more-complex analyses that can be undertaken. The material can only be suggestive; references indicate where the reader may study a more extensive presentation similar to the illustrations. Work to date represents a limited exploration of the archive. It is clear that considerable innovation both in methods for handling missing data and in estimation from panels of cross-section data will enhance future analyses on the archive (Maddala, 1971; Nerlove, 1971; Swami, 1970).

Independent, Representative Cross-Sections

Since each year's data represents the universe of taxpayers, the most natural organization of data would be to develop estimates independently from successive cross-sections for groups of interest. Figure 3-2 illustrates that approach. Male taxpayers born in specified periods were isolated in each year's collection of tax returns. Income estimates and filing rates for a succession of years were then combined to give the series plotted in the chart. Mobility into and out of the Wisconsin population implies that the estimates apply to a group of individuals that changes slightly over time.[2] Thus the estimates from successive cross-sections, though representative, do not reflect the experience of identical persons.

Panel Data on Indivuduals

To obtain statistics pertaining to identical individuals, the data can be organized into panels of k years' duration. Table 3-4 indicates the number of

Table 3-4

Distribution of Number of Tax Returns Filed by Males in Wisconsin Within Birth Cohort, 1947-1959 (Cumulative Percent in Italics)

Number of Years Filed	1860-1894	1895-1904	1905-1914	1915-1924	After 1924	Un-known	All
1	7.5%	4.7%	3.2%	5.4%	17.3%	18.9%	9.6%
	(7.5)	*(4.7)*	*(3.2)*	*(5.4)*	*(17.3)*	*(18.9)*	*(9.6)*
2-3	13.9	6.5	5.6	9.3	21.3	18.6	13.0
	(21.4)	*(11.2)*	*(8.8)*	*(14.7)*	*(38.6)*	*(37.5)*	*(22.6)*
4-5	12.1	6.1	6.9	8.9	18.0	14.2	11.5
	(33.5)	*(17.3)*	*(15.7)*	*(23.6)*	*(56.6)*	*(51.7)*	*(34.1)*
6-7	11.3	7.3	7.5	9.2	14.1	11.9	10.5
	(44.8)	*(24.6)*	*(23.2)*	*(32.8)*	*(70.7)*	*(63.6)*	*(44.6)*
8-10	18.2	14.2	14.6	15.8	14.7	14.3	15.3
	(63.0)	*(38.8)*	*(37.8)*	*(48.6)*	*(85.4)*	*(77.9)*	*(59.9)*
11-12	12.3	12.8	14.1	15.4	8.3	10.0	12.0
	(75.3)	*(51.6)*	*(51.9)*	*(64.0)*	*(93.7)*	*(87.9)*	*(71.9)*
13	24.7	48.4	48.1	36.0	6.3	12.1	28.2
	(100.0)	*(100.0)*	*(100.0)*	*(100.0)*	*(100.0)*	*(100.0)*	*(100.0)*
Number	1571	1567	1845	2069	2908	974	10,934

years between 1947 and 1959 for which identical taxpayers have filed returns. The percentages shown in italics reveal the attrition in sample size that occurs when analysis is focused on panel data with increasing numbers of tax records for each individual. Men who were born in 1895-1924 were established in their careers during the period of observation and filed returns for consistently lengthy periods. That cohort was at least 23 years of age and under 65 during the period 1947-1959. Table 3-4 also shows that when a minimum of four years of data are required for analysis, relatively little loss in sample size occurs; and there is correspondingly little danger of bias in the remaining panel.

The richness of the panel data embedded in the tax record sample is illustrated by Table 3-5. Three successive tax records for each individual were required to produce each observation. The table reports change in income for those who changed residence or occupation between the time of filing one tax return and the next. The first row in each panel indicates the change in income from the year prior to the indicated mobility to the year in which residential or occupational change occurred. The second row indicates the change in income between the year of mobility and the year following. The column labelled *gain* indicates the relative improvement in earnings experienced by mobile persons relative to nonmovers for the year following a change and for the two-year period including change.

Note that a single taxpayer may be included in this tabulation as many as

Table 3-5
Two-Year Changes in Earnings Associated with Annual Mobility Within Birth-Year Cohorts, 1948–1959 (Wisconsin Males)

Birth-Year Cohort	Earnings Change from	Occupational Mobility, Year t			Residential Mobility, Year t		
		None	Change	Gain	Within County	Intercounty	Gain
1860–1894	$t-1, t$	$ -27	$-132	$	$ -98	$-362	$
	$t, t+1$	-122	-109	+13	-135	-107	28
	2-years	-149	-241	-92	-233	-469	-236
1895–1904	$t-1, t$	130	99		125	28	
	$t, t+1$	99	121	22	97	213	116
	2-years	229	220	-9	222	241	19
1905–1914	$t-1, t$	218	217		225	-247	
	$t, t+1$	182	243	61	184	506	322
	2-years	400	450	50	409	259	-150
1915–1924	$t-1, t$	302	259		303	169	
	$t, t+1$	245	363	118	244	657	413
	2-years	547	622	75	547	826	279
1925–1959	$t-1, t$	468	356		449	431	
	$t, t+1$	350	478	128	379	315	-64
	2-years	818	834	16	828	746	-82

Source: Schroeder and David, 1970, Table 7.
Note: Table includes only those tax records for which both a prior return and a subsequent return were available.

eleven times. Thus a taxpayer who reports for five years and changes occupation once would be classified as follows:

Year	Occupation	Table Classification
1	A	—
2	B	Occupation change
3	B	No change
4	B	No change
5	B	No change

The means in the table reflect the average over eleven years for all taxpayers who reported at least three times in the period 1947–1959.

The individual may not be the proper subject for study. For federal tax problems, the computation of income in a joint return requires data on a marital unit consisting of husband and wife.[3] Considerable interest also attaches to family income that includes earnings of minors. To study incomes for married couples, the data must be organized so that sums of income sources, the total number of dependents, and total deductions can be computed from two separate tax records for a given year.

Tax records for husbands and wives were linked for a period of five years to produce Table 3-6. The table was developed to assess the significance of averaging provisions in the 1964 Tax Reform Act (David et al., 1970). Thus averages were computed in such a way as to simulate the effect of the law wherever possible.[4]

Panel Data Combined with Current and Retrospective Interview Data

Still another technique for organizing the archive is to relate the time series of income information to the personal interview data collected in 1965. One study (Brown, 1973) is proceeding along these lines. Characteristics of income change are being related to the age at which a home is first purchased, expenditure on purchased housing, and the level of mortgage commitment obtained. Clearly, many other analyses along these lines can be undertaken, with the precision of tax-record information supplemented by recall data and benchmarks obtained in 1965 from direct interviews.

Tax-Record Data Linked to Other Archives of Microdata

The most involved formats for presenting data within the archive relate to those instances in which observations from several sources at the same point in

Table 3-6
Net Taxable Income Fluctuation for Married Taxpayers, 1958: Percent of Units in a Given Row (AGI bracket in 1958) Whose Fluctuation Places Them in a Given Column (1958 NTI Less Prior Average)

Adjusted Gross Income, 1958	1958 Net Taxable Income Less Four-Year Average (in dollars)[a]											Number of Sample Tax Units[b]
	-5001 or Less	-5000 to -3001	-3000 to -2001	-2000 to -1001	-1000 to -1	0	1 to 1000	1001 to 2000	2001 to 3000	3001 to 5000	5001 or More	
$1000 or less	3.3%	5.8%	6.7%	18.3%	41.7%	24.2%	0.0%	0.0%	0.0%	0.0%	0.0%	120
$1001–$3000	0.9	3.0	7.0	10.4	37.0	24.4	17.0	0.3	0.0	0.0	0.0	643
$3001–$5000	0.5	1.6	3.1	9.7	31.7	9.4	34.6	8.1	1.2	0.0	0.0	1221
$5001–$7000	0.1	0.8	2.7	4.6	22.5	1.8	43.9	17.5	5.0	1.1	0.0	1353
$7001–$10,000	0.7	1.0	1.2	2.7	13.4	0.1	32.0	30.5	11.5	6.2	0.6	819
$10,001–$15,000	1.2	1.6	1.2	2.5	5.7	0.0	19.5	27.2	19.5	13.8	7.7	246
$15,001–$20,000	7.9	0.0	0.0	0.0	9.5	0.0	12.7	14.3	14.3	15.9	25.4	63
$20,001 or more	7.2	2.4	1.2	6.0	1.2	0.0	7.2	8.4	10.8	8.4	47.0	83
All income groups	0.8	1.6	3.1	6.7	24.4	7.2	31.9	14.8	5.3	2.6	1.7	4548

[a]Negative income excluded and capital gains included in full in net taxable income.
[b]Assuming joint returns and reconstruction of income where applicable.

time must be coordinated to answer the question addressed to the archive. One such question that might be raised concerns the degree to which social security benefits enhance income from other soruces. Table 3-7 shows the number of years in which tax return and beneficiary data overlap for the population that ever received benefits. (Lack of overlap can be ascribed to migration out of the state at retirement, failure to receive cash benefits in the last year of labor force participation, lack of entitlement under one's own social security account number, and perhaps mismatching of the files.) The table indicates the extent to which tax data and benefit data can be meaningfully aggregated for a given year.

Perhaps the most ambitious task of linking information from a variety of sources at a single instant in time was undertaken by Bussman (1972). He decomposed the information on corporate equity assets into a file identified by asset, by taxpayer, and by date. This information was linked to a separate file containing the prices and other pertinent data on corporate securities. The result could be aggregated for each taxpayer to determine a rate of return on his portfolio and the variance of that return. We shall return to some of the logical problems entailed in this operation in Chapter 5.

The brief review of alternative structures for presenting the data in the WAIS archive indicates clearly that a conceptual framework must be used to organize the information in the archive. Some frameworks require a sequence of information on identical individuals; others do not. Some frameworks require a matching of married taxpayers, or a matching of tax-record information to other files of microdata. At the same time enormously useful information can be derived from extremely elementary conceptions of the data as a random sample of information gathered about individuals over a span of 18 years.

A parallel concern with conceptualization applies to the manner in which relationships among variables are to be studied. Some discussion of our experience in that area follows.

3.3 Defining Explanatory Variables

So long as microdata are collected at a single point in time, the definition of homogeneous population groups for study is relatively straightforward. The available information includes (a) contemporaneous behavior variables, (b) recall information on past behavior, and (c) fixed characteristics such as birth date and sex. As soon as a time series of data are available for the individual, it becomes possible to have both recall information and contemporaneous measurement of some behavior in the past. The choice of a classification principle is not trivial, since both types of data may include measurement errors.

Furthermore, many variables that tend to be treated as fixed in the analyses of single cross-sections (occupation, marital status, residential location) are in

Table 3-7

Linkage Between Tax-Record and Social Security Beneficiary Data

Historical Relationship of Tax and Beneficiary Records	1946– 1951	1952– 1955	1956– 1959	1960– 1965	Total
Gap between last tax year and first receipt of social security benefits					
6 or more years					
Men	0	3	24	83	110
Women	0	6	41	96	143
4–5 years					
Men	0	11	29	86	126
Women	0	9	20	70	99
3 years					
Men	3	2	15	122	142
Women	5	5	21	67	98
2 years					
Mcn	7	12	11	158	188
Women	1	11	11	78	101
1 year					
Men	10	32	30	157	229
Women	5	20	22	63	110
Number of years in which the tax returns and social security benefits are linked in the archive[a]					
1 year					
Men	17	62	76	77	232
Women	7	27	46	36	116
2 years					
Men	23	39	125	–	187
Women	4	18	81	–	103
3 years					
Men	15	20	96	–	131
Women	2	7	55	–	75
4–6 years					
Men	36	117	138	–	291
Women	11	69	77	–	157
7–10 years					
Men	50	82	–	–	132
Women	23	31	–	–	54
11 or more years					
Men	38	–	–	–	38
Women	14	–	–	–	14
No tax-record data[b]					
Men	5	3	5	189	202
Women	61	110	258	483	912
Total					
Men	204	383	549	872	2008
Women	133	313	643	893	1982
Percent					
Men	10.2	19.1	27.3	43.4	100.0%
Women	6.7	15.8	32.4	45.1	100.0%

[a]The number reflects potential overlap in the two data sources. Some years for which linkage exists contain no tax records as a consequence of the sample structure.

[b]These individuals enter the sample through its extension to beneficiaries of taxpayers. See pp. 19, 59.

fact the endogenous outcome of processes of career development and socialization which change for some individuals from time to time (Blau and Duncan, 1967). Under the circumstances, it may be desirable to consider both present and past values of occupation, marital status, and other explanatory variables in developing analyses of the behavior of recognizable population groups. Quite clearly, no general rules can be given for how this is to be done. Nevertheless, a few observations may be helpful.

Figure 3-2 makes clear that it is sometimes extremely useful to trace the history of a fixed group of individuals (defined by birth date in this case) through the archive. This can be done by examining a group for whom a given characteristic is known at some fixed point in time (e.g., occupation at the time of entry into the labor force), rather than a group who may have that characteristic at a later date.

An extension of this technique is to locate individuals whose characteristics have remained the same over the entire period of observation under study; it thus may be of special value to study individuals with unique occupations, persons who are continuously married, and persons who maintain a fixed residence (Miller and David, 1971, p. 242).

The logical complement of individuals with fixed demographic characteristics includes persons whose behavior has changed in some notable respect and who are therefore an interesting population for study. Particular types of changes can be enumerated and form another basis for classifying individuals with a given time series of information. Marriage, retirement, and change of employer are thus all events that can be usefully studied in relation to a panel of earnings data. Comparison of Tables 3-8 and 3-9 indicates that the extension of a static

Table 3-8
Mobility Rates by Marital Status and Dependents

| | | Mobility Rates | | | | |
| | | Geographical | | Occupational | | |
Marital and Dependent Status	*Fre-quency*	*Intra-county*	*Inter-county*	*Change*	*Into Labor Force*	*Out of Labor Force*
Zero dependents						
Single	11,107	2.5%	32.%	8.3%	2.3%	2.3%
Married, wife without income	13,595	2.0	1.7	3.8	0.6	2.3
Married, wife with income	9,190	4.2	3.6	7.5	1.0	1.8
One or more dependents						
Single	2,092	2.7	2.7	7.5	0.2	1.0
Married, wife without income	29,865	2.9	3.3	6.1	0.3	0.2
Married, wife with income	10,916	3.4	2.9	7.6	0.4	0.4

Source: Schroeder, 1971.

Table 3–9
Mobility Rates by Changes in Marital Status

| | | Mobility Rates | | | | |
| | | Geographical | | Occupational | | |
Marital Status Change	Fre-quency	Intra-county	Inter-county	Change	Into Labor Force	Out of Labor Force
Remain single	12,494	2.4%	2.9%	8.0%	2.0%	2.0%
Remain married						
Wife continues without income	39,482	2.4	2.4	4.9	0.2	0.9
Wife continues with income	15,578	2.9	2.4	6.4	0.6	0.9
Wife starts income	3,221	3.9	3.5	9.4	0.4	1.2
Wife terminates income	3,212	4.6	5.6	9.8	1.2	0.6
Become married						
Wife with income	728	9.1	10.0	12.1	3.3	1.6
Wife without income	1,246	14.3	12.3	17.3	2.8	2.0
Marriage terminated						
Death	705	5.5	7.1	11.1	1.0	4.0
other	101	4.0	3.0	5.0	0.6	2.4

Source: Schroeder, 1971.

life-cycle code to one that considers year-to-year changes reveals some important feature of occupational and locational mobility.

Another device for summarizing characteristics of an individual that may change over time is to extract measures of central tendency from the available time series. In the case of occupation, the modal occupation may be of interest. Mean receipts from capital gains or mean property income may be of special interest as indicators of a person's wealth and portfolio practices. The value of the latter type of classification is illustrated in Table 3–10.

Alternatively, it is sometimes useful to isolate groups who report a given type of behavior at any time during the period covered by the archive—again, the reporting of capital gains is an example. Indications of earnings for married women, and indications of self-employment income are also of special interest for particular analysis purposes.

3.4 Multivariate Analysis

A detailed discussion of structural model building and estimation would be out of place in this monograph. What would appear helpful is to review briefly several possible approaches to reducing the volume of data in an archive such as WAIS to tractable proportions.

Table 3-10
Distribution of Mean Gains by Mean Dividends Received During the
Filing Period

Mean Capital Gain (in dollars)	Mean Dividend				
	None	$1-100	$101-300	$301+	All
Less than −100	1.8%	3.3%	3.1%	6.8%	2.2%
−100 to −1	3.8	7.5	10.4	11.3	4.7
0	78.2	52.0	33.3	16.9	71.4
1 to 100	8.4	18.5	18.8	17.7	10.4
101 to 200	2.7	5.6	9.4	8.8	3.5
201 to 500	3.1	9.4	11.5	12.0	4.5
501 to 1000	1.4	2.9	8.3	11.3	2.1
1001+	0.6	0.8	5.2	15.3	1.2
Total	100.0%	100.0%	100.0%	100.0%	100.0%
Number of Filers	3001	5.1	96	124	3740

Source: David and Miller, 1972, p. 276.

Note: Sample comprises male taxpayers who filed at least four pairs of consecutive tax returns, 1947–1959.

Microdata available represent measures that are replicated over individuals, and progress in a time series for each individual. Thus, three types of data reduction are possible:

i. Aggretate data over homogeneous groups of individuals and analyze the resulting time series.
ii. Aggregate data over time and analyze the resulting summary statistics in relation to characteristics of the individuals.
iii. Specify a model of the data that pools information over time *and* individuals; then estimate the dynamic and individual effects simultaneously.

All three approaches have been used on the archive.

Aggregate–Then Analyze

The first approach is typical of much economic analysis, as for example, the analysis of variations in labor force participation over the Standard Metropolitan Statistical Areas of the country. A WAIS study of mean earnings and their rate of growth gave insight into the age profile of earnings (David, 1969). Table 3-11 indicates the result.

A somewhat more sophisticated approach is to analyze the aggregates of each cross-section as a time series and incorporate variables that reflect the

Table 3-11

Rate of Growth of Real Earnings for Selected Occupation Groups Within
Birth-Year Cohorts (Wisconsin Male Taxpayers 1947-1959)

Occupation	Birth-Year Cohort				
	1925–1964	1915–1924	1905–1914	1895–1904	Prior to 1895
Professional	.0233	.0671[a]	.0294[a]	.0039	.0202[a]
Semiprofessional	.0777[a]	.0471[a]	.0047	.0012	.0072
Managerial	.0668[a]	.0624[a]	.0337[a]	.0118[a]	–.0039
Self-employed businessman	.0216	.0053	.0055	–.0232[a]	.0351[a]
Farmers	.0188	.0095	–.0219	–.0413[a]	–.0437[a]
Clerical	.0459[a]	.0454[a]	.0191[a]	.0212[a]	–.0119
Sales	.0671[a]	.0538[a]	.0235[a]	–.0082	.0005
Skilled	.0522[a]	.0428[a]	.0252[a]	.0160[a]	–.0257[a]
Semi-skilled and unskilled	.0414[a]	.0299[a]	.0186[a]	.0167[a]	–0219[a]
Service workers	.0195	.0349[a]	.0271[a]	.0186[a]	.0280[a]
All occupations[b]	.0438[a]	.0414[a]	.0179[a]	.002	–.0432[a]

Source: David, 1969.

[a]Rate is significantly different from zero with a probability greater than .99.

[b]Including retired and occupation unknown.

changing environment in which the household or taxpayer makes the decisions
that are reflected in the available data.

As an example we present an attempt to relate realization of capital gains
to interest rates and aggregative measures of yield (see David and Miller, 1972).
The regression was generated by regressing the probability of realizing capital
gains for specified birth cohorts on the variables indicated in Table 3-12. The
probability was computed for each of eight birth cohorts for each year from
1947 to 1959. In this particular instance, macrovariables did not significantly
explain realization behavior.

Summary Statistics for Each Individual

The second approach is frankly descriptive and is illustrated by Table
3-13. However, the technique can be related to random coefficients models. The
mean coefficients and the variance-covariance matrix give insights into the
interpersonal variation in behavior as well as the systematic effects of outside
forces (David, 1971b; Swami, 1970). Given that there is considerable likelihood
that individuals respond differently to economic events, the random coefficients
model may prove particularly helpful in dealing with the data available in an
archive such as WAIS.

Table 3-12
A Model of the Realization Propensity of Wisconsin Taxpayers 1947-1959

	Regression Coefficients (t Ratio)	
	Men	Women
Constant	-.00495	-.0986
	(-0.30)	(-4.23)[a]
Birth-cohort variables		
Age	.00130	.00262
	(8.21)[a]	(13.3)[a]
Wealth proxy	.00105	.000487
(in thousands of dollars)	(4.48)[a]	(5.00)[a]
Labor and self-employment income	.00658	.00994
(in thousands of dollars)	(2.60)[b]	(2.56)[b]
Market variables		
Baa bond rate	-.480	.392
	(-1.06)	(0.62)
Accruing capital gains in the household	-.0000935	.0000485
sector (in thousands of dollars)	(1.27)	(0.46)

Notes: Age is measured by the difference between calendar year and the average birth year of the cohort, except for those born 1860-1874 where age is measured by the difference between the year and 1872.

Baa bond rate is Moody's index of yields on corporate bonds (*Source:* Economic Report of the President, 1971, p. 265).

Accrued gains are those reported by Bhatia (1970).

[a]Significant at the $P = .01$ level.
[b]Significant at the $P = .05$ level.

Direct Regression on the Archive

The third technique, direct estimation of parameters in a statistical regression model, is familiar to most readers. A complex problem of strategy in estimation remains. Since interactions between personal characteristics and behavior responses are often postulated, estimates are desired for population subgroups. Furthermore, lag structures relating responses at different points in time are seldom fully specified by theory.

As a consequence there is always a temptation to search the data. Some observations on the problems involved in data searching and model building are reported in Lansing and Morgan (1971, pp. 332-343). The reader may also wish to consult Sonquist, Baker, and Morgan (1971).

We illustrate the regression technique by some simple equations fit to earnings and change in wealth (David and Miller, 1969). Some results appear in Table 3-14. The statistical model used was dictated by a theory of consumer behavior and the process by which households adjust to disequilibrium.

Table 3-13
Mean Income Position and Mean Trend Coefficient

	Individuals with a Unique Occupation				Individuals with One Major Change in Occupation[a]						
					Occupation of Origin			Terminal Occupation			
	No.	$\bar{Y}$	$\bar{b}$	Average Degrees of Freedom	No.	$\bar{Y}$	$\bar{b}$[b]	No.	$\bar{Y}$	$\bar{b}$[b]	Average Degrees of Freedom
Professional	127	$8404	.0574	6.9	20	$4059	-.0559	22	$4581	.0548	5.7
Semiprofessional	46	7611	.0147	7.0	10	4619	.0165	14	3427	.0284	6.5
Managerial	106	8865	.0582	7.9	32	5364	-.0125	63	5669	-.0034	3.1
Self-employed											
Business	152	3876	-.0460	7.6	36	3912	.0045	54	4043	-.0354	8.0
Farmers	3.2	2304	-.0272	7.5	62	2519	.0138	32	2614	-.0191	7.8
Clerical	52	3909	-.0115	6.6	37	3943	.0003	24	3626	.0021	7.5
Sales	83	5586	-.0131	7.6	33	4697	-.0297	22	4762	-.0312	6.7
Service	60	3435	.0052	7.0	23	2983	-.0353	34	2500	-.0214	5.8
Skilled	304	4544	-.0095	7.8	85	3404	-.0236	115	4106	-.0094	7.4
Semiskilled	650	3502	-.0214	7.0	249	3404	-.0236	144	3096	-.0062	7.7
Not in labor force	20	715	.0361	7.2	15	3154	.0715	76	2315	-.0773	7.4
All	1912	4292	-.0096	7.4	602	3666	-.0171	611	3656	-.0171	7.3

Source: David and Miller, 1970, p. 109.

[a]More than 20 percent of time spent in second job.

[b]$\bar{b}$ is the average trend in relative income. Relative income is defined as the ratio of adjusted gross income for the individual to the mean income of his birth cohort for each year.

Table 3-14
Regressions of Earnings and Wealth (Wisconsin Males Under Age 65,
Non-Self-Employed, and Born Prior to 1905, Tax Years 1948-1960)

	Coefficients of Regression	
	Money Earnings Net of Tax (t Ratio)	End-of-Period Wealth (t Ratio)
Independent variables		
Consumer price index	6.484	1.522
	(10.3)	(.236)
Wage rate	-.0785	-.0397
	(5.76)	(.285)
Potentially disposable wealth and value of tax deductions	.0008	.9240
	(1.96)	(209.)
Number of Dependents[a]	.1961	-2.160
	(1.88)	(2.02)
Money value of asset gain or loss	-.1783	-.6993
	(20.3)	(7.78)
Unemployment rate	-44.22	-47.48
	(8.15)	(.855)
Medical expenses[a]	.1300	-0.913
	(2.71)	(.1862)
Lagged earnings, adjusted for this year's tax rate and wage level	.9457	.2209
	(269.)	(.035)
Standard Error of Estimate	$966.6	$9890.
R^2	.911[b]	.850[b]
Mean of dependent variable	$2822	$4959
Number of observations	8773	8773

[a]Times the price index. This interaction was specified on theoretical grounds to eliminate money illusion.
[b]Computed as 1 minus the ratio of the error variance to the variance of the dependent variable.

The model is of interest because it exhibits the strong dependency of current earnings on their value in the prior period and a correspondingly strong relationship between beginning and end of period wealth. In addition, unemployment and dependents shift these strong time interdependencies in theoretically predicted ways.

3.5 Conclusions

In this chapter we have attempted to illustrate the wide variety of analytical uses offered by a large archive such as WAIS. We have discussed simple statistics that can be generated from such an archive, and illustrated the products of more complex statistical procedures.

The citations of analyses already published are intended to assist the reader in finding the details behind the illustrations and the context in which alternative analytical techniques were used.

Taken together, the statistics presented demonstrate how the same information can be organized to reveal alternative facets of the archive. Each can be used to answer a question about the social system from which the archive was collected. In the presentation of simple cross-section aggregates (Table 3-1), we observe the evolution of incomes over more than a decade of history. In Figure 3-2 these same data have been provided with the richer meaning of a life history for particular individuals. Table 3-5 shows how assembling data for several years for one individual provides better understanding of the consequences of his mobility for income. The same material is presented in a regression model whose functional form was determined by elaborate theoretical argument (Table 3-14).

In addition, the material presented indicates that considerable attention must be given to both the question of the unit of analysis—individual or tax year—and to problems of dating the explanatory variables. Obtaining useful measures when occupation or other demographic characteristics change may require either selecting modal types (e.g., principal occupation) or focusing on rare events that may be repeated a sufficient number of times to generate useful findings (e.g., realization of capital gains).

With these illustrations in mind, it will be easier to understand the motivation behind the record linkages undertaken and the problems of data development and organization described in subsequent chapters.

4

The Nature and Nurture of
Linked Information

In reviewing the overall structure of the data collected in the WAIS archive (Section 2.3), we alluded to the significance of information from the Social Security Administration (hereafter SSA). SSA earnings records provide badly needed data on the birth date of taxpayers and some indications of earnings in years for which no tax returns may be available. Social security benefits are known to be the principal source of income for retired persons; thus SSA beneficiary records cover the statistically largest source of nontaxable income.

Linking the SSA data to the tax records proceeded in three stages: (1) Earnings records (hereafter ER) were matched to the tax archive. (2) Benefit data were assimilated. (3) Other Wisconsin data were scanned to find birth date. The benefit data collection could not proceed until a valid social security number (hereafter SSN) had been established in step 1. There was no point to scanning other sources of birth information in the third step until the information available in the first two steps had been determined. Tax records of parents, death certificates, and motor vehicle operator's licenses were scanned for birth dates in the third step. [1]

Linkage between these sources of information raises two problems of methodology: First, characteristics of the records and their physical structure determine the processing that must be undertaken to link the two sources of information. And second, once linkage is complete the content of the linked files raises analytical questions. If the data in the component files overlap, use of the information to reduce biases of measurement error is indicated. If the data in the component files do not overlap, problems arise in using information from one file to impute missing data into the second file.

The *content* of the data sources will be discussed in the following section to make the power and objectives of data linkage clear. The *method of linkage* and concepts involved in executing a meshing of data generated by different techniques are discussed in the remainder of the chapter.

4.1 Substantive Characteristics of the SSA Records

Age and Birth Date

The need for information on age of taxpayers provided the chief motivation for linking the ER to tax records. Age can be derived from the birth dates shown on the ER. The combination of age and detailed income information on the tax record make it possible to determine (1) the extent to which sources of income change over the life cycle, (2) the degree to which older taxpayers are inhibited from liquidating their assets in capital gains, and (3) the extent to which taxpayers cease to earn income at later points in their lives.

Social Security Data as Proxies for Earnings

The ER contains a substantial amount of information in addition to birth date. Annual earnings reported to the SSA were available for each year from 1951 to 1962 on the extract that WAIS received from SSA. Such information provides a validation of tax data when both sources are available and earnings reports are not truncated by the ceiling on wages taxable for federal payroll tax purposes (Table 4-1, case 1).

When only social security information is available, reported earnings can be used to derive a proxy for the missing tax information (Table 4-1, cases 5-7). This is particularly useful when the individual's tax records are interrupted by a gap which may represent years of out-of-state residence. In fact, the SSA has long had algorithms to arrive at estimated earnings by extrapolating from the earnings reported in successive quarters. This procedure can be approximated for the WAIS archive by using annual earnings summaries and quarters in which taxable wages are reported, both available on the extract.

Both the ceiling on taxable earnings and the gaps in coverage of the social security payroll tax imply that in many instances tax records will show larger amounts than the ER (Table 4-1, cases 2-4).[2] This phenomenon provides an interesting source of microdata concerning the effective coverage of the payroll tax.

Table 4-1
A Comparison of Information Available when Tax Records and Wage Earnings Records Are Linked

Distribution of Individual's Earnings	Individual Tax Record Is	
	In WAIS Sample, Year t	Not in WAIS Sample, Year t
All earnings in covered employment:		
less than wage ceiling	(1) $E_{805} = E_{TAX}$	(5) E_{805}
Greater than wage ceiling	(2) $E_{805} < E_{TAX}$	(6) E_{805}
Some earnings in covered employment	(3) $E_{805} < E_{TAX}$	(7) E_{805}
No earnings in covered employment	(4) E_{TAX}	(8) No data

$E_{805} \sim$ earnings reported to SSA.
$E_{TAX} \sim$ earnings reported for tax purposes.

Social Security Benefit Information

During the period for which tax record data are available (1947–1964), government transfer payments ranged between 6 and 8 percent of personal income. Over the same period payments under the social insurance program increased from approximately 10 percent to more than 40 percent of the total government transfers to persons.

Under the circumstances, it is clear that a significant insight into the non-taxable income of persons can be obtained by adding information on social security benefits to whatever information is available in the tax return. It is also of interest to ask to what extent the social insurance system served the function of replacing earnings of workers at retirement. After-the-fact surveys of retirees provide a less solid base for inferring prior income than do the time series of data actually available in the Master Tax Record File (MF). Table 4-2 illustrates the complementarities between the MF and the available benefit information.

Because some clue concerning the wealth of the taxpayer is available in tax information filed prior to retirement, the use of benefit payments as a lower bound on income for retirees becomes especially valuable. Thus a failure to report interest and dividend information during working years combined with the failure to file current income tax returns becomes strong evidence of a lack of adequate retirement income.

Summary

Linkage of social insurance records to tax records extends the history of individual income information by including data on periods not covered by the original sample. The extension includes like kinds of income (earnings) that

Table 4-2
Complementarities Between Social Security Beneficiary Data and Tax Record Data

	Individual Tax Record Is	
Retirement and Beneficiary Status of the Individual	*In WAIS Sample, Year* t	*Not in WAIS Sample, Year* t
Not retired, not eligible for benefits	Tax information, no benefits possible	No data
Retired and eligible for benefits	Benefit payments supplement tax information	Benefit payments constitute a lower bound on income
Retired and not eligible for benefits	Tax information, no benefits possible	No data

were not discovered because of jurisdictional limitations and filing regulations that determine the number of tax records available for any given individual. The extension also includes nontaxable transfer payments under social insurance.

These additional items of information do not produce a neat structure within which income amounts from the two sources can be readily merged; the value of the additional information and its particular use must be determined in terms of the particular analysis that is being undertaken. For example, the relationship between benefits and total income for persons who continue filing tax returns can be arrived at easily because the enlarged data set includes benefit payments (see Table 4–2). Only a qualitative bound on that relationship can be estimated for persons for whom no tax record is available. The data linkages thus challenge the analyst to increase the sophistication of missing data algorithms. Rejecting the information at hand because it does not come in the form of a neat rectangular array of data on the same variables over a period of time is a counsel of despair.

4.2   General Features of the Data Linkage

Many of the problems of handling a data archive arose in the process of integrating SSA records with Wisconsin tax information. It is thus useful to describe in some detail the procedures involved in that operation before discussing general principles of file management. [3]

Five features of the integration operation represent problems that recur in the handling of the data archive and deserve careful and general planning in any archival operation:

Batches. Data were received in batches and considerable periods of time elapsed between the receipt of different batches. In some cases editing and error correction in the WAIS files was a prerequisite to the collection of additional data, since data received at later points in time often included information extending into later time periods.

Units. The logic of the data collected implied that records had to be developed on a variety of units; some data were received for individuals, some for the transactions in an individual's benefit account.

Record Correspondences. Logically, when two files are linked it is possible to find (a) a one-to-one correspondence of records, (b) several records in the secondary file for each record in the primary file, (c) several records in the primary file for each record in the secondary file, or both (b) and (c). The linkage between ER and tax records disclosed multiple correspondences of both kinds. Devising techniques for integrating records, i.e., eliminating multiple correspondences or preserving conceptually important multiple correspondences, proved to be an important part of the linkage operation.

Sample Extension. The linkage of social security data to the tax-record sample extends the type of information available. The administrative procedures entailed in the social security system also result in an extension of the original taxpayer sample to include individuals that were outside the original sample universe. The death of a Wisconsin taxpayer whose wife and children are entitled to survivor's benefits generates social security beneficiary accounts for the wife and children. None of those individuals need ever have filed a Wisconsin tax return to appear in the WAIS archive. Indeed, the wife may move to Florida following her husband's death so that tax records associated with her income could fall entirely outside the sample.

Change of Identifier. The collection of data from social security records also reveals one of the most difficult and persistent problems that have complicated the process of data integration. In some cases the identification number assigned to a particular individual did not identify him correctly as a dependent or head of a family unit. Such incorrect assignments of identification numbers could lead to the failure to integrate all the tax records in an individual's file; incorrect assignments might also lead to incorrect estimates of income for joint returns or families.

In Chapter 5 we shall generalize these concrete problems and show how they recur and relate to other aspects of the data processing and analysis pursued by WAIS. The succession of similar problems, tackled with programming languages of increased sophistication and computers with increasing possibilities for remote and interactive applications, lead to some global conceptualizations and techniques which can be better understood by looking first at the details of at least one of the linkage operations completed by WAIS.

4.3 Collection and Linkage of the Social Security Earnings Records (ER's)

The process by which the ER's were linked to the MF illustrates three of the problems of integration discussed above. The information was received in two separate *batches*. ER's received corresponded to individuals, while data in the MF included separate *units* of observation on each individual in a series of years. Multiple *correspondences* arose both because particular individuals have more than one SSN and because individuals in the tax-record sample had been purposely assigned two identification numbers by WAIS staff if a household dependent became head of a separate household in later years. [4]

Figure 4-1 shows the division of labor involved in linking ER to the tax

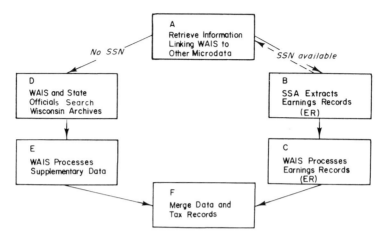

Figure 4-1. Basic Steps in Linking Birth Data to Tax Records

record: WAIS staff were required to retrieve linking information and forward SSN's to the SSA (step A). Remaining taxpayers were identified by current address; that information was used cooperatively by Wisconsin state officials and WAIS staff to search a variety of administrative records (step D). The SSA operations produced extracts (step B) that required further processing (step C) and merging with the MF (step F).

Details of operations involved in the collection of ER's for persons filing tax returns in Wisconsin during the period covered by the first collection (1947–1959 or 1960) are shown in Figure 4-2. Letters on the large boxes correspond to Figure 4-1. The procedure was relatively simple. All SSN's associated with the tax records had been recorded in the ID file. An extract of name, address, most frequently used SSN, and WAIS identifier was created from the ID file producing File 1. The SSA manually checked the account numbers against its master file of account numbers (SS-5 file). This produced the five files numbered 2-6 shown in the center of Figure 4-2.

Associated with valid SSN's recorded in the WAIS files were 14,627 ER's (File 4) and 2,733 identified cases of claims on those accounts (File 3). There were multiple SSN's for one individual for 344 of the ER's; listings of those accounts were provided (File 6). Files 2-6 were returned to WAIS in March 1964. Subsequent checking of 1,407 account numbers identified as invalid by SSA (File 2) produced a new list of 181 SSN's associated with WAIS records; additional SSN's were located in the state tax roll for 1964. An extract of WAIS identifiers and SSN's corresponding to File 1 was returned to SSA, thereby permitting SSA to repeat its operations. The second round of the operations shown on the right-hand side of Figure 4-2 yielded a second installment to Files 2-6.

The left-hand side of Figure 4-2 entails two major steps: (1) reformatting

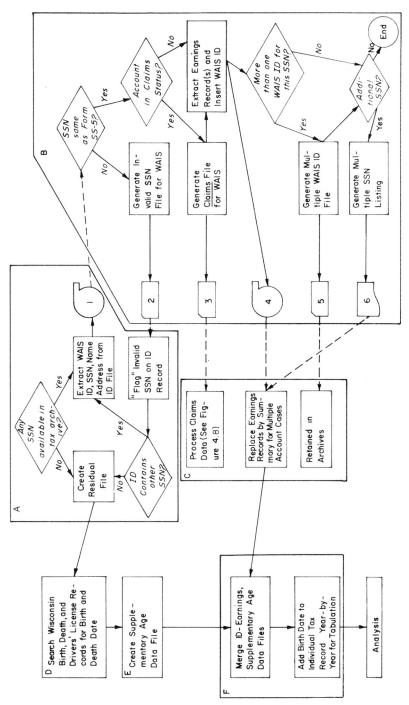

Figure 4-2. Flow of Operations in Processing SSA Earnings Records

and consolidation of multiple ER's. The original data for each individual included numerous subrecords for ease of tabulation and display of the ER information. The records were reformatted and consolidated into one logical record per individual for the WAIS archive. (2) Instances in which an individual reported earnings under more than one SSN were hand coded to consolidate the reported earnings for each year into a single aggregate. These hand-coded records were then merged with the other records and portions of the ID to produce a single file. [5]

The two collections of data from the SSA produced earnings information for 15,971 individuals in the WAIS sample. An additional 95 ER's could not be matched to valid WAIS identifiers, probably because of changes in the WAIS identifier between the initiation of the request for account information and the merging of the two files (see Table 4-3). [6]

The 5,497 individuals for whom no ER's were available were likely to be older and in self-employed occupations. The aged may never have worked in a covered employment, as coverage was initially limited; the self-employed and farmers, who received coverage beginning in 1951 and 1955 respectively, were the last groups to be covered.

We have little evidence on the rate at which earnings and tax record files are matched erroneously. The most frequently reported SSN, used initially to establish the link between the two files, proved invalid for 1863 cases, roughly 10 percent of all individuals. (Out of that 10 percent, one-tenth of the 10 percent also reported a correct number at some time on their tax returns.) We feel the careful SSA check on the validity of the SSN precluded most mismatches. However, individuals with common names could conceivably have an incorrect SSN on the tax form that was valid for another individual in the sample; such an event would produce mismatches.

The only evidence of mismatching between taxpayers and ER's lies in discrepancies between sex of taxpayer (assigned by WAIS coders) and the sex indicated on the ER. There were 128 cases in which the WAIS ID indicates one sex and the ER the other. It is difficult to evaluate the meaning of those discrepancies. The rate of mismatching is smaller to the extent that WAIS coding is in error. WAIS identifiers are likely to be in error whenever a first name is ambiguous as to sex and the taxpayer is not married. However, it is also the case that mismatches could occur without giving rise to a discrepancy in the sex codes. By this latter argument, 128/15,971 understates the rate of mismatching. At the moment, we feel that WAIS coding is the primary source of discrepancies.

4.4 Supplementary Age Data Collection

An attempt was made to locate age data for the individuals who lacked a SSN or whose SSN was declared invalid by SSA.

Death records kept by the Office of Vital Statistics of the Sate of Wisconsin

Table 4-3

Information Received from the Social Security Administration and Reconciliation with WAIS Matches

	File 4 Total Earnings Records Received	File 5 Identical Earnings Records (for WAIS Multiple ID's)	File 6 Multiple Earnings Records for One WAIS ID	File 2 Invalid SSN in WAIS ID Records
Inputs from Social Security Administration				
A March 6, 1964	14,627	695	344	1,407
B September 2, 1965	2,375	41	58*	456
Total information received	17,002	736	402	1,863
Reconciliation of matches				
Subtract:				
Duplicate ER reported by SSA	−736	−736		
Multiple ER integrated into combined records	−202		−402	
Net ER to be matched to unique individuals	16,064			
Number of records Integrated under valid WAIS ID's in August 1967	15,971			
Discrepancy	95			
Invalid SSN				
Subtract valid SSN located for (A)				−181
Number of individuals whose only SSN available 1947–1960 is invalid				1,682

*Estimated from the rate in the first shipment.

were manually checked against the name and address available in the ID File (see D, Figure 4-2). The same extract was also transmitted to the Motor Vehicle Department to check for persons who had renewed licenses in Wisconsin between 1962 and 1966. Also, birth dates of children who received survivor's benefits were obtained from the Beneficiary File described in Section 4.5.

The operations indicated in the left-hand side of Figure 4.2 show that this supplementary age information was merged with the age and earnings data of the WAIS ER File. The merged file provided age data as follows: [7]

Age obtained from earnings record	15,971	75%
Age obtained from supplementary data	3,087	14
Age not ascertained	2,410	11
Total individuals	21,468	100%

The completed file clearly meets the original objective of providing birth data for the individuals in the tax-record sample. In the final step of operations, age data from the combined WAIS ER File were transferred to each year's tax record available for the individual in question. Age or birth date could then be used for substantive studies.

The different search processes produced new information for 3,087 taxpayers: [8]

a.	Cross-checking of benefit files and age of dependents internal to the WAIS archive	1,479
b.	Checking age recorded on death certificates	673
c.	Obtaining age from motor vehicle license records	935
	Total supplementary age data (SAD)	3,087

In 207 cases the death records indicated two persons with identical names; matching was done on the basis of occupation recorded in the tax record. The only clue to the reliability of this process is that 26 inconsistencies were detected for age of death data coded independently in a and b, implying an error rate of less than 1.5 percent.

4.5 The Structure of the Social Security Benefit Data

The processing of the social security benefit data affords an opportunity to observe the extension of the original sample and trace the development of a complex record structure. Section 4.1 indicated that the primary objective of obtaining the benefit data was to supplement annual data on income in the tax record or provide a lower bound for income of persons who filed no tax return. In order to understand how the record linkage was executed, it is necessary to understand the relationship between social security accounts and beneficiaries. It is also necessary to understand the nested structure of WAIS tax records. After these ideas are treated in this section the details of processing benefit data will be described in Section 4.6.

The Logical Record System

The structure of information available in the benefit records reveals that information is received for a nested set of units. The *account* of the insured is the source of the information. (The account corresponds to a taxpayer in the origi-

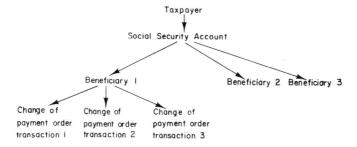

Figure 4-3. Nested Units of Observation Associated with Accounts in Claims Office

nal sample.) Several individuals may make claims on the account, thereby becoming *beneficiaries*. The earnings of beneficiaries, changes in their age and marital status, and changes in the law regarding benefit payments all create *transactions involving change* of benefit-payment levels. These transactions are naturally ordered by date for any particular beneficiary. The structure is illustrated in Figure 4-3. The transactions information must be integrated over a period of time to provide the annual benefit information that is comparable to the data in tax records.

*Logical Linkage of Benefit Data and
Tax Records*

The link between the 1 percent sample of Wisconsin tax records and SSA benefit records was the SSN that appears on the tax records. That link provided the basis for identifying social security accounts. During the history of an individual's account, records must be kept of earnings that are credited to his account; subsequently, information in the ER is used to compute a Primary Insurance Amount (PIA) that determines the level of payments to be made to the beneficiaries of the account.

As a consequence, linking the ER to tax records augments the tax information by using other data on the same individual. The linkage provides a cycle from individual's tax records to account and then back to those same records.

Proceeding from the SSN of a taxpayer to the data on benefits paid to beneficiaries of the account provides a connection from the individual's tax records to a number of beneficiary records, one of which *may* represent the original individual. Other beneficiaries may themselves be taxpayers. Linking a taxpayer to benefit records and linking those benefit records to taxpayers may create a chain that involves tax records other than those with identified SSN's. For example, consider a wage earner with a *rentier* wife. The earner's identified

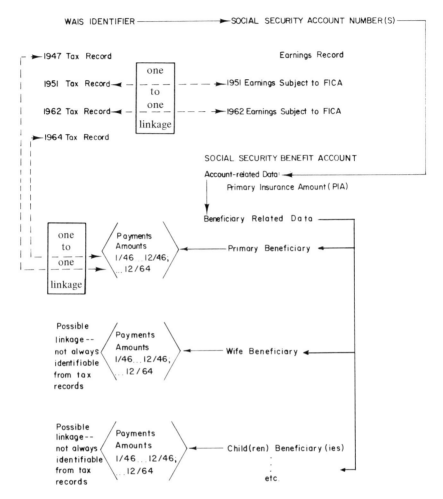

Figure 4-4. Record- and Unit-Linkage Involving Social Security Data

SSN may entitle his spouse to benefits; her tax return may not include a valid SSN. Linkage of beneficiary records to the taxpayer sample may involve individuals outside the sample of tax records (children and wives who never received income reported for tax purposes). See Figure 4–4.

Thus the benefit data posed a problem unlike any other part of the WAIS archive. The data created an extension of the original sample—an extension which could not be ignored. Individuals in the sample extension "represent" a group of beneficiaries included in the sample itself—namely, persons in the tax record sample who received benefits from an account excluded from the name-group sample. For example, a widow who moves to Wisconsin need never report the SSN of her husband on her Wisconsin tax returns. Thus we have no way of knowing that this woman is receiving widow's benefits. Yet it is quite possible that other income is reported on Wisconsin tax returns. These ideas are sketched out in Venn diagrams in Figures 4-5 and 4-6.

The fact that none of the three universes—taxpayers, SSN holders, and beneficiaries—includes all members of the population is made clear in Figure 4-5. Linking beneficiary data to samples of tax records implies tht WAIS samples universe I with the extension into III that we have just discussed. However, the problem is equally serious if linkage had originated in II since a number of persons never obtained their own SSN but might well be members of I or III. The intersection of II and III delimits the population of potential primary beneficiaries. [9] Linkage of a sample of I to that intersection establishes the one-to-one correspondence of records alluded to in Figure 4-4.

In Figure 4-6 the complexities of the actual samples drawn are illustrated by elaborating the basic idea of Figure 4-5. The straight lines indicate the division of the population according to the status of the SSN:

Those with no SSN fall below line A.

Those with no identified SSN fall below line B. (The difference is due to response error).

Those identified accounts which paid benefits (according to SSA records prior to 1966) fall below line C and above line B (sample groups 3, 9).

Samples of tax records yield the component samples 1-8 (corresponding to I in

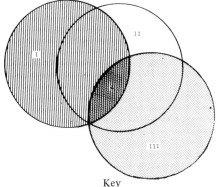

Key

I.   Taxpayers
II. Ever registered for a
     social security account
     prior to 1966

III. Legal beneficiaries of
     social security account
     numbers

Figure 4-5. Extension of WAIS Sample Through Beneficiary Population

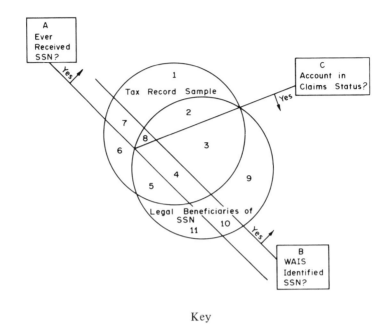

Key

1–8	Tax Record Sample	1–3	ER matched to tax sample
1–4, 7–10	Adults who applied for SSN prior to 1966	4, 7, 8	Unknown SSN of tax-payers; also taxpayers not matched to valid ER
3–4	Accounts in claims status, or terminated prior to 1966; also primary bene-ficiaries of the accounts	4	Taxpayers who are un-known to be primary beneficiaries
2, 5, 8, 9–11	Other legal beneficiaries of 3–4	8, 10	Unknown beneficiaries who are legally entitled from 4
		2, 5	Taxpayers who are known beneficiaries of other SSN than their own

Figure 4-6. Extension of the WAIS Sample Through Beneficiaries of Identified SSN

Figure 4-5). Sample 9 corresponds to only a portion of population III shown in Figure 4-5. Persons who can not be linked to a taxpayer have been excluded. Samples 3–4 include primary beneficiaries while sample 4 indicates missing data for primary beneficiaries linked to the tax sample. The remaining groups are described in the key to Figure 4-6.

Because of the extension of the sample, some beneficiaries lacked an identifier assigned through the tax-record sample. Even if an identifier had been assigned, it was not always the one associated with the account number that generated the beneficiary information. As likely as not, it would be beneficiary information for the spouse of the man who held the account—but which spouse?

Clearly a careful process of identifying the beneficiaries and checking their characteristics against data available in the ID File was a prerequisite to the processing of data.

The logic of links between the record universes and the samples drawn and the earlier description of the structure of information obtained from SSA provides the background necessary to understand the processing of the benefit data.

4.6 Processing the Social Security Benefit Data

The SSA identified 3217 SSN's as accounts in "claims status." That is, some individual had received or was entitled to receive benefits on the account. This information is shown as File 3 in Figure 4-2. Figure 4-7 shows the manner in which data on the payments made to the beneficiaries was collected by SSA.

The data collected cover payments from January 1, 1946, through a variable closing date, which depends upon the date the data were extracted by SSA. All information prior to 1962 was hand-coded from records kept in the regional benefit payment centers. This information was supplied on Form 9249. In addition, accounts that were not terminated prior to 1962 were reported on a standard listing taken from the SSA current beneficiary master file after the December 1965 entries were made.

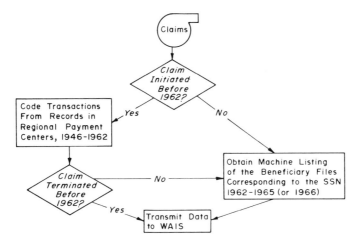

Figure 4-7. SSA Operations in Collecting Benefit Data

Once data had been received by WAIS, processing proceeded according to a familiar pattern described in detail in Figure 4-8:

a. Data were logged.
b. Identifiers were assigned.
c. Records were coded, keypunched, and verified.
d. Card images were edited.
e. Inter-record checks were performed.
f. Annual benefit payments were computed from the completed records.

Some comments on these steps are presented below.

The SSA sent benefit data in small groups. Summary information was punched in logging cards to provide a tally of data received and the portion of the file processed. The first data were received in May and June of 1965. As of June 1, 1966, benefit data for 2810 claims cases had been received. The final installment of the remaining cases was not received until September 1967. Benefit data were ultimately received for 3208 identified claims.

Given the logic of the relationships between beneficiaries of the account and changes in benefit payments, it was necessary to provide for varying numbers of *beneficiaries* and varying numbers of *transactions* in recording the claims history associated with any given account. [10]

After precoding and ID assignment, the benefit data were keypunched directly from the SSA forms. The matching of beneficiaries to tax record ID's and assignment of new ID's to the additional individuals encompassed by beneficiary records are explained in Appendix B.

Single Card Edits

The general card edit program (see Chapter 6) was used extensively for checking errors in the benefit data cards. The program checked the internal validity of the following data and control items:

Study number	SSA beneficiary ID codes
Card number	Date of birth
Sequence number	Date of entitlement
Blanks in the record	Sex
WAIS ID numbers	Type of claim

Other Edits

In addition to checking the internal consistency of the several types of cards, it was also desirable to check the consistency of all the cards associated with an

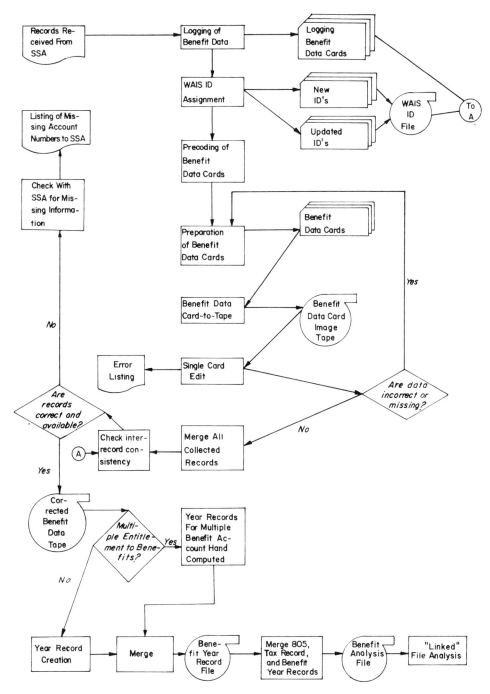

Figure 4-8. Flow of Operations in Processing Beneficiary Data

account or with a beneficiary. The following checks were completed and the resulting errors corrected:

Consistency checks involving only benefit data:
  Duplicate cards in a sequence.
  Missing cards in a sequence.
  Proper chronology of history entries.
  Last history entry for beneficiaries consistent with account data.
  Correct number of beneficiaries.
Consistency checks involving other WAIS files:
  Benefit data must exist for each account logged in. (Check against the Logging File.)
  Benefit data must exist for each individual who is assigned an ID and who is identified with an account in claims status. (Check against the ID File.)

Year Record Creation

The basic reason for transforming the benefit data into year records was to make a record that could be related to the annual tax data collected by WAIS. The process of creating year records involved five basic steps:

a. The data unit was transformed from a nesting of records by SSA beneficiary account numbers to a nesting of records by WAIS ID's.
b. Change of payment transactions were cumulated over time and reinterpreted as monthly accruals over the entire period.
c. Monthly payments were aggregated according to encoded data which were required to convert records from benefits accrued to cash.
d. Year records were then created for each beneficiary for each year that he received benefits during the 1946–1964 period. Months-beneficiary-worked during the year and the beneficiary codes that describe the relationship of beneficiary to primary beneficiary were transcribed from the transactions entries and the beneficiary records to the benefit-year record.
e. The final step in creating the benefit-year records involved much the same problem as that of constructing ER's for persons with multiple accounts. About 125 persons were receiving benefits through both their own account number and their entitlement to husband or wife benefits. The total annual benefit from both accounts was computed by hand. The resulting amounts were then encoded in the format of benefit-year records and were merged with the computed benefit-year amounts available from the remaining cases. [11]

The last stage in the data integration was the creation of a single record for each individual; this record contained a summary of data extracted from individual tax-year records, the WAIS earnings record, and the benefit-year data. (The identifier for this file is BNAN.)

4.7 Summary

In this chapter we described two aspects of data linkages: The nature of the information linked and the concepts underlying the process of building linked records.

Discussion of the substance of the data linked indicates that different measures of the same phenomenon provide consistency and validation checks. Vexing problems arise when one measurement is truncated or missing altogether, so that information available for a particular person becomes a nonrectangular array.

The process of building the data archive clearly illustrates several problems. Receiving data in batches over a period of time implied a need for iterative processing. Errors in the data files required recycling and correction of records. Changes in identifiers that link records for the same person in different files required both sophistication in error correction and some theory about record correspondences. The latter involved analysis of sample extension.

Several of the problems encountered in handling the social security data are sufficiently universal to warrant further discussion. The following two chapters are devoted to both a history of the data correction techniques used in the archive and a discussion of the strategies used for building linkages and optimal storing of data in permanent files.

5 The Methodology of Data Development

5.1 Concepts for Data Handling

In this section we describe aspects of the data that will later be used to suggest some general principles for handling large data archives. Three concepts—recycling, data descriptors, and convenient data linkages—are central to the discussion. They are interrelated and best described jointly (and briefly) at the outset, then separately and in detail.

The essential ingredients of the *recycling process* are outlined in the flow chart in Figure 5-1. This chart was formulated in 1964 in connection with the development of the first collection of tax records. [1] The process envisaged storage of information in sequential order on magnetic tape. (Storage of information on disk modifies the approach but retains the basic concept of recycling. We discuss economies of disk storage later on in this chapter (see also Dodd, 1969).

The ingredients of the process described are not novel by any means. Every business accounting operation must have the same capability of updating files as that of the cycle illustrated. In a business application, error correction messages (or transactions) become new information about an account; and records that are recycled because of changes in the identifying number might reflect changes in the structure of accounts due to consolidation or reclassification of account information.

The unique aspect of the recycling process pictured in Figure 5-1, even at this early stage in our development of recycling capabilities, was the generality of the software that had to be developed. Software had to deal with a variety of different file formats and accept changes in the data file in *any* identified field. The fact that errors could occur in any portion of the file in turn implied that some unique system would have to be created to describe data elements.

To aver that each datum should be uniquely named is trivial. What requires sophistication is to assure that such names are legible to program compilers, clerical staff, and analysts. Furthermore, the algorithm for assigning names must assure that identical data from several points in time are related by their nomenclature while identical measures from different data sources are adequately differentiated.

In their initial approach to nomenclature, WAIS programmers revealed the difficulties that follow from a laissez faire approach. Programmers named data according to character positions and variables in a long array. Errors were cor-

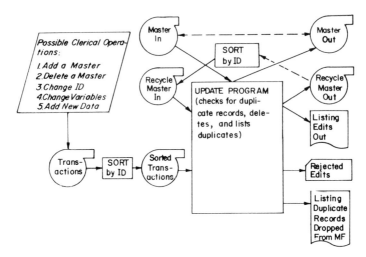

Figure 5-1. Edit and Master File Updating Run

rected by naming the index of the appropriate element of the array. In practice, this system led to numerous failures. Programmers could easily err in the assignment of an index in developing programs to detect errors. Coders could easily transpose the digits of an index or otherwise introduce errors into their instructions for correcting a record. And if coders *were* correct, the keypuncher could still fail to reproduce the coded forms accurately. Finally, identical information in two different files would almost never have the same array identifier.

As a consequence, the early practice of using array positions or character positions to address the field undergoing correction was soon dropped. In its place the staff developed standard mnemonics, *data descriptors,* that were used to locate fields at every stage of data development and error correction. The use of standard mnemonics did not limit programmers in any way, since equivalence assignments could always be used to take advantage of treating information as arrays. [2]

Since several distinct physical files contain information about the same individual, the process of error correction immediately introduces the possibility that part of the file is corrected while another logically related part in a different file is uncorrected. The worst aspect of such a "partial correction" process occurs when the identifier or sequence number on one file has been altered, while the identifier in another file remains in its original form. [3] The best solution to this problem is to retrieve records "in parallel" from the several files while corrections are being made. Such an approach requires direct access (disk or drum) storage. With sequential media, failure to note the status of the different files could clearly lead to great confusion. Thus, some kind of housekeeping is required to insure that all corrections to the files are made to keep the different types of records about an individual in compatible form. This notion was conveyed in the *file status*.

The file status was incorporated into the label of each machine-readable file. Each time the file was corrected and altered the file status was incremented. Thus BNAN (1) was the original analysis tape produced by integrating the data described in Chapter 4; BNAN(2) was a corrected successor, etc. [4]

Another aspect of the existence of several files is the fact that it must be possible to determine what types of records exist for any given individual. This information needs to be readily accessible so that any matching of records between files can be double checked. (Often the process of merging files will result in omitted records due to the intervention of computer operators, improper programming, or difficulties with system procedures for handling the end of a reel of tape. In this case a catalog of the number of correct matches that should have occurred is an extremely helpful control on the data processing).

Linkage of records through a retrieval system becomes necessary as soon as the amount of information exceeds that which can economically be stored in a single file. The existence of asymmetries in the type of information available (itemized deductions for some individuals, standard deductions for others), different units of analysis (individuals versus tax years), and missing data all imply that an exhaustive array of all potential data is extremely inefficient for storing information. The need to compact the file brings with it the need to recreate a vector containing appropriate data for editing and analysis. With sequential media this can be done by extracting, transforming, and merging information from several files into a single record. The extracted record provides information that is redundant with parts of the original file but is accessible. Alternatively, direct access media and pointers can be used to link the basic files and access desired information without redundancies. This alternative is discussed at length in Section 5.4 and Chapter 8. For the moment, we will deal with the problem of organizing the file so that records can be reliably extracted. To that end *record indicators* were designed and collated.

The most obvious location for record indicators pertaining to an individual appeared to be the ID File. However, several problems arose in conceptualizing how much information should be included as a record indicator associated with the ID File. One problem arose from the various stages of progress in processing the file. The record information for the first collection had been completely edited by 1967, while information for the second collection was not even in machine-readable form at that time.

In addition, the open-ended character of the WAIS archive created a second and related problem. Until final edited versions of the basic files in the archive were available, it was not possible to determine how many records of a given type were nested within the individual's record. For example, dividend data for a given year would provide a clear indication that information on particular assets should be present in the Property File; however, that information would not indicate how many different types of holdings might be reported.

A third problem was tactical: the effort that was required to construct a set of record indicators describing file structure might be almost as large as the effort required to create simple analysis extracts combining the information in various files. Unless savings are realized from the repeated use of record indicators in retrieving data, no purpose is served by creating record indicators. Indeed the rational limit to the resources that can be invested in the creation of record indicators is determined by the savings of computer and staff time expected in applications of the indicators. This consideration forces simplicity on both the programs creating indicators and on the information included in the indicators. Fortunately, even simple indicators proved worthwhile in the development of analysis files; programmers were delighted not to have to worry about the logic of matching records—all of that information was included in the record indicators.

To meet the requirements of the record indicators, the concept of a History Selection File (HSF) was developed. An abstract of key information from each of the seven basic data files was recorded in a single HSF that served as reference to the major files:

File	Datum Recorded in HSF	Name of Indicator
ID	ID; SSN	$ID; SSN$
MF	Record available, year t?	x_t $t = 1 \ldots 18$
P	Record available, year t?	y_t $t = 1 \ldots 18$
ER	Valid earnings record matched?	e
BN	Benefits paid this person?	b
IN	Interview sample? Interview taken?	z
AD	Asset diary left? Completed?	d

The intersection of values for $x, y, \ldots, d$ could then be used to define relevant subsets of the total file. [5] In addition to the indicators listed, the HSF included a subset of basic data on each file. The HSF also provided coded explanations of missing records for an individual whose data were incomplete.

With this brief discussion of recycling, data descriptors, and linkage and retrieval systems in mind, we return to a more complete discussion of each, beginning with the evolution of the WAIS recycling capabilities.

5.2 Recycling

The first collection of tax-record data was processed almost entirely by means of special-purpose programs written in machine assembly language for the IBM 1410 (in spite of the fact that the IBM 650 was the machine available at the outset of the project). Effective use was made of IBM's available sort and merge routines for file handling, but the operation of introducing corrections into the file was specific to the original file formats developed for the tax record. The discovery of 29 cases in which originally coded fields were exceeded implied a need for modification of the maintenance program to deal with larger fields. While assembly language programming optimized the speed with which the data were processed, it proved rigid and could only be used by the particular individuals who developed the program.

Beginning in 1965, the availability of COBOL on the IBM 1410 made it realistic to think of expanding the format-specific program, whose general features are diagrammed in Figure 5-1, to deal with generalized files. The result of this generalization was UPDATEAL. The flexibility and legibility of a program designed in COBOL had to be weighed against the limitations of a generalized file maintenance program. As compared to a special-purpose routine, generality is likely to imply higher set-up costs, increased execution times, and the need for more attention to program parameter cards. However, a generalized routine is also susceptible to increased checking since it is executed in a number of different circumstances. It can relieve staff from burdensome mechanical chores of checking character locations and BCD character structure, and hence give them free time to consider more substantive problems.

In our view, the appropriate level of generality for a file management system used the power of COBOL file descriptions to advantage and provided a limited number of specific capabilities. Thus UPDATEAL was conceived and executed with the following general principles in mind.

General Requirements

In all cases where a data file is so large that file regeneration *de novo* is more expensive than maintenance by a special-purpose system, the system must allow for the following types of changes:

a. Add records.
b. Delete records: either (i) delete all observations for a particular unit, or (ii) delete only specific observations for a particular unit. The type of deletion may be made conditional on the existence of duplicate records for a particular observation or individual.
c. Delete variables within all observations.
d. Add variables to all observations (provided that these variables can be constructed by specific operations on already existing variables).
e. Change the contents of specific variables in specific observations.

The Concept of the "Double Identifier"

Another essential feature of a file maintenance system results from the necessity to safeguard against the application of changes to the wrong records due to mispunches, clerical errors, etc. The "double identifier" concept simply means tht a unit for which observations are contained on the file is identified by two fields on the record instead of one. Many of the WAIS files already carry this feature in the form of the WAIS ID (the "primary" identifier) and the SSN (the "secondary" identifier) for the same individual. The apparently redundant secondary identifier must be used by the file maintenance system in the following way:

a.   The maintenance program locates the "status" record, indicated by the primary identifier, on the affected file. (This file has been sorted on the primary identifier.)

b.   The program tests, on that record, the contents of the secondary identifier which is also indicated on the "change-generating input" record:

    (i)   If the test fails, the change is not made, and a message to that effect is produced on the printer.

    (ii)   If the test passes, the change is made.

Record of Changes Made

As an extra safeguard against the introduction of additional errors due to improper error correction, a field maintenance program should produce a printed version of the affected record, before as well as after the change was made. For very small files, where it is desirable as well as possible to maintain a printed version of the current file, this device will allow the researcher to "update" his printed file at a very low cost and with a minimal time lapse after his file has been updated. In general, such printouts allow for some feedback to ensure that the change was made correctly. They may also be used effectively in investigating the consequences of the change for other variables in the same record.

Activity Date

Not only do files require a file label containing information on the file status, individual records require a similar label. When a record is changed by the maintenance program, the activity date field on the new record should reflect the date, or the number of the updating cycle, when the last change was made.

Especially for files undergoing many changes in relatively short periods of time, this feature helps to trace the status of specific records in previous stages.

General Description–UPDATEAL

UPDATEAL is a set of generalized file maintenance programs, that can be adapted to virtually any sequentially arranged tape file by a few parameter changes in its COBOL source decks.

It has the capability to execute the changes described in General Requirements a–e above. The program can also be used for creating new tape files or portions of files from cards.

The records to be changed or added are specified on input cards together with the kind of action to be taken and the data to be used. No specific format for a transaction or detail file needs to be designed. The input data cards are subjected to intensive validity checks, and detailed diagnostic messages are provided during the four phases of the job. A detailed description of the program follows. The reader should note the relationship of the program to Figure 5-1.

Files to be maintained by UPDATEAL should be made up of BCD records between 25 and 999 characters in length. (If the record already has a terminating record mark, 1000 characters is the limit.) The file needs to be sorted in ascending order (based on the computer's collating sequence) on at the most 18 characters. The sortfield(s) [control-field(s), or sort key(s)] can be located anywhere in the record and their number is limited only by the total sortfield length of 18 characters.

UPDATEAL consists of four phases. In phase 1 the input cards are checked and the data are set up in the format of the file to be updated. If any serious errors occur in the input cards, the job will be interrupted at the end of this phase. In phase 2, the records set up in phase 1 are passed against the file and the specified action is taken. If at the end of phase 2 no changes to the sortfield(s) of a record have been made, the job is completed. Otherwise the records with the changed sortfield(s), which were put out on a recycle file, will be sorted in phase 3, and then in phase 4 merged with the updated file from phase 2. The detailed program structure is in Appendix D. An evaluation of the program's effectiveness is our next concern.

Evaluation

The concepts behind UPDATEAL were identical to the original assembly language recycling program. All changes in the file were in the form of "transactions." A batch of transactions was used to operate on records in the file, selectively producing listings of the action taken. Nothing in the UPDATEAL program provided: double checking on the record to be changed; assurance that the correct field was designated for change; or assurance that all the changes intended were actually executed. These double checks could be obtained only by a process that included reexamining the output file for the types of errors that were to be corrected, generating a new list of transactions, and processing through UPDATEAL for a second and perhaps a third time.

The cost of any one transaction was high. To establish a unique record required ten characters of identifying information since the ID, and the year of the record were all required. In addition to identifying the record, the field length and character position had to be defined by another four characters. As a consequence, a high volume of cards were generated for an extensive change, such as adding a record. Many minor changes required more information about the change than the actual information being changed. (For example, only one character of a field might be in error.)

The batch orientation of UPDATEAL programming implied that the entire file had to be processed whenever changes were made. The cost and inertia involved in this procedure implied that frequent emendations to the file were uneconomical in terms of staff time, computer time, and dollars. This created further problems when errors of one type were identified and later additional information on the same record had to be changed for another reason. Finally, problems experienced in changing identifiers lead to the notion that both ID and SSN should be included in the sorting field.

Evolution of Recycling Capabilities:
A First Iteration

The first step in solving these problems was to envision the processes of error detection and correction as a unified flow (as in Figure 2–2). The process of error detection should isolate problem records; correction should proceed on the problem file; and files should be merged only when completely updated. These ideas are conveyed in Figure 5–2.

A second step in improving error correction was to eliminate the possibility of error in the correction process. This was accomplished by requiring the *incorrect* datum as the key information needed to *perform* a correction. Until the values in the existing file were presented to the computer by the person editing a file, no changes could be made in them. This insight enabled us to check that the record and the field that was to be changed within the record were correctly identified.

The final step was to provide names for data that could be used in the development of programs and would uniquely identify data for the clerical staff.

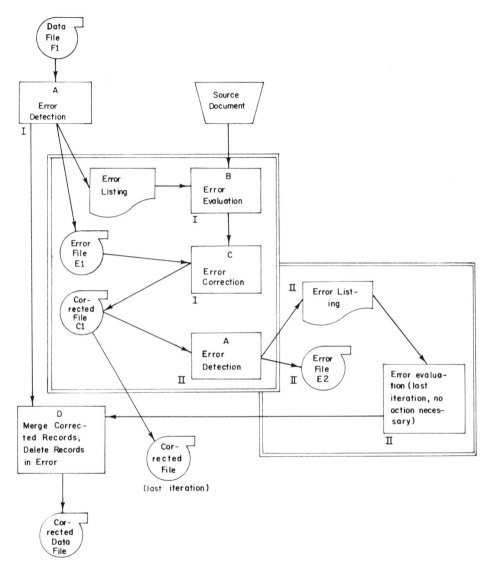

Figure 5-2. Basic Scheme for Error Correction

The names were independent of the particular file in which data were embedded. Those names were called *data descriptors*.

With this introduction, we proceed to discuss Figure 5-2 in detail. [6] Figure 5-2 illustrates two aspects of the correction process that were not made

explicit earlier. (1) The error detection process must be repeated until no further action is deemed necessary. Successive iterations insure that corrections
have been properly executed. (2) Most correction processes involve a stage of
evaluation where decisions are made outside the original programming framework through which errors were detected. (This phase of the problem was not
shown in Figure 5-1.) The repetitive nature of error correction is suggested by
the double box which includes a module of operations. Those marked I are required to complete the first iteration of corrections. The error detection marked
II is necessary to assure that the corrected file is satisfactory. If not, output becomes input in the next iteration of error evaluation and correction. The module
of operations in the double box can be repeated until acceptable error tolerances
are reached.

A natural further development is to increase the ease with which error
detection can be applied to offending records. This is accomplished by segregating such records into an error file at the time errors are detected. Correcting
and manipulating a few records in an error file is clearly less costly than embed-
ding the process in an environment of correct records that need not be interrogated. (In the framework of UPDATEAL error records were not segregated.)
Iterative application of the correction process produces a sequence of error
files. With each iteration a smaller number of records will be segregated as error
records. Until acceptable error tolerances are reached, changes are made *within*
a record (operations 3, 4, and 5 in Figure 5-1); only when correction is considered satisfactory are the corrected records inserted in place of records
originally in the data file (operations 1 and 2 in Figure 5-1).

Evolution of Recycling Capabilities:
A Second Iteration

The immediate problem that generated UPDATEAL concerned a general
capability for file maintenance. The limitations of programs specific to particular files or structured to use only one type of hardware led us to focus attention
on a general program written in a language adaptable to several computer en-
vironments. In the process, programmers focused on the efficiency of certain
techniques: checking the transactions file; sorting and merging the corrected
files; and maintaining control over the entire process through adequate documentation, diagnostics, messages to the computer operator, and contingency routines.

Like Ponce de Leon, we had no sooner discovered one fountain of efficiency than visions of others beckoned us onwards. The processing of the second
batch of tax records led us to realize that a serious communication problem had
developed between the programming and the clerical staff. This problem was
resolved by the use of the data descriptor. At the same time the unwieldy
character of updating files stored on sequential media led us to exploit disk
storage, interactive data entry, and direct-access files.

UPDATEAL embodies a technique for handling sequential files in a batch orientation. It is a capability that must be used when software does not conveniently, and inexpensively, handle interactive file manipulation. Where system procedures exist for efficiently allocating secondary storage and retrieving data, great economies can be realized from altogether different approaches to file maintenance. These approaches are discussed in the following chapters. We shall see that interactive correction (Section 6.2), file segmentation (Section 7.6), and file linkage (Section 5.4) all contribute to a more efficient approach to data management. Unlike the sequential mode of operation that characterizes UPDATEAL, an interactive program can avoid regeneration of large parts of the file that are not in error. The development of recycling and error correction capabilities following these discoveries will be described in some detail in Chapter 6.

The next section describes in detail the role of the data descriptor in processing data. The chapter concludes with discussion of the data linkage problems and solutions (Section 5.4).

5.3 Data Descriptors

Basic Concept

A data descriptor is an acronym for a longer word or phrase. It must be unambiguous and expressive of concept and meaning. Data descriptors are frequently used in special-jargon conversations and by programmers attempting to make their program "understandable." They arise spontaneously, but seldom develop as a standard set shared by even a small group concerned with the same project. A set of data descriptors defines the logical record. The set element corresponds to the data elements comprising the logical record within the computer. The merits of standard data descriptors are numerous:

New researchers in the group can be more easily initiated and face less liklihood of finding undocumented concepts in programs.

Programmers, specifically, can incorporate data descriptors throughout all programming efforts.

Outsiders can be easily oriented in their search for information, which minimizes their frustration.

Group communication is less cumbersome.

Analysis has a standard tool for specifying procedures.

The value of the descriptors will be illustrated by WAIS experiences.

At the outset, WAIS used abbreviations like NTI and AGI which derived from tax return terminology (i.e., net taxable income and adjusted gross income). These mnemonics were not too formidable. However, cross-tabulation programs required many more abbreviations. Adding to an already complex situation, different analyses and different individuals used different abbreviations. At the same time file maintenance programs, such as UPDATEAL, were oriented to character positions, making preparation of correction transactions tedious. Furthermore, correcting errors required identifiers different from error evaluation, thus producing minimal feedback to the correction process. Though standardization appeared useful, the failure to adopt data descriptors at the outset suggests that benefits were evidently not perceived initially as greater than the cost and burden involved. Standardization carries with it inflexibility and an overhead cost required to train workers to use the standard descriptors. However, intelligent choice of mnemonics using clues from source documents can minimize these costs.

WAIS concluded from its early experiences that a standard set of data descriptors would greatly facilitate processing the second collection of tax records.

A set of abbreviations for all variables on the MF was prepared when the second collection of MF data was still in card form. These abbreviations were in lieu of character position in error detection and correction. A priori, the data descriptors appeared superior to character or array positions since clerical staff were to correct errors by sending messages to the computer through on-line teletypes. The descriptors maximized the common features of the tax record as a document and the names of variables in machine-readable form. One of the specifications of our on-line correction program was that the data descriptors were used to identify data elements within the computer record.

Recent Applications

Following the application of data descriptors to error correction, the descriptors were consciously incorporated into the planning of all data processing. They were used in COBOL file descriptions and ALGOL error detecting programs. Use of descriptors increased the legibility of programs, since mnemonics standardized variable name creation for new fields created by a program. Programmers used the data descriptors directly or at least as roots. Armed with a set of data descriptors, the programmer was free to establish equivalences. This enabled him to use more powerful indexing procedures on the array. At the same time, the equivalences provided an automatic dictionary of the indices that might be used and made it possible for the programmer to locate any specific element in the array without counting or incrementing an index. In files as complex as ours, this proved a tremendous timesaver. Thus, AGI, the twentieth element in an array being processed, could be addressed directly since the inclusion of equivalences between array elements and data descriptors was set forth automatically at the outset of the program. [7] On the other hand, the rounding of all fields to the nearest $100 could still be executed by a single routine indexed over the entire array.

While planning a complex program, it is most natural to use descriptors rather than specific array designators, especially in the flowchart stage. The descriptors also can be used as the basis for ALGOL (or COBOL) label and procedure declarations. For example, the computer was directed to the procedure labeled AGIOK whenever the computed value of AGI, labeled AGI1, corresponded to the coded AGI value. Similarly, the procedure AGICHECK contained the tests on AGI. This labeling made reading of the program much easier.

The descriptors were very helpful when expanding on the program after a few days absence. Instead of relearning the array positions of various fields, the programmer could return almost directly to the coding. In addition, changes in the list and format were much easier than changes in array positions. Changing one subscript requires that all subsequent positions be changed. For example, though the four-digit field containing age of dependents was originally designated AGE, it could be decomposed into four one-digit fields without changing complex programming for remaining fields of the record.

Data descriptors not only provided common nomenclature, but they also automatically provided good housekeeping. The specified width assured appropriate interpretation of BCD characters, and in COBOL automatically provided editing for signs and alphabetic characters.

Still another aspect of the data descriptor is that particular mnemonics can be derived from the descriptor to deal with specific values. TERR9 is an easy device for defining those instances in which the content of TERR equals 9. This device has been particularly useful in dealing with missing data codes. Such codes represent information about data quality that must often be coded in a content field to warn the unsuspecting user who might otherwise interpret a blank field as legitimate and null data.

5.4 Predecessor and Successor Relations Among Data Descriptors

Use of the data descriptors rapidly evolved from identifying information to identifying the structure through which information was processed. A logical extension of the latter was to use the data descriptor as the basis for file documentation. The information identified by a descriptor ultimately has its source in one of the underlying documents or files received by WAIS. The process of derivation from those files could clearly be presented as a directed graph in which the original elements of the document become combined by mathematical functions into complicated variables (Harary et al., 1965).

The use of a graph to present the sources of information is particularly important since tax records come from a variety of legal forms in the various years under study. The variety of forms not only reflects the vagaries of administrative process, but also shows subtle changes in income definition that are sometimes lost in the process of attempting to integrate information about several years. For example, the nondeductible portion of medical expenses was changed from $50 to $75 in 1954. The field designated "medical expense deduction" on the master tax record does not include a caveat indicating the different interpretation that must be placed on the information. The use of a directed-graph to describe the origin of data makes it possible to define such changes in the meaning of machine-readable information. Over the period spanned by the MF, changes in social patterns—divorce, unemployment, and home ownership—necessitated modifications of specific entries on the tax document to respond to changes in the prevalence of alimony, unemployment compensation, and mortgage interest.

An illustration may serve to make the use of data descriptors and predecessor-successor relations more concrete. Figure 5–3 indicates the derivation of one datum that appears in the MF. WAGE1 is its data descriptor. The content of WAGE1 is the largest amount of wage or salary income reported by the taxpayer. The information was derived from a specific location on each tax document. In fact, those locations can be described by four classes that cover the possibilities on all types of tax documents used from 1946–1964. In the case of wage and salary income a specific entry was made on each tax return in each year; for other items the situation is not so simple. Unemployment compensation, for example, was taxable as part of state net taxable income throughout the period covered by the WAIS archives. However, the state tax authorities included a special entry for this type of income only in 1964, making it likely that the item could appear almost anywhere on the tax document in other years, if it was reported at all.

The datum WAGE1 is an input to the consistency checking program that identified logical errors in the relationship among the items of information reported by the taxpayer. In some cases the errors were committed in the processing of the data; in other cases errors were due to the arithmetic inconsistencies actually on the tax document. The inconsistency was flagged by TERR and the item WAGE1 was altered when the error could be unambiguously attributed to WAIS or taxpayer errors; otherwise the error was allowed to remain in the completed MF (see Chapter 6). This error correction process indicates that the graph for the definition of a datum may often include a cycle in which original entries to the file are modified by a process that reviews the original documents and overrides the original entry.

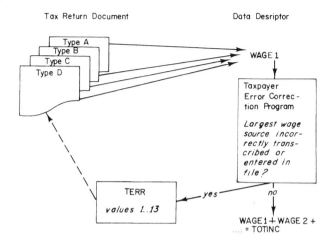

Figure 5-3. A Graph of the Source, Feedback, and Successor Relationships Implicit in the WAGE1 Field of the Completed Master File

Figure 5-4 indicates how the items of information in the file are logically related by what we have termed predecessor and successor relationships. The figure illustrates the relationships for a particularly simple instance, the case in which taxpayers filed "short forms" in 1963 or 1964. Thus the figure only deals with one of the four classes of documents shown in Figure 5-3. Other graphs pertain to the other types of documents. The graph describing the origin of the datum WAGE1 is now embedded in a larger graph that describes the source and logical relationships that affect TOTINC. Five items of information are required to test the consistency of TOTINC on the tax document. These are the predecessors of TOTINC—namely WAGE1, WAGE2, OTHWGE, OTHERY, and UNEMP. In turn, both the amount of STNDED and NTI depend directly on the amount of TOTINC. Hence, these items are shown as successors to TOTINC in the graph.

The A-card intervening between the tax document and OTHERY indicates that coders were asked to make special note of information about income sources described as "other income" to permit the classification of that amount by type. In most cases, however, classification was impossible and OTHERY represents a conglomeration of small amounts of dividends, interest, and any other miscellaneous income sources accruing to the taxpayer.

Once the graph for each data descriptor has been drawn (as in Figure 5-4) we obtain a complete system of documentation for the process by which the datum in the final file was derived. Only the relationships indicated by the heavy lines need to be shown for the graph of TOTINC since the remaining relationships will be included in the graphs for other data descriptors. The consistency required of TOTINC is implied by the fact that the two heavy arrows enter *A;* the predecessors of TOTINC are the nontrivial constraint on values of A. The

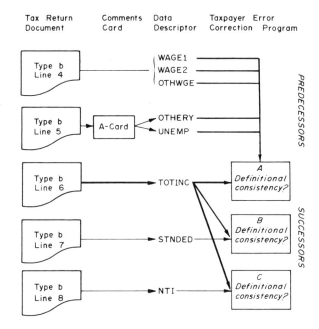

Figure 5-4. A Graph of Source, Predecessor, and Successor Relationship to TOTINC

consistency implied by TOTINC is represented by the successors to TOTINC.

The graph can be compressed into a compact notation by representing the relationships through a list:

WAGE1, WAGE2, OTHWGE, OTHERY, UNEMP, 1, STNDED, NTI

The key element in the list is the number 1. It is a code describing the manner in which information in the data descriptor being documented was generated. The complete *variable classification* code used includes these values:

1 transfered directly from the tax document
2 transferred subject to the interpretation of a coder or keypuncher
3 transformed from other machine-readable data without reference to source documents
4 coded on the tax document or other codesheets prior to keypunching
5 undefined and not available in the source document

The data descriptors preceding the source variable classification are predecessors. The descriptors following are the successors of that descriptor. Relationships in the data that are implied by these first-order relationships among the data descriptors can be seen by chaining together the lists for several data descriptors. (Such chaining together of information about several data descriptors is illustrated in Figure 5–4 for the predecessors of TOTINC.)

Appendix E indicates the layout of documentation for data descriptors that define the source-of-income portion of the MF. In addition to the list of predecessors and successors that we have just described, each page includes three additional items of information: content qualification, file definition, and a narrative description. The first indicates where the user should look for information about the validity of the field; the second defines the physical location of the information in the permanent archive; and the third gives a brief summary of the internal memoranda that are pertinent to content and use of the datum in question.

The foregoing discussion has made clear that concepts initially tied to nomenclature and communication about items of data rapidly developed into a paradigm for thinking about the process of building a data archive. What had initially been a tool to aid clerical staff in dealing with the computer (and with programmers) became a technique for the designers of the archive to conceptualize what was to be done and what had been done—linking planning, execution, and documentation. The structure of data descriptors could be described by predecessor-successor relations quite apart from the mechanics of which computer or what clerical mechanism was used to generate and refine machine-readable data.

The description of data structures developed here will be useful in understanding the discussion of data linkage that follows.

5.5 Convenient Data Linkages

The problem of retrieving data from the WAIS archive was clear enough—logically related types of information needed to be assembled at low cost for statistical studies and verification with source documents. The unsolved question was whether a generalized system for retrieval could increase the speed, reliability, and completeness with which related items of information could be assembled from the basic archive. Design and maintenance of a system for retrieving data proved more complex than we had initially imagined.

The retrieval system devised entails the use of both record indicators and pointers. While record indicators provide information on the data structure, they must be embedded in a software system before the component parts of the archive are linked for substantive study. Pointers provide immediate access to the information that they reference and require a minimal software system to make use of linked data.

Our first concepts of retrieval were strongly influenced by the computer environment of the time. Limited computer memory, data stored on magnetic tape, and restrictions on the number of files that could be processed at any one time implied that retrieval could be achieved through a controlling file, the HSF, and record indicators. Some of the problems with this technique are outlined in the next section.

The limitations of the HSF led to a better conceptualization of the retrieval and linkage problem. At the same time, the availability of disk memory made it possible to concentrate on mechanisms for retrieving and linking data for an individual rather than on the mechanisms for handling blocks of identically formatted data for a large number of individuals. When attention was focused on the microcosm where information was to be retrieved, it became apparent that several types of references between the component items of data would be useful. In addition to the obvious linkage or cross-reference items of information for the same individual at the same point in time, there were both analytical and mechanical advantages in retrieving information on several individuals with common characteristics at one point in time, or information about the same individual at several points in time.

This section discusses the conceptualization of record linkages. The section concludes with illustrations of linkage successfully completed. (Those links were required for the analyses discussed in Section 3.2.)

File Integration on Sequential Media

One of the major mechanical problems in dealing with a large and diverse set of data files such as WAIS is that each of the basic files contains a different number of "observations," so that several records in one file may correspond to one record in another file. For example, several years of tax records in the MF correspond to one entry identifying a person in the ID File.

In order to facilitate the integration of these files, the HSF extracted indicators of the information available for each person. HSF contained all pertinent identification numbers and enabled the user to cross-index data available on a given individual. Using the entry recorded in the HSF, it was possible to select people by SSN or by the ID number that WAIS assigned. It was also possible to determine whether entries existed for those persons in the MF, Property File, or Benefit File, etc. The HSF thus cross-referenced ID numbers and records based on different units of analysis and different data collection techniques. Data could then be retrieved in parallel fashion from several files.

Keeping the HSF up-to-date proved to be a major problem. By the time one set of information was updated, another set of edits would reveal inconsistencies that had to be corrected. As a result, an early concept of the HSF that included details of record structure and some descriptive variables, was dropped in favor of a less ambitious objective. The cross-reference provided by the file was limited to Boolean variables; each variable indicated the existence of information in the corresponding file. These variables were added to the basic ID at the time that identifiers in the various files were checked against the identifier available in the ID.

Concepts of Links Between Files

The difficulties with extracting and maintaining the HSF in a useful form indicated a need for conceptualizing the retrieval problem and specifying the gains to be obtained from alternative systems of data linkage. The effort required to maintain the HSF could not be allowed to prevent substantive analysis from proceeding.

The most primitive notion of linkage is to assemble those data which have a common identifying number from the various subfiles. While this approach capitalizes on the most obvious feature of the data, its limitations are extreme. The mechanical matching of data with common identifiers offers no principle by which multiple records in one file can be easily merged with another. Absence of data in one of the subfiles also leads to immediate problems. Thus it does not seem obvious that assembling all the data for a single identifier has particular merit. The simplistic representation shown in Figure 1–1 must be developed. Logical relationships between elements in the subfiles must be brought to bear on the problem if missing data and multiple observations are to be correctly interpreted.

A second concept of linkage is to generate a rectangular array of the information available. The array incorporates the principles of replication responsible for the observations at hand. In the case of the tax archive, individuals constitute one dimension in which observations are replicated; years in time constitute a second; and types of assets, a third. We can conceive of storing all the available information in a large matrix indexed over individuals, time, and assets. The difficulty with this type of linkage is that much of the matrix will be empty. Many taxpayers have no portfolio assets; many individuals are not filing tax returns in some of the sampled years; and some assets are not in existence at different points in time. Thus the large array creates as many problems as it solves. Some points in the array are impossible (because the world is not really a neat Euclidian space); and some points are null or missing data.

Furthermore, indexing much of the information in the archive by asset type creates useless cross-referencing of information. It may be relevant to know a taxpayer's occupation in order to analyze his demand for a particular type of asset, but it is not at all clear that the level of charitable donations is required for that analysis. Similarly, there is no clear reason why detailed information on portfolio holdings is relevant to a study of geographical mobility. Thus some items of information that will be related (at great cost) by this matrix approach to linkage do not appear to be important or useful.

These two naive approaches to data linkage—compacting data under a common identifier and arraying data in the space determined by the replications underlying the observations—are clearly straw men. Nonetheless, their deficiences make clear that linkage is not a trivial problem and an analysis of the data structure allows substantial economy in retrieving information.

Gains from Data Linkage

At the risk of belaboring the obvious, we remind the reader of the gains to be achieved from data linkage. Substantive gain results from the ability to link information in the various records included in the archive and analyze the relationships implicit in the data structure. Without linkage the value inherent in the several data bodies cannot be exploited. A well-designed retrieval system also increases the reliability of record matching from the various subfiles and facilitates merging of data from the various records assembled in the archive.

A second benefit from linkage is the ability to use data in one file to validate and correct data in other files. This benefit can only be realized if information is both easily retrieved and easily stored in the original files. This two-way communication with the underlying records is more demanding of computer resources and systems planning than the one-way retrieval required to extract and assemble data for statistical analysis.

A third benefit of linkage results from the ability to relate records that share common features. Establishing such a link may greatly enhance the efficiency of computer computations. Two examples illustrate this principle.

The assembly of joint tax returns from the available data requires knowledge of the tax information from both partners. Unless the file has been carefully organized for that purpose, the income information may be difficult or impossible to assemble. For example, if the marriage partners are not identified by a retrievable key, no matching is possible. [8] Alternatively, if the records are randomly placed in a large file, the cost of finding the information for both marriage partners may be extremely high, even though matching is possible.

Another example of the gains from a retrieval system that links records with common features is seen in the valuation of assets held by individual taxpayers. Tens of thousands of different assets are owned by a large number of taxpayers. Price and yield data in a separate file of information classified by asset identifiers must be linked with information on the individual's holdings. How this can be done efficiently is not clear. Some price and yield information will never be needed to value the sample at hand; other information may be required for the majority of portfolios. Since it is not possible to have *all* the price and yield data or *all* the portfolio holdings information in the computer memory at one time, it is necessary to exploit the relative frequency of holdings to keep the most needed information in the computer. We shall return to this problem later. For the present disucssion, we need only observe that some information about the portfolio of individual *j* may be relevant to programming decisions that must be made when individual *i*'s assets are being valued.

With this motivation for linkage in mind, we return to the problem of conceptualizing the linkage. One tool that is useful is a graph of the relationships among the data elements.

A Graph-Theoretic Description of Data

In any case in which data elements are related one-to-one or one-to-many, the structure of the data can be described as a tree with varying numbers of branches. The only instance in which a more complicated relationship applies to the WAIS files is the benefit data that have been described earlier. The tree is an adequate device for dealing with varying numbers of observations. The observations may be replicated over persons, or over other observational units.

It thus appears logical to describe the tax-record data for a given household in the manner shown in Figure 5–5. The picture can be extended to include asset-year records for the individual and the ER data (Figure 5–6). Indeed, for many analysis problems it is likely that data outside the archive must be brought to bear upon the analysis, and a data structure like that in Figure 5–7 will be required. (This data structure has been used extensively in several of the analyses on the file.)

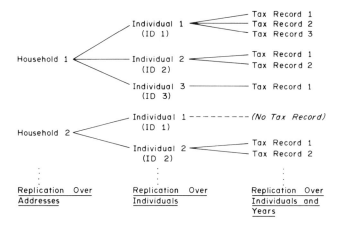

Figure 5–5. Nested Records Shown as a Data Tree

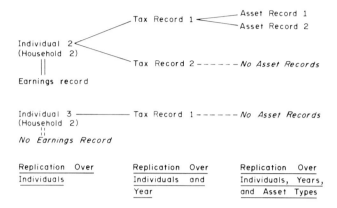

Figure 5-6. Extension of the Data Tree for Assets and Earnings Records

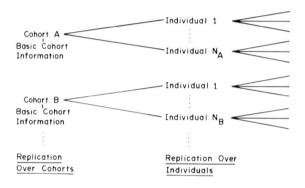

Figure 5-7. Extension of the Data Tree for Aggregate Information

Record Structure vs. Logical Structure

The illustrations make clear that the existence of some records may imply the existence of information; at the same time, records of that information may be missing from the archive and unavailable for analysis. For example, in Figure 5-6 one individual is associated with ER data; the other is not. (Section 4.5 indicated that more than a quarter of the individuals in the archive lack an ER.) The double bonds between files indicate a one-to-one correspondence of records. Thus no more than one ER is included in the archive for each individual for whom there would be an ID record.

Nonetheless, the physical record structure may hide some of the underlying logic of the data structure. The ER consists of four types of data. Some quantities are fixed for a particular individual, for example birth date (type A data). The remainder of the record consists of dated quantities: earnings that are repli-

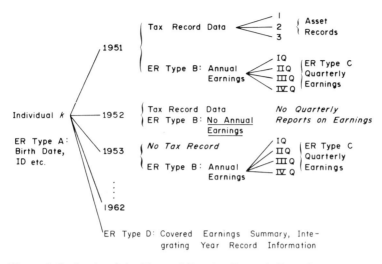

Figure 5–8. Logic of the Tax and Earning Records Data Structure

cated annually (type B data); quarterly information on covered earnings that are replicated every three months (type C data); and summary information that gives the total covered earnings at the time that the record was extracted from SSA files (type D data).

Knowledge of the logic of this data structure implies that the appropriate data tree for analysis purposes would appear as in Figure 5–8. Parallel observations of annual earnings recur in both the tax-record and ER files. The quarterly earnings data represent a radically different principle of replication within the ER than the replication associated with asset records.

Clearly, using the form of information storage found in the original data source is a course of action that commends itself only as a course of least resistance. Although record indicators such as those established in the HSF indicate the presence of relevant information in several files, assembling data within each file on an appropriate unit of replication is still a logical problem. The complexity of that problem can be alleviated by storing information according to the unit of replication: all cohort data in a cohort file; all individual data in individual files; all individual yearly data in a set of annual files, etc. Information using the same unit of replication need not be integrated in one file; several files of a like kind can be identified and cross-linked. The details and limitations of such links will be discussed below.

Storing information according to the logical unit of replication has an additional advantage. Data need only be recorded physically at one point in the archive of files. The computer can relate the component files of the archive just as one can trace back through the branches of the trees in Figure 5–8 to relate data to the groups within which they are nested. However, eliminating redundancies may decrease the reliability of file structure. For example, linkages or other critical information can be lost through parity errors.

In addition, redundancies may make it possible to retrieve information more quickly. Birth year provides an instructive example. Birth year is a fixed datum for the individual. Inserting birth year on the tax-record file requires four characters. Almost any retrieval system that would require linking tax records to the ER File would require so much computer effort and storage that it is not worth accessing the ER File for that one datum.

A third reason to eschew storage of all data according to its unit of replication is that some minimum of information is required in the subfile before it is worth the additional accounting required to keep track of identifiers, record counts, and linkages between the files. It would clearly be a waste of effort to store quarterly earnings codes (one character per quarter) in a subfile that would require yet another character to identify the quarter of the year to which the code referred. In such a case repetition of similar fields can be employed to economize storage. The order (position) of the elements yields the information as to the "quarter" of the earnings.

Sequential vs. Direct-Access Media

Nearly all the comments on data linkage that have been made up to this point are based on the assumption that data must be stored permanently on magnetic tape. In that case the ordering of physical records in sequence by identification number forms an implicit linkage between the information for different individuals. Often, the unavailability of tape drives and the unreliability of reading from tape constrains the number of files that can be manipulated simultaneously.

If information can be stored on disk or drum media, both the constraint of physical sequencing and the constraint of number of input devices are eliminated. The computer can visit locations where data are stored in any order, and provided that appropriate links are established, it can assemble information from a large number of files. [9] It is too early to guess what implications disk might have for an archive such as WAIS, but it is clear that we have been able to use disk media to great advantage for correcting and updating individual records. The value of disk for statistical analyses in which each datum is scanned only once is less clear, but potentialities are explored in Chapter 8.

Special-Purpose Solutions to the Retrieval and Linkage Problem

Before proceeding further, it may be wise to discuss how some special-purpose files were created for particular analyses. Each file establishes links among the eight basic files. The linkage in turn implies a distinct treatment of missing data and a unit for statistical analysis.

The most elementary analysis file (EXT 03) was created by extracting information about the major sources of income from the tax record and tagging each record with the birth year of the taxpayer. The resulting file treats each available tax record as a unit of observation and imputes no meaning to the absence of tax records.

A more elaborate analysis was undertaken for persons with at least four pairs of consecutive tax records. In this case the records were again tagged with the birth year. However, all the information in the tax records of a particular individual was summarized so the individual becomes the unit of analysis. This *longitudinal* file suppresses information about the timing of particular events. Moreover, persons observed for five consecutive tax records received equal weight in the analysis with persons observed for twelve. Again, no meaning was attributed to gaps in the filing of tax records or to the absence of records.

A third analysis was undertaken to investigate the problem of missing tax records by assembling an array of data from the tax record, the ER, and the benefit-year records. In this case any element of the rectangular array of feasible observations can be used as a datum; the time series observed for particular variables can also be studied. This flexibility permits analysis by both types of units mentioned above—individuals and individuals in a given year. The missing data in the array must be interpreted before statistics can be computed. If missing data are suppressed, the results are identical to those of the EXT 03 File described above; if values are attributed by missing plot techniques, more refined estimates can be obtained.

The fourth special-purpose file was created to simulate joint tax returns for individuals in 1958. The unit of observation was therefore the joint-return tax year. However, the computations required references to tax returns filed in four preceding years. Missing data was clearly a problem, and was imputed in some cases. A more serious difficulty arose from the fact that the same tax information might be required for two different tax computations when a woman leaves her husband and remarries.

These special-purpose analyses revealed a number of features of the data that are important for the creation of an efficient general-purpose retrieval system:

a. It is extremely useful to have the entire time series of data for a particular individual accessible for study and manipulation (seriatim ordering in a sequential file or double linkage with pointers in a direct-access file).

b. Substantial compaction, albeit with corresponding limitations on the analyses, can be achieved by segregating income-source information from other aspects of the tax record and asset files.

c. Efficiency in constructing extracts can be increased by preceding the time series of data with a vector describing the availability of information for that individual and his spouse.

    d.   A general approach to the missing-data problem in this file is still too complex to be tractable, and appropriate decisions on how to treat missing data must be handled separately for each analysis problem.

In the section that follows, we illustrate how these ideas influence the current file structures and linkages in the archive.

Implementation of the Logical Tree in the
Data Archive

Up to this point we have said nothing about the technique whereby the logical relationships between data elements exhibited in Figure 5–8 can be represented in the computer to provide linkage between the basic records of the data archive.

At the beginning of this section we indicated that record indicators cross-reference each of the six data files. The indicators on the file establish whether information exists in each of the six data files for each individual identification number. Those indicators are necessary to assure that the original files are properly matched, but they are not sufficient for most analysis purposes. In the four files that contain dated information—ER, Property, Tax Record, and Benefit—information is also required on which years include simultaneous measurements. If we are to know anything about the combined incomes of husband and wife, information is also required on the information available for the spouse.

A solution to this problem has been developed for the tax record. (The Property File poses more serious difficulties and will be discussed below.) A summary record for each household number is developed from the sequence of available tax records. The heart of each summary record is an array whose rows correspond to the individuals in the household and whose columns correspond to years from 1946 to 1964. [10] The entry in each cell of the array contains the following information:

	Code	
Tax record availability:	0	Available
	1–9	Reason why return is unavailable (inferred from prior or later years)
Marital status:	0	Single
	1–2	Married
	3–5	Changes in marital status
	6	Taxpayer died during the year
	8–9	Other

This array of information serves three functions:

a.   Availabilty of specified combinations of tax-records information for
     the husband and wife can be determined without reading the records
     themselves. This aids in extracting special-purpose samples.
b.   The marital-status information becomes the basis for determining in
     advance whose returns are to be combined for joint incomes. Typically,
     some returns are available for both the husband and his wife in years
     prior to their marriage; returns pertaining to those years can be treated
     as separate tax units.
c.   Reasons for not filing a return can be interpreted to indicate which
     years reflect points that are outside the sample universe (i.e., a deceased
     taxpayer) and which reflect a deficiency in the data-gathering process.

With the summary record available as a control in data processing, it is
easy to set indexes in advance for preparing summary information or for locating tax records in a file. By combining the summary information with the ID
File and its indicators, complex sub-populations of the archive can easily be
selected for study. (Extensions of this idea are discussed in Miller and David,
1971.)

In the context of a summary record of this type, data linkage consists of
a program that calls for information from each file. Special-purpose programming
is necessary to assemble the desired data for analysis. We will discuss later the
way in which more general programming can be used repetitively in connection
with pointers (Chapter 8).

Pointers in a System of Data Linkage

One further example of file linkages should be discussed, even though it
has not yet been fully implemented. In processing the Asset File, it will be
highly desirable to prepare a summary record similar to the summary record
described above for the Tax Record File. Each summary record will inventory
the types of assets reported by each taxpayer. The summary records can then be
"chained" together by adding a reference to the next taxpayer with a particular type of asset holding. The references link taxpayers with common elements
in their portfolios. A typical set of links is shown in Figure 5-9.

While other types of references across the file can be imagined, they do
not have as clear a payoff. For example, each asset-year record could be tagged
with the next year for which that asset appears in the portfolio. Continuity of
holdings implies that this information is automatically given for most taxpayers
in a large percentage of cases. The physical sequencing of records in the sorting

	Asset			
Individual (index i)	General Motors	Nabisco	Oshkosh	Xerox
1 Own Holding	100	–	–	–
Next Holding i =	*2*	–	–	–
2 Own Holding	10	10	–	50
Next Holding i =	*i*	*l*	–	*3*
⋮				
i Own Holding	5	–	500	–
Next Holding i =	*j*	–	*none*	–
⋮				
l Own Holding	–	100	–	–
(Last Individual)				
Next Holding i =	*none*	*none*	*none*	*none*

Figure 5–9. Asset-Type Linkage Required for Portfolio Evaluation

order which is determined by individual identifier, asset identifier, and year, will compact all references to a particular type of asset for a particular taxpayer in a limited physical area. The same cannot be said of the linkage to the next taxpayer holding that asset. The fact that this problem cannot be escaped by varying the sorting sequence of the file is what makes the need for a cross-referencing of taxpayers critical.

For example, sorting the records in the order determined by asset type, year, and taxpayer makes it trivial to link price data to the file. However, any cross-reference to previous-year holdings or next-year holdings of a given asset becomes as difficult in the resorted file as the cross-references between taxpayers were in the file organization suggested above. Such cross-references will be necessary to identify assets that have been held for part of a year (see Miller, 1969; Bussman, 1972).

5.6 Conclusions

In this chapter we have described three aspects of data handling that are critical to all information archives. Linking information in different physical records, correctly identifying data elements and their transforms, and updating information found to be incorrect are general problems that were related to the specific details of the WAIS archive.

Experience in WAIS has shown that large payoffs result from considering the interrelationships of these three elements. Data descriptors used in programming and file descriptions both clarify the nature of the file structure so that the logical organization of information can be exploited in retrieving data. Experience has also shown that the paradigm for correcting erroneous records has powerful features that can be extended to acquisition of new information and the extraction of information from the file for analysis purposes.

A second aspect of the discussion of recycling, data descriptors, and data linkages is that the evolution of the computer environment has profoundly affected our concepts of the archive and the manner in which the data in the archive can be usefully related. Direct access media made it possible to view information in a manner altogether different from the concept of the linear array stored on cards or magnetic tape. This in turn led us to the notion that data structures could be represented by a graph. The graph of a data structure constitutes an extremely powerful device for exploiting the information available without excessive redundancies. Such graphs emphasize the manner in which observations are replicated. While it has been convenient for us to display only a portion of the logical structure that binds the individual datum to the complex of information available in the entire archive (Figures 5-3 to 5-9), the computer is not limited to dealing with such a small picture of the structure at any one time—indeed, it can be made to respond to a variety of relationships that are expressed in pointers that instruct a program what information to retrieve next (Knuth, 1968, Chapter 2.3). Once such pointers have been established, they may be used in whatever manner promotes the analytical purpose at hand and only part of the actual complexity of the archive need be interpreted. (We shall explore these ideas further in Chapter 8.)

The third aspect of this discussion that bears mentioning is that the discoveries that we have made (albeit by reinventing the wheel in many cases) are applicable not only to data development and maintenance, but also to the problem of obtaining information from a complex archive for a management information system. In contrast to the view expressed by Aron (1969, p. 233), we do not feel that it is possible to anticipate the analytical questions that will be asked of the archive; a basic description of the information using the techniques we have outlined in the system will provide both the flexibility and the systems framework for asking a wide variety of questions of the data set. Concentrating on the structure of information will produce dividends in retrieval, and will also make it easier to understand whether the archive is capable of producing answers to a particular question. Finally, a careful analysis of the microstructure of the data will make it clear what information must be added to the archive and how it must be added to relate the archive to questions it cannot yet answer.

In Chapter 6, we will discuss the details of the error correction process to indicate more clearly how advances in the concepts underlying error correction and detection influenced thinking about use and storage of the files.

6 Error Detection and Error Correction

6.1 Refinements in the Concepts of Recycling

The essential concepts that lead to greater efficiency and accuracy in the process of error correction were already presented in the discussion of recycling in the last chapter. One basic concept is the implementation of an error detection and correction system that can be applied repeatedly to generate a succession of files containing fewer and fewer records in error. The data descriptor constitutes a second basic concept. These ideas can be applied to sequential files within a batch-processing framework.

Additional flexibility and efficiency in the error detection and correction process used in the WAIS archive stem from the application of these error detection and correction concepts to an interactive computer environment, and the use of direct-access storage media rather than sequential files stored on magnetic tape. The combination of interactive processing and direct-access storage greatly increases the flexibility and efficiency with which the recycling processes sketched out in Figure 5–1 can be applied.

In this section, we will discuss the refinements due to disk storage and interactive error correction, and their implications for error correction. Implications of these refinements for error detection are explored in the next section. We give examples of the flexibility possible with interactive computing and direct-access storage in Section 6.3.

Remote Access to the Computer

A remote teletype terminal manned by clerical staff trained by WAIS eliminates a number of intermediaries that exist in a batch-oriented error correction process. Keypunchers, verifiers, and computer operators—intermediaries who were essential to the batch-oriented correction system—no longer form a part of the chain of operations that lead to error corrections. With interactive error correction, outsiders are not required to interpret the manually corrected error listings. Time and computer costs associated with false starts, omissions, and abortive production runs due to the failures of the computer can be minimized. In addition, staff time need not be used for the mechanical details of submitting data, picking up cards, and moving files from place to place. The remote terminal also conserves research staff effort since queuing can be reduced.

Once the problem posed by an error has been solved, the only impediment to data correction is inability to have access to the computer. Waiting time for the delivery of error correction cards and listings that must be produced elsewhere can be obviated. Furthermore, any clerk or coder capable of typing can use *both* an understanding of source documents and knowledge about record structure while records are being corrected. By contrast, the keypuncher generally does not have the training or interest to assess the validity of his codesheets—documents that will appear identical for operations involving radically different data structures.

The increased accessibility of the computer to clerks engaged in evaluating and correcting errors makes clear why data descriptors become so important in an interactive error correction process: First, data descriptor labels for fields in error generated by the error detection program are used by the coding staff in scanning the source documents. And, second, the descriptors then become a means for addressing the computer while changes are being made.

Direct-Access Disk Storage

It is cumbersome to maintain information outside the computer between correction operations. Records must be written sequentially on tape. The middle or end of a file is not readily available. Furthermore, every operation on a tape file entails the overhead cost of mounting tapes and the physical problems of reading information.

Disk storage has proved desirable for both reasons. The middle of a file is available at a moment's notice. Files residing on a disk are instantaneously available, without assistance from an operator. The elimination of operator intervention in the mounting of tapes and the intrinsic reliability of the disk reduces parity errors, tape drive problems (broken tapes, etc.), and false starts or relays due to operator errors. [1]

The accessibility of data on the disk creates an environment in which error correction operations can be partitioned into small volumes of changes spaced over an extended period of time. The cost of accessing a specific record in a tape environment tends to concentrate error correction into large volumes executed at one point in time.

A third and extremely important aspect of disk storage is that records can be corrected one field at a time. On sequential media, a change of one character is sufficient to require rewriting an entire set of records, i.e., an entire reel of tape.

Phases of the Detection-Correction Process

Figure 5-2 indicated four major phases to the error detection-correction process: (A) detect errors, (B) evaluate errors, (C) correct errors, and (D) merge corrected records. The operations A–C can be repeated until desired error tolerances are obtained; this fact was stressed by the error correction module highlighted in Figure 5-2.

Decision points that control the iterative application of the error correction module are explicitly shown in Figure 6-1. Operations are labelled A–D to correspond to the less detailed picture in Figure 5-2.

A. *Error detection* is a machine process in which a main data file is input or an updated error file is cycled through the error detection program. The program produces an error file and an error listing. The error file consists of extracted logical records thought to be in error. The error listing documents the detected inconsistency and provides as much information as possible regarding the nature of the problem. Each field in error is named by a data descriptor. Aggregate summaries of error types are tabulated.

The error detection process can be controlled to create: (i) a file of records in error and printed documentation, or (ii) only printed documentation. Alternative (i) can be used on an initial pass when the volume of data is large. Alternative (ii) can be used when the error file anticipated is sufficiently small so that the cost of merging the error file and the main file (phase D) exceeds the costs of finding records in the main file. We shall discuss this option in greater detail when we comment on the flexibility of the interactive error detection process (Section 6.3).

B. *Error evaluation* proceeds manually, and in two steps. A review of aggregate error rates for all types of records may indicate sufficiently low error rates to permit immediate wrap-up of the correction operations (including a merger of previously corrected records in phase D). If aggregate error rates are not satisfactory, an evaluation of individual records against source documents must be undertaken.

A coder uses source documents and the error listing to determine if corrections are appropriate. If corrections are needed, data descriptors, old contents, and new contents are coded on the error listing; otherwise, the logical record is marked "O.K." on the listing. [2] The process requires supervision to assure that cost or quality tolerances are met. Staff must check-edit clerical decisions. If check-editing reveals a problem, it may be necessary to revise a procedure and repeat the error evaluation (phase B2) with new instructions. Alternatively, analysis of errors may show that larger error rates must be accepted since available source documents do not provide clear answers to the consistencies demanded by the error detection algorithm.

C. *Interactive error correction* combines manual and machine processes.

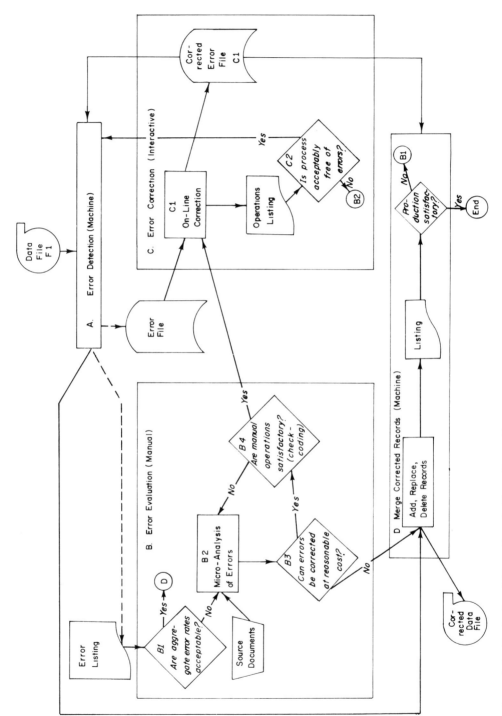

Figure 6–1. Control and Operations in Error Correction

Two options are available: Clerks can interact directly with the data file via the correction program. Alternatively, "transactions messages" can be keypunched and transmitted to a batch-oriented recycling program. The possibility for error in the latter process makes it quite objectionable. WAIS staff communicated interactively with a Burroughs 5500 via a standard teletype installation.

During the error correction the teletype operator initiates a program and then proceeds to update the error file, using the error listing with notations. This involves changing individual fields in each logical record. Coders and teletype operators will make mistakes in this process. In Chapter 5 it was pointed out that requiring data on the incorrect item that is to be changed prevents errors of commission; errors of omission, however, are still possible. Quality control of the error correction phase may take two forms. Initially it will be necessary to return to phase A, the error detection process. However, as the characteristics of on-line correction are relatively invariant over different files, monitoring the teleprinter output can be used to supplement phase A processing. Clerks who experience difficulties in using the correction program, or omit desired corrections, can be quickly spotted from their teleprinter output.

Interactive Error Correction

The WAIS error correction program uses an error file stored on a magnetic disk. The program provides:

Two techniques for locating records:
  (a) Binary search
  (b) Relative sequential search
Data element addressing by data descriptor [3]
Execution time sortfield definition
The capability for adding records

A more general program would also delete records and sort files, but this is not essential if add, drop, and merge capabilities are separately available (phase D). A more general program could handle different logical and physical record sizes without program modification. These generalizations are possible, but did not seem advantageous to WAIS.

The remainder of this section describes the interactive error correction in detail. The description concludes with a discussion of possible interactive programs and a comparison with batch systems.

For those unfamiliar with remote-interactive programs we present the following definitions:

Program initiation—all necessary control information is provided.

User Supplied Messages	Program Responses
1??EXECUTE GENERAL/EDIT480; FILE INFILE = GATES/OUTFM1; FILE DESCRIPT = GATES/DESCRIP; STACK = 200; CORE = 1400, END←	
2	8:GENERAL/EDIT480 = 01 BOJ 2105 FROM 01/12 SHALOM
3	# OF RECORDS IN FILE 00000000239
4	PLEASE DEFINE YOUR SORTFIELD SUCH AS 001 010 WHEN YOU ARE FINISHED TYPE DONE
5 002 005←006 011←DONE←	:
6 #1	0801280060
	:
7 #-100←	0702119960
	:
8 0801280059←	NO RECORD
	:
9 0801280060←	:
10 TERR 7 9←	:
11 NH 1222222222←	BAD FIELD LENGTHS
	:
12 COL11 9←	
	CHK ENTRY
	:
13 COL1 1 9←	2
	CHK ENTRY
	:
14 *SPILL←	COL1 1 1 NH 2 11 TERR 9 9
	:
15 *QUIT←	# OF RECORDS IN FILE 00000000239
16	GENERAL/EDIT480 - 1 EOJ 2109

Figure 6-2. Execution of Data Correction Program

Program execution—the actual interaction between user and program.
Program termination—the user has signaled his desire to the program
   to terminate interaction.
←indicates the end of a message from the user.

Proper initiation requires information—illustrated in area 1 of Figure 6-2—regarding the program name (GENERAL/EDIT480), the data file (GATES/OUTFM1), and the data descriptor file (GATES/DESCRIP). The data descriptor file in our implementation resides on B-5500 disk and is of the following format:

<data descriptor> <begin column> <end column>

A set of descriptors defines the logical record. The descriptor file is read by the program immediately after initiation and its contents are stored in a program array. (The array is limited to a maximum of 99 descriptors, but the actual number of descriptors in the file may vary. The maximum size of the data element is ten characters.)

While in use, the program builds the data element addressed by the user character-by-character and matches it against original contents also typed in by the user. This aspect of the program is described in greater detail later. The computer *system* response to program initiation is in area 2. BOJ stands for "beginning of job."

The *program* responds to the initiation of the program with two messages:

A. # OF RECORDS IN FILE
    <integer>
B. PLEASE DEFINE YOUR SORTFIELD SUCH AS 001 010
    WHEN YOU ARE FINISHED TYPE DONE

The messages can be seen in areas 3–4 of Figure 6-2. The number of records is typed to the user upon initiation of the program and again upon termination so that he may verify that records have not been added inadvertently.

Area 5 is the user's sortfield definition. The example illustrates that the sortfield may be defined in more than one part. In this case the first part of the sortfield lies in columns 2–5 and the second part in columns 6-11. The order could just as well have been reversed if it would make sense so far as the organization of the file is concerned. Failure to define a sortfield results in the following program message: [4]

C. BAD ENTRY . . . ENTER AGAIN

Program recognition of the sortfield produces the program response : indicated in the right-hand column of Figure 6-2, area 5.

Areas 6-7 are examples of relative sequential addressing. The user's syntax is

$$<\#> <\text{integer}>   <\leftarrow> ,$$

where the integer is positive if unsigned and negative if preceded by a minus sign. The *program* finds the desired record and responds by giving the sortfield of the record that is available at that location. The information in that record is then available and work may proceed. Messages from the program are terminated by the punctuation : , carriage return, and line feed.

The relative sequential search locates the record relative to the last record located plus or minus the integer specfied. This move may be in a positive or negative direction, i.e., towards the end of the file or its beginning, respectively. Ordinarily the user is interested in addressing the next or the previous record.

Using this mechanism, records may be added by addressing beyond the end of the file.

The binary search for specific records is illustrated in areas 8–9. In area 8 the user has entered a sortfield; the program performs its binary search and responds with the message:

D. NO RECORD

Area 9 alternatively illustrates a successful binary search where the programs response is the   : , carriage return, and line feed.

Binary search requires that the file is sorted sequentially before it is loaded onto the disk. The search procedure consists simply of dividing the entire file in half, determining which half contains the desired record, and iterating the procedure on the portion of the file containing the desired record. If N is the number of records in a file and b is the smallest integer larger than $\log_2 N$, a maximum of b tests will be required to search a file using a binary search technique. The number of tests required is minimized in the error correction program by comparing the desired address with the address of the last record used. [5] This initial interrogation thus reduces the number of times information must be obtained from the disk.

Figure 6–3 illustrates binary search on a file of the following 7 records:

Records on disk	#1	#2	#3	#4	#5	#6	#7
Sortfields	11	26	38	40	52	67	71

Record available in core: #3
Record requested by identifier: 52

As successive records are examined against the required identifier the size of the remaining file that must be interrogated decreases. This is illustrated by the succession of values N_0, N_1, and N_2 in Figure 6–3. (The corresponding b_1 and b_2 indicate the maximum number of searches that remain.) If all remaining searches are completed without success, the program informs the user that no record with the indicated identifier is available. This is the logic underlying the test $b_i > 0$?

Error correction using the program is illustrated in areas 10–15 of Figure 6–2. The syntax that appears in entries 10–13 is

<data descriptor> <original contents> <new contents> <←>

To accomplish a correction, the user types in sequence the following: data descriptor, at least one blank, the present or original contents of the field, and the contents he wishes to have in the field. Area 10 illustrates successful correction. The program response of   :   followed by carriage return and line feed indicates that the change has been accomplished.

Areas 11–13 indicate program responses to invalid attempts to correct

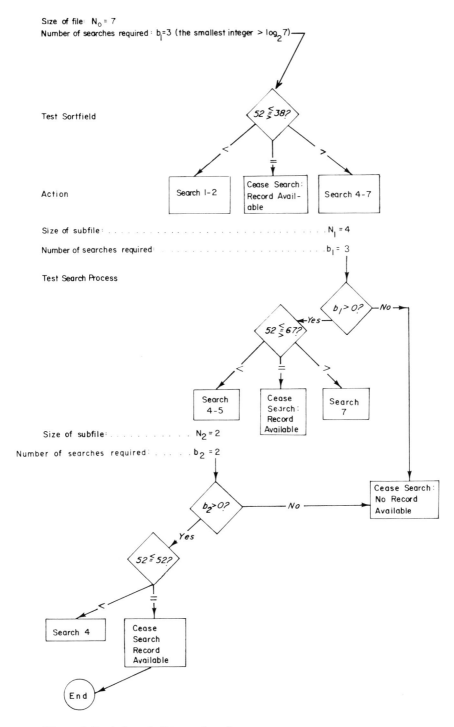

Size of file: $N_0 = 7$
Number of searches required: $b_1 = 3$ (the smallest integer $> \log_2 7$)

Test Sortfield

$52 \lessgtr 38?$

Action

Search 1-2

Cease Search: Record Available

Search 4-7

Size of subfile: . . . . $N_1 = 4$

Number of searches required: . . . . $b_1 = 3$

Test Search Process

$b_1 > 0?$ —No→

←Yes—

$52 \lessgtr 67?$

Search 4-5

Cease Search: Record Available

Search 7

Size of subfile: . . . . $N_2 = 2$

Number of searches required: . . . . $b_2 = 2$

$b_2 > 0?$ — No → Cease Search: No Record Available

Yes

$52 \lessgtr 52?$

Search 4

Cease Search Record Available

End

Figure 6-3. A Sample Binary Search

107

records. Failure to use identical field lengths for the old and new entries produces program message E.

E. BAD FIELD LENGTHS (area 11)

Invalid data descriptors or incorrect information produce message F.

F. <old contents>
CHK ENTRY (areas 12-13)

Area 12 illustrates an invalid descriptor; area 13 illustrates incorrect contents. Under some circumstances display of information on the file would not be desirable, and hence we have operated the program without the display.

Note that the data descriptors control the correction process. Their use insures that the user is in the proper column and that the field to be edited has a predefined length. The user must know the data descriptor and the original contents of the data element before any change is effected.

The user command <*SPILL←> causes the display of all data descriptors for a particular record and of the first and last character to which each refers (area 14).

Area (15) is the user's command indicating he wishes to terminate interaction. He types <*QUIT←> and the *program* responds with a count of the records. The *system* then terminates the program use, giving the program name and time of termination.

Performance

The remote-interactive correction of records is less costly than is error correction in a batch environment. Moreover, the interactive mode provides qualitative benefits of accessibility, immediate feedback on problem cases, and an automatic record of the clerk's understanding of the correction process for supervisory review and later verification. The retrieval of a record and correction is practically instantaneous. The rate of correction from the teletype is approximately 250 per hour assuming one eight-character edit per record of 480 characters.

Several possibilities exist for program generalization. It would be convenient to remove character limitations on sortfields and data elements. It would also be convenient to incorporate a check on improper sortfield definitions through the data descriptor file. Ability to handle different logical and physical record sizes and modify record length at execution time would also be an asset. It might also be convenient to have an option for visual display of the record on a cathode ray tube. Finally, search costs could be reduced by storing records according to an algorithm based on the identifier. [6]

6.2 Detection of Errors

Technique of Error Detection

Up to this point, little has been said about the planning and techniques used to detect errors and generate the error listing (and error file #) described in Figure 6-1. The technique has evolved in much the same way as data recycling. Initial error detection work was executed in assembly language programming. The program was oriented to a specific file (the MF), a specific physical record, and fields defined by character positions. The desirability of more powerful editing techniques was obvious. For example, the "transactions" required for error correction in the original recycling program had to be edited piecemeal to avoid "failures."

In 1963-1964 assembly languages were the only languages which were efficient and flexible enough to permit reasonable and economical editing. By careful analysis of the particular file one determined a set of potential errors that could exist and then proceeded to write a program to carry out the detection. Generalizing this process was economically unfeasible given the computing hardware then available, except on a small scale.

A second attempt at editing thus took the form of an 80-column card-editing program which could be controlled to provide checks on:

a. Admissible characters
b. Values smaller or larger than a predefined interval
c. Values within a prescribed interval

The programming was again developed in assembly language. The generality of the format gave this program considerable flexibility, and allowed us to check card images in the second collection of tax records before they were assembled into a 400-character record.

The value of a simple card-editing program was clear, but the initial execution left a great deal to be desired. Careful bookkeeping on the total volume of cards processed was not available. The control cards required to specify checks desired were cumbersome. The program did not permit one specified check to be used on several fields. Complex relationships among fields in the card could not be checked without a separate program.

By 1967 it was apparent that a more general procedure should be used; the capabilities of scientific computer compilers were sufficiently powerful to handle most editing applications quite easily. Rather than creating a special language to control edit procedures, both FORTRAN and ALGOL could be more easily specified *in toto*. At the same time, standard procedures for decoding a card image efficiently, and procedures for displaying error messages, needed to be programmed once as part of a system to avoid time-consuming and redundant programming efforts.

The first result of these ideas was a FORTRAN program capable of some simple character checks, but which also provided access to a subroutine that could be programmed by any user (see Figure 6–4). The program was extensively used on the CDC 1604 and 3600, with both cards and card-image tapes. Despite the speed of the program and its advantages relative to earlier specific efforts, several difficulties became apparent in repeated use of the program from 1968–1969: (1) The program was character-oriented; that is, each position in the physical record had to be interpreted by the user. (2) Planning could not be simplified by data descriptors. (3) Debugging and specifying the correct logic for tests proved to be difficult and cumbersome. (4) Every test required submission of the entire program, data, and the test subroutine. (5) Preliminary investigation of checks that were likely to produce high error rates could not easily be accomplished. (6) The program was oriented to card images and rigid formatting. (7) The program produced an error listing, but not a segregated file of cards in error. (8) Finally, the inherent unreliability of handling large volumes of cards made it likely that cards would be lost, mislaid, or damaged during the processing.

The deficiencies of the FORTRAN card-edit program were largely overcome in editing the second collection of master tax records. Principles learned in error correction were applied to error detection:

Both the planning and programming for error detection relied on data descriptors.

The assembly of a large editing problem was interactive.

The power of scientific compilers was used to generate the logic of the consistencies required.

Testing of the error detection routine used both fabricated data and actual records stored in disk files.

Interactive development of the error detection process speeded the completion of error-free programs and reduced computer costs. At the same time, the general strategy developed in the FORTRAN card-image error detection program was carried over into the interactive application.

Interactive development of error detection proceeded as a specific routine to check the second collection of MF tax records. The records were assembled as a 480-character logical record prior to checking. As before, each record represented one tax return for one individual.

During the program development a test file of records was maintained on

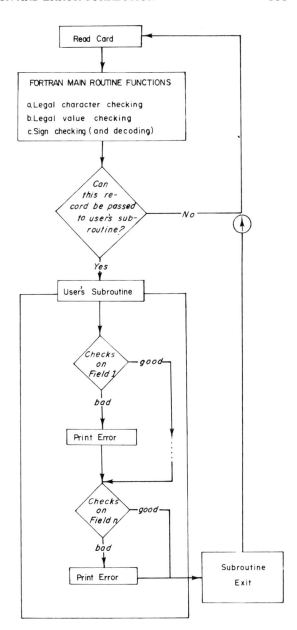

Figure 6–4. Subroutine Users Flow Chart

the B-5500 disk together with the existing program. Programming was in ALGOL owing to the historical accident that FORTRAN was not available on the B-5500 when the program development began. The use of ALGOL in an inter-active mode proved to have numerous advantages:

The syntax of ALGOL implies that the completed program can be thor-oughly self-documenting (a FORTRAN routine would not be).

Names of fields, procedures, and statement labels can be given English or ready identified mnemonics.

Each step in the flow chart of planned edits could be quickly compiled and tested on the disk. Immediate steps could be taken to correct both errors of syntax and mistakes in underlying logic that became apparent as valid data were displayed as being in error.

Programmer time saved in transmitting the problem, cost of resubmitting valid parts of the program and test data, and the reduction of turn-around time from twenty-four hours to one or two minutes, all indicated quite clearly that the cost of the interactive program development used was far less than the cost of conventional program development using the earlier EDIT program (Gold, 1969).

Planning Error Detection

Perhaps the most important aspect of the error detection process is suffi-cient planning before any coding occurs. If codes and data descriptors are devised such that all fields can be checked for valid entries contingent upon at least one other field, machine testing of data can be complex. For example, per-haps the code in field C must equal 1 whenever the codes in fields A and B are identical. Such a contingency may easily be tested. Or, if the following are pre-defined formulas—$D + E = F$ and $F - G = H$—one can utilize the logic displayed in Figure 6-5 to determine which, if any, fields are in error. [7] The figure illustrates how the presence of identities or redundancies in the data structure can be advantageously used to improve the quality of data. In the tax record, data errors introduced by keypunching and coding (which accounted for al-most a third of the inconsistencies detected in the data) could easily be checked by the redundant information on the return. The total of itemized deductions must add to the total deduction taken, etc.

Correction of fields can proceed in one of three fashions:

a.   The validity of certain items of information can be asserted, and the

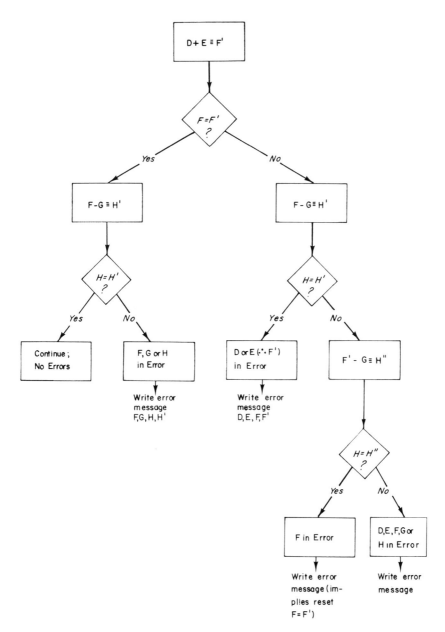

Figure 6-5. Logic of Error Detection and Machine Error Correction

record can be made consistent with the implications of the fields asserted as valid.

b. The nature of the inconsistency can be noted on the record so that future analysts can be alerted to the problem. (This can be recorded in a documentation system, such as that shown in Appendix E.)

c. Source documents can be evaluated to assess the validity of fields and relationships in the source record.

Processes (a) and (b) can be programmed as part of the error detection process; (c) requires the recycling discussed in Section 6.1.

The flow chart in Figure 6-5 clearly indicates how the underlying logic of the data can be tested. It is less clear how information about errors should be transmitted to persons for correction. The standard adopted was the following:

> Actual value
> Check (or computed) value
> Name of the field
> Name of the procedure in which the error was identified
> Record identifier

If errors were machine corrected, the check value and action taken were recorded in a "taxpayer error" code. (The codes could readily be added to the portion of the MF stored on the magnetic disk.)

Documentation of edits completed on the second collection of tax records appears in Appendix F.

6.3 Flexibility in Error Detection and Correction

The previous discussion of error detection and correction programs does not make clear the enormous flexibility and adaptability of the procedures discussed. *Interactive program development and record correction have made possible a tailoring of the job to fit constraints imposed by data availability, the cost of error evaluation, and the time required for producing output.*

Use of disk storage makes it possible to segment a large file into blocks that are convenient in relation to available computer time and the time required to complete the error correction cycle. For some files, segmentation may be unnecessary since the files are too small. Even for small files, however, processing segments may have the advantage of permitting the correction of batches of data while additional data are being collected or received. Furthermore, the error detection program can be designed to produce an even smaller error file if that is economical relative to the cost of maintaining the entire file on disk during correction.

As long as data are stored on the disk, the logic of error detection can be applied in any piecemeal fashion that may be consistent with the development of insight into the nature of errors on the file. Thus, in early batches the staff may wish to experiment with a number of different consistencies or data checks that prove to be unimportant when actual information is processed. Such trivial checks can later be dropped from the processing of the file. Alternatively, if early checking reveals inconsistencies that cannot be resolved by manual interpretation of the data, the error detecting program can be reset to flag problem cases without bringing them to the attention of clerks engaged in manual checking operations.

Finally, the whole process can be inverted so that data entry onto the computer occurs simultaneously with the evaluation and checking of the data. Up to this point, the discussion proceeded on the assumption that a file of machine-readable data was already created. However, there is no reason why a machine-readable record cannot be created by precisely the same type of entry process that we have used for error correction. All that is needed is a small change in the program to signal to the teletype operator which field is to be entered next.

If the logic of the error detection program is then added to the control program signalling for data entry, the information that is being added to a record can be simultaneously edited for consistency. Any errors can be immediately reviewed by the teletype operator without any search for documents. Finally, check-editing can be accomplished on all or part of the record by simply repeating the data entry and collating the results.

To summarize, the general strategy embedded in error correction and detection as we have described it lends itself to a wide variety of applications. The ability to decompose a large data processing problem into small blocks of data which are analyzed by logic that is sequentially developed and tested makes it possible to achieve production results in situations that might easily be impossible because of human errors. Focusing on an entire logical record on disk facilitates checking procedures that are unwieldy and expensive when the data processing is oriented to individual card files on sequential media.

Chapters 4–6 have indicated the sophistication with which a complex data archive must be treated if research results of any value are to be realized. The iterative nature of the data collection and of error correction make it clear that some process must be available for updating the file by rewriting old records or adding new ones. (This is the recycling facility that we described in Chapter 1.) As we mentioned earlier, the need for such capabilities arises from the need for data management, not from the substantive information structure that is being assembled.

Concern with the data and their manipulation also generates concern with a number of housekeeping operations that require careful conceptualization and solution. The WAIS archive includes an inventory of over 200 tapes which requires constant attention to insure that the location, responsible person, and description of the tape are always available. "Debugging" of programs requires easy access to test data and fabricated pathological records which can be used in program testing, while maintaining basic data files intact. Output of the processing runs has to be stored in retrievable form, whether the output is a record of successful production runs or listings that form the basis for error correction. Finally the skill of a staff of excellent programmers in dealing with various phases of the data processing leads to the need for quick, accurate program documentation. These ideas are mentioned here because development of our methodology for handling the data went hand-in-glove with improvements in these housekeeping operations. A detailed report on housekeeping problems follows in Chapter 7.

7 Housekeeping and Documentation

Chapters 2–4 surveyed the structure of a large and changing data set, while Chapters 5–6 provided insights into the techniques for handling the processing of pieces of the archive. This chapter describes the network of documents and procedures that have evolved to control the data processing and provide a permanent record of details involved.

7.1 Functions and Standards for a Housekeeping System

The ultimate objective of a housekeeping system is to provide a complete and precise description of the data that generate a set of statistical estimates. This description is a *document* and the housekeeping system must assume that the documents are written and retrievable on demand. When the process of producing a data set is as involved as in the WAIS archive, clearly intermediate phases of data processing must be documented if the ultimate objective of describing the data structure in analyses is to be reached.

In addition, the intermediate documentation serves a number of valuable functions in improving the quality of data processing:

Intermediate documentation serves as a means of communication among staff members who are associated with different parts of the archive.

Intermediate documentation provides a benchmark that is valuable in recovering from errors in the process of transforming, manipulating, and merging data files.

Finally, intermediate documentation can and should make data processing algorithms function independently of the programmers who originally created them.

A housekeeping system must meet a number of requirements. The ultimate objective of precisely describing material used in statistical analyses is to create permanent, complete, and legible documents. The intermediate objectives of staff communication and coordination, recovery from errors, and universality of programming effort entail record keeping and documents that may be less permanent, legible, and complete. Staff communication and coordination require that documents be produced as quickly as data processing steps are completed. Moreover, documents produced must direct readers to details that can be quickly and reliably retrieved from a mass of listings and computer related documents. Recovery from processing errors entails the need to keep obsolete data and related formats even when they have been superseded by more satisfactory data structures.

Housekeeping may also be regarded as the means to control, record, and organize transitions in the creation of a data system (see Figure 2-2). Control requires orderly recording of all pertinent information. Organization must be imposed to make retrieval of data and information about data possible.

Pertinent information is sometimes trivial (e.g., card counts) and is lost because the need for it is not foreseen. The archival team must always review what has been done to insure against failures in hardware and software and to preserve information so that both the methodology and the substance of data can be retrieved in the future.

A housekeeping system is a minimal management-information system, rather than a data-management system. The data-management system controls the form and development of data. A housekeeping system involves more than people interacting with the computer system. A management-information or housekeeping system is required to characterize fully the nature of the man-machine interaction. Information about the system and its performance must be available to plan future developments and control action taken in the present. Thus we view a housekeeping system as the rudiments of the management-information system within which programmers, researchers, and the data librarian can find answers to questions about the processing of the data archive.

7.2 Documentation and Process

The development of any empirical research can be characterized by the sequence of events: idea, algorithm, output. The fallibility of human nature makes it wise to allow for errors both in logic and in execution, so that a more realistic sequence might be characterized as: idea (1), algorithm (1), error (1), idea (2), algorithm (2), . . . , idea (k), algorithm (k), output (k). In this representation the information from errors feeds back to the conceptualization of the problem and output is realized only at the kth iteration of the process.

Ideally, permanent documentation is required only for the kth iteration. *Idea k* will include a description of reasons why earlier conceptualizations of the problem were inadequate; *algorithm k* provides the information on how estimates were derived from data sources; and the *output k* contains the desired results. However, it is unlikely that the documentation at the kth iteration will be correct if no documentation of earlier stages was developed. Thus any documentation system must have the capacity for tracing the implications of errors in earlier documents. Since the kth iteration cannot be identified at the outset, it is inevitable that some documentation will become obsolete as data are processed.

In some cases errors can be located but cannot be corrected, as when two data sources indicate inconsistent information about a particular event. In this case, documentation about errors identified prior to the kth iteration may be a desirable part of the permanent file of documentation.

The sequence of events suggested above also points to a useful partition of documentation: (i) a portion that deals with the conceptualization of the problem; (ii) a portion that describes the algorithms used to transform data into estimates; (iii) a portion that deals with data, inconsistencies, and information required to interpret machine-readable data; (iv) a report on successful output. The characteristics of each type of documentation can be adapted to meet the requirements set out above. This can most easily be seen by following an analysis problem through its processing in a typical WAIS operation. Figure 7–1 illustrates the documentation associated with the process and the procedures used to maintain access to these documents.

Any problem must start with a statement of theory and method. As this statement will utimately (when corrected) become part of the final research product, permanent and legible documentation is required for this phase. Consequently, a file of "concept" papers was established early in the history of WAIS. The content of the papers was general in character. The papers required little programming knowledge and were expected to be self-explanatory. Where references to other papers were required or where the problem had already passed through several iterations, cross-references to earlier conceptualizations were included (to the extent humanly feasible).

The file of *WAIS papers* was organized serially by date. Accessibility was maintained by regularly indexing papers according to subject matter, the pertinent data file, and author. The latter was useful since different staff members developed areas of special expertise and an item of information could sometimes be located more easily by scanning his contributions to the paper series than looking under the several subjects where information might conceivably be indexed.

In Figure 7–1 the cross-indexing required to maintain access to WAIS papers is indicated by the circled 1 in the box to the right of the document itself. The document is designated a type 1, or conceptualization, document. The instrument for retrieval, R1, is a simple catalog.

As program development proceeds, documentation of the algorithm and its treatment of the data is clearly needed. The program generates test documentation that must be preserved when a satisfactory algorithm has been developed. To this end WAIS staff developed a procedure for program documentation that would provide a reference to the sources of information about the program and

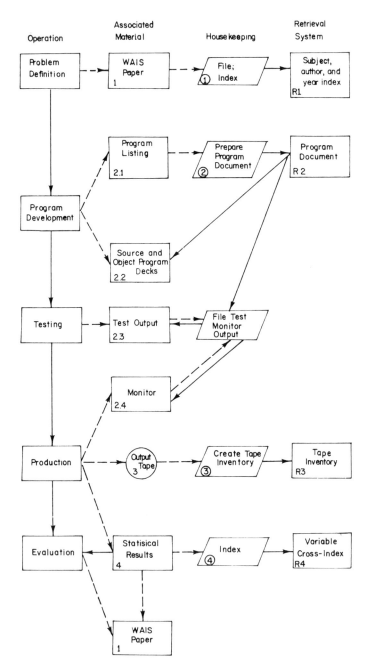

Figure 7-1. Flow of Operations and Documentation

test runs. The resulting *program document* was organized in a looseleaf form and indexed according to the applicable data file and computer. Clearly it is a retrieval instrument, R2. Programming techniques must be relied upon to make the program listing (2.1) as self-documenting as possible. WAIS papers supply the remaining documentation needed. It is worth pointing out once more that data descriptors and procedure labelling conventions make the program listing far more complete than it would be if programming effort were not disciplined in that manner.

The program document also provides a ready index to the information about the actual processing of data shown in the testing and production phases of Figure 7-1. Location and identification of program decks, documents monitoring the production process, and the structure of key parameters controlling the process were also included in the program document.

The only aspect of data that could not easily be referenced by the program document was the stock of data and its physical form. Typically, a given file could be input to a number of programs, so that an independent record-keeping structure seemed reasonable. In fact, the *tape inventory* (R3) that was developed served primarily mechanical functions for retrieving reels of tape. The inventory established the location, the physical record structure, and the person responsible for the tape. If the file was permanent, a record of format and codes was established as a WAIS paper for reference and legibility. (Indeed it is mostly likely that the paper had been written in advance.) The tape inventory was organized according to the pertinent data source, using a classification identical to that provided for program documentation.

In the last stage, output is evaluated. The resulting document becomes a part of the permanent paper file. If statistical output will be widely referenced it may also be desirable to index (R4) the statistics available so that several analysts do not needlessly repeat the same statistical studies.

This brief discussion of the process by which data are converted into statistical results motivates the three major forms of documentation that have appeared in the WAIS archive. The paper series has permanence and legibility; the program document is not self-sufficient, but has the merit that it can be produced at the same time that work is processed. Similarly the tape inventory is not complete documentation of the interpretation to be given to the content of a tape. However, it provides sufficient information to permit anyone to read the information on the tape and to locate further information about the file when it is needed.

The three files are interrelated. Major concepts in processing data will become part of the paper file. Conversely, WAIS papers contain the information required to locate individual program listings and test data in the document archive.

In the following sections the program document and tape inventory are described in detail. Characteristics of the paper files are relatively obvious and will not need elaboration.

7.3 Program Documentation

Two types of questions motivate a study of program documentation. A user may wish to determine whether a particular algorithm solves a problem in which he is directly interested. Alternatively, an analyst may wish to determine whether the algorithm dealt satisfactorily with the logical possibilities in the original problem statement.

To use an existing program without modifications, a programmer must have accurate and complete information about the parameters that must be supplied when the routine is executed. He must also be able to locate the flow chart and source code for the program (in the form of a listing), and the object program (in machine-readable form). A review of the source code and flow chart is necessary to determine what the program accomplishes. If the algorithm is compatible with the projected application, the object program provides the most efficient means of reinstating the instructions on the computer.

In the program document, parameters required for execution are given in full. A sample of parameter statements actually used is included. The names of the source program and of the object program are given so that machine-readable versions of those programs can be extracted from files of cards or magnetic disk. The source program name also provides a key to the permanent listing of program code, test data, and test output which are filed with the program document whenever possible.

The information required to use a program, described above, is sufficient to meet the needs of the programmer who wishes to undertake modifications to an existing program. The only difference is that in the latter case the programmer will need to make more intensive studies of the source listing and the flow chart to determine where changes in the algorithm are required.

Since most programs are functionally related to specific files, we applied a digital scheme to subclassify programming efforts. A four-digit number is assigned to a program that has been written; the program deck, program listing, and program document have the same number attached.

The program document was modified after its creation. Originally, a line called PROGRAM SERIES was included for programs constructed in a chain or to be executed sequentially. It was used very seldom and the narrative section PURPOSE AND DESCRIPTION OF EXECUTION now serves in its stead. Also, the original concept was to apply only to the B–5500. The success of the B–5500 documentation led us to use the document system for all computers; we added COMPUTER and PROGRAMMER so that the document would be universal. We now document all programming by this means. It was originally hoped that the DESCRIPTION section would include timing data. As descriptions seldom covered performance, the request for PERFORMANCE ESTIMATES AND TIMING DATA was explicitly added to the document. This section is very important because one does not care to execute an unfamiliar program without any insight into its possible costs.

PROGRAM DOCUMENT NUMBER
AND DECK NUMBER 1032

COMPUTER: *B-5500*   PROGRAMMER: *B. Gates*

SOURCE NAME: *GATES/TTT480* OBJECT NAME: *MASTER/MERGE*   DATE: *12-8-69*

FILE DECLARATIONS:
INPUT-TAPE1, INPUT-TAPE2, OUTPUT-TAPE, DISK-FILE, MESSAGES
Production line printer output will be filed with the program listing,
generally.

DATA FORMAT DECLARATIONS:
Tapes are 480 characters blocked 10; Disk error file is 480 unblocked;
Standard line printer file. (Batch, see sample with program listing.)

SAMPLE EXECUTION CONTROL CARDS:
?EXECUTE MASTER/MERGE; FILE"INPUT-TAPE1" = A/B;
FILE "INPUT-TAPE2" = C/D; FILE "OUTPUT-TAPE" = E/F;
FILE "DISK-FILE" = GATES/DUP2M4

RELATED PROGRAMS: *SCHILB/TTT480, GATES/NOLABEL*

PERFORMANCE ESTIMATES AND TIMING DATA:
Read/write 23674 records consume most of execution.
PROCESS = 94 secs ELAPSED = 7 min. IO = 8.3 minutes
Cost = $18 under present prices. The IO > ELAPSED is because there
are four IO channels.

PURPOSE AND DESCRIPTION OF EXECUTION:

To merge separate form types of the new Master data and duplicate check on
ID number, thereby creating an error file on disk for future correction. On
the error file the second record is the one on the Master File for each pair of
duplicates.

Figure 7–2. Sample Program Document

Essential to successful collection of information about programs is the realization that no one (especially a programmer) cares to execute an unfamiliar program. At the same time, even extensive program documents are not likely to be complete and are very unlikely to be filed in a timely manner. Therefore minimal program documentation with references to the program decks and source listing is a good strategy for maximizing the usefulness of special-purpose programs. A sample program document is shown in Figure 7–2.

"Insertions" were an extremely helpful addition to the program document looseleaf. Each of those documents reflected discoveries about particular modes of operating the computer for general classes of problems that were likely to be encountered by most staff members. For example, techniques for handling multi-reel files or patching programs on disk were covered by specific insertions.

The program document provides an easy device for integrating the efforts of a number of staff members and automatically organizing permanent records in a useful fashion. The minimal character of the document itself and the looseleaf organization implies that the various individuals using programs can be quickly informed of the completion of different program efforts. Finally, the document provides a basis for the division of labor between the data librarian, secretaries, and programming staff. This insures that vital information is accessible to research analysts and clerks and is not buried in some programmer's heap of completed (and therefore trivial) assignments.

The last point should be underscored. The housekeeping system that produced the program document naturally provides a division of labor *and* checks to assure that documentation is properly developed. The data librarian controls tapes; he files cards and listings. This delegation of responsibility is a great convenience to programmers. At the same time, the librarian always knows when material is checked out for use elsewhere. Thus he can anticipate new program documents, creation of new files, and press for corresponding documents. It will be easier to see these interrelationships after we have discussed tape inventories.

7.4   The Tape Inventory

The creation of a tape inventory was made necessary by the same pressures that led to the program document. A number of individuals working on different aspects of the WAIS archive needed information on the data to be input to their algorithms. Editing and file updating implied, for example, that the reels of tape that might be required for a given analysis extract would change and would be likely to change their location. The basic function of the tape inventory is to assure that the stock of tapes in use by WAIS programmers and staff can be located and used by any staff member.

The inventory serves two additional functions. The inventory minimizes the number of scratch tapes in use, and provides a convenient device for removing obsolete files from the archive.

The inventory is maintained in machine-readable form. As a result, listings of the complete inventory or portion of it can be produced on demand. This characteristic of the file is essential to providing up-to-date information for the programming staff. Maintaining the file in machine-readable form provides the opportunity to exploit interactive computing capabilities. Immediate and foolproof modifications of the tape inventory are entered on disk as work is processed. In the following paragraphs we describe the format of the inventory and its relation to other documents. We then provide illustrations of the interactive use of the inventory.

The tape inventory record provided the following information on a standard 80-column card:

   a.   Serial
   b.   External label number

   c. Location
   d. Number assigned to the tape in the location
   e. Responsible person
   f. Tape label and other pertinent information

The machine-readable record is augmented by a document that supplies enough additional information to assure that the tape can be read by any user. The paper document also indicates the permanence of information on the file (see Figure 7–3).

The serial assigned to each tape identifies the file area with which information on the tape is associated. The same decimal system that is used classifying programs is used here. Location is critical information, since tapes can be permanently stored in the data library or at the computing center; also, tapes might temporarily be in transit or in use at one of several other locations. Because a tape rack number was assigned to each tape as it was entered into the computing center, knowledge of the number was essential to calling for tapes in use on that system.

A free-formatted portion of the 80-column record was used to give as much information as possible, including the creation date and record counts.

The file of machine-readable tape inventory records can be placed on the disk of the B–5500 computer. EDITOR and general sort programs can then be used to modify, add, and delete records from the file. Furthermore, the command SCAN can be used to locate all files whose description included key words, such as "Master File". Under this scheme, it is trivial for a programmer to indicate that he has logged in a set of tapes at the computing center or created a new set of permanent data files. This information can be entered in the tape inventory records at the time that the program is submitted for execution.

The combination of the simple card record and the paper document works well to maintain control over the physical inventory of tapes in the WAIS archive. Programmers cannot evade the responsibility for tapes by asserting they have been moved to another location. The record clearly identifies all tapes that are not in the possession of particular staff members. (We were led to this system by the mysterious "disappearance" and scratching of a data tape for which no one claimed responsibility!) The system could be elaborated, but works well in its present form both on the computer and manually on peripheral equipment.

The program document and tape inventory complement each other. Any major operation requires both *access* to existing permanent files and new tapes for permanent storage of processed data. [1] (The system was even further enhanced by computer file cataloging facilities on the B–5500 and Univac 1108.)

The data librarian controls permanent files, new tapes, and the corresponding tape inventory. He is thus in a position to supervise completion of the necessary documents. The programmer is asked for material that is readily accessible and is not *required* to produce a marvel of pedagogy to instruct future program

LINKAGE AND RETRIEVAL OF MICROECONOMIC DATA

WAIS Tapes Form

Date_____ Name_____

UWCC Tape Rack Number	Person Responsible (Initials)	DPLS or SSRI Number	Length (3, 12, or 24 hundred feet)	Tape Label	Date Created	Reel Number	Record Count	Characters Per Record	Records Per Block	Parity* (O or E)	Backup or Scratch Status (Circle and complete where applicable)	Description of Data	Program Used
											1. Prime—Backup Is _____ 2. Is Backup to _____ 3. Scratch_____		
											1. Prime—Backup Is _____ 2. Is Backup to _____ 3. Scratch_____		
											1. Prime—Backup Is _____ 2. Is Backup to _____ 3. Scratch_____		

*Even parity results from running COBOL nonstandard, or ALGOL ALPHA specifications. Odd parity results if the program does not specify nonstandard or ALPHA. Binary tapes are written in odd parity. Most of our work is in even parity.

Figure 7-3. A Sample of the Tape Document.

users. This conserves his energies yet enables staff to recover needed details of special-purpose programs.

7.5 Systems Procedures, Interactive Computing, and Housekeeping

Every computer has its own housekeeping system. That system can be used to complement the document we have discussed. Under ideal conditions the documents desired can be produced within the computer's system. Control of housekeeping for the data archive can then be delegated to the computer's executive and utility programs.

We are still far from that ideal. However, two examples indicate that an appropriate computer systems environment makes many housekeeping functions easier: tape labelling; and disk store and dumps.

If the executive system of the computer recognizes tape labels across all compilers and initiates proper labelling at the beginning and end of files, much of what is required in the tape inventory is embedded in the tape in machine-readable form. Thus the name of the file, density, blocking factors, number of physical records, date of creation, and permanence can be automatically recorded in COBOL labelling procedures on the B–5500. If these elements can be interpreted and used for control under other compilers, the labelling system fills many of the needs that dictated the creation of a tape inventory. However, when different languages or machines do not find these labels compatible, and do not automatically respond to information located there (providing a fail-safe procedure against erasure, for example), the user can be disasterously misled and must supply control from the outside, as we have done.

When data being processed can be stored on disks, the need for extensive listings as a device for detecting errors in algorithms can be eliminated. In place of a program document that directs the user to tape dumps, specified input and output records on the disk can be retrieved almost instantaneously on the remote teletype. This feature enables the staff to be extremely selective in picking only that class of records in which they are particularly interested. Dumps produced routinely for documentation and monitoring may contain few of the pathological cases that raise questions about the performance and accuracy of a step in data processing.

7.6 File Segmentation and Secondary Memory Media

As the volume of data in an archive grows, the size of data files eventually increases to the point where physical and management constraints must be considered. Growth results in the following: The data files cannot be accomodated on a single reel of magnetic tape. The time required, the number of tape drives, and the needs for printed output for elementary operations on the file exceed the limits for jobs that can be given high priority. Elapsed time for operations on the file rises. In fact, elapsed time rises quite out of proportion to the increased demands. System failures, operator errors in handling multi-reel files, and problems with tape drives occur with sufficiently high probabilities that the likelihood of successful completion of jobs falls dramatically once the volume of data processed requires more than one reel of input tape. [2]

If no explicit decision is made on how to deal with multi-reel files, data are assigned to tapes by the computer system. An implicit decision has been made to segment the file. As tapes vary in length, there is no guarantee that the same decision will be made again, even if all that is done is to copy the file. As the file is segmented according to physical records, information that may be required at one time (all tax records for one person) may be on different reels. Furthermore, our analysis runs have shown on several occasions that the reflector spot on the end of the tape cannot always be relied upon to initiate the request for the second reel of a multi-reel file. Another problem that arises when files are implicitly segmented is that the optimal capacity of disk storage and the physical capacity of tapes are not identical. Implicit segmentation of files may lead to the need to read a single reel of tape more than once in connection with a job that makes use of disk storage.

The solution to all these problems is to establish explicit principles for segmenting the data file. If the structure underlying the data is considered, the file can be segmented in a manner that makes it highly unlikely that data from more than one reel of tape must be read at the same time. In the case of the WAIS archive, all the information for the husband and wife (or wives), for example, should clearly be on a single reel (see Figure 5-6). In the WAIS archive, the boundary points of the surname clusters used in sampling served as convenient logical points for segmenting the file. In other samples, geographic boundaries or other key explanatory variables could be used to segment the file.

When the file has been explicitly segmented, housekeeping chores increase to the extent that more units of tape are required for storing the file segments. However, the cost of such housekeeping may be justified by the substantial benefits of an explicit segmentation:

a. The segments can be limited to a size that is convenient to load on disks.
b. The segments can be limited to a size that will copy on all tapes (despite random variation in tape length).
c. The content of the first and last records in each segment can be listed as a housekeeping procedure which provides direct verification that programming errors have not truncated the file.

d. For many operations, the record count of the input and output files as well as the first and last record identifiers should be identical. Hence, housekeeping chores are reduced by the foreknowledge of this constancy.

e. Systems problems, and low priority in the queue of computer operations can be avoided by keeping the size of segments small. Turn-around time for processing a job falls correspondingly.

*Segmentation and Its Relation to
Disk Storage*

A further benefit in both housekeeping and data processing derives from the use of the segmented file in connection with disk storage. Table 7-1 provides a paradigm of a typical operation involving the use of a tape file segmented in a manner that can be economically stored on the disk. Loading of the data onto the disk can be handled by systems routines without special-purpose programming, the likelihood of format errors, and the cost of suboptimal tape handling. Systems procedures automatically provide housekeeping information on the file. Production can be initiated either in batch or interactive modes. As we have already pointed out, use of the disk as a storage medium offers the flexibility of random access to records. (In Chapter 8 we will indicate that it also provides the ability to call up subpopulations without retrieving every record.)

Upon completion of the production operation the data remain on the disk until the operation has been evaluated. The evaluation is enhanced by the fact that records in both the input and output files can be retrieved almost instantaneously in response to queries about some aspect of the performance of

Table 7-1
Overview: Segmented Processing

Operation	Comments
1 Load data from tape to drum or disk (save until 3)	System commands utilized for efficiency in handling and housekeeping.
2 Production	Utilize advantages of random access. Interaction possible.
3 Evaluate production Satisfactory output—Go to 4	Random access check of records possible.
4 Purge file Unsatisfactory output—Go to 5	System commands handle disk to tape as well as dumping.
5 Modify production program— Go to 2	

the processing program. If necessary, the process of production can be repeated, with a minimal data-handling cost. Moreover, the queue for reinstating the process entails less wait than if data must be read from the tape. When the operation has been successfully completed, the file can be purged from the disk. Systems procedures and housekeeping will again provide automatic documentation for the data archive.

This discussion of segmentation and disk usage was introduced to indicate how a conscious decision about the way files are to be stored increases both the efficiency of housekeeping and the speed of data processing. Focusing the attention of programmer, data librarian, and the computer system on macro-units of data which are segmented according to the logic of the data structure, can routinize and simplify the chores of keeping track of the details of a large archive. At the same time, the decision to segment a file is an important data management strategy that makes it easier for researchers and programmers to deal with the inevitable failures of the computer, software, and storage media.

Appropriate segmentation can make good use of systems procedures to provide essential documentation on the character of files. Documentation becomes both automatic and more reliable. At the same time, the purpose of housekeeping—maintaining adequate control over the record archive—is enhanced by easier access to individual items of information that can only be retrieved at great expense when files are compactly stored on sequential media.

7.7 Conclusions

A number of different types of documents are required to support a major archive such as WAIS. The accuracy and availability of such documentation is critically dependent on attention to the housekeeping system in which the information is generated and the rubric within which the documentation is classified.

In the case of WAIS, it became obvious after a minimum of processing that a system of easy entry and quick retrieval was required to update the description of the program and tape inventories. On the other hand, major items of permanent documentation designed for general review could be easily filed and catalogued within the framework of any system well adapted to some, but not extensive, subject-matter classification.

The system devised appears complete, self-supporting, and legible. Its main deficiencies result from the fact that we have yet to devise a system for automatically identifying obsolete WAIS papers, eliminating superseded tapes, and destroying inefficient programs. These tasks must be undertaken periodically, and for the moment rely excessively on the memory of persons well-acquainted with the character of the archive and its data processing needs.

One other area has proved troublesome—indexing of statistical findings and published results does not integrate readily with the WAIS Paper Series. It should perhaps be the responsibility of the data librarian to record the sequence of WAIS papers that are predecessors to each publication to assure that interested persons can easily find their way into the working documentations associated with the scientific product of the file.

For the time being, little energy has been spent in cross-indexing the intermediate statistical products of the archive. This is because each product reflects the idiosyncratic needs of a particular researcher, and also because it is difficult to devise a system of indexing such output that is sufficiently general to handle a broad variety of statistical materials and deal with the many variants of a dimension that may be represented in the statistical results. Our one modest step in the direction of indexing has been to classify n-dimensioned tables on the first file collection by the names of the variables used to define the table. This at least makes basic information on the frequency of particular kinds of events available to the researcher who is attempting to define a new problem for analysis.

8

On the Horizon—Some Recent Experiences and Their Implications

In Chapter 5 we alluded to the improvements in archive organization that arise from the use of pointers to describe the linkages among the basic records of the archive. Implementation of the pointer concept was not described, nor was the relationship between pointers and the manner of storing data fully explained. In Section 8.1 of this Chapter we undertake a brief explanation of the techniques that must be implemented to assure efficient retrieval of archives stored in several distinct classes of records within the direct access memory of a computer. This material is discussed elegantly in Knuth (1968) and Berztiss (1971). It may be omitted by those who are already familiar with the concepts of pointers.

Section 8.2 indicates how the use of pointers simplifies programming of analysis problems and subsequent retrieval of information for further processing. Section 8.3 explains random storage of records in a hashed file. The remainder of the chapter is devoted to an explanation of how pointers, hashed files, and the file organization that they make possible have been exploited in merging the first and second collections of tax record data, and in the development of further simulation analyses related to tax averaging.

8.1 The Use of Pointers to Link Records in an Archive

Typically, the processing of information obtained by replicated measurements produces a series of documents that are identical in format. The processing of the documents assigns an order to the series. [1] The order becomes a conventional manner of presenting the records to the computer as they are interpreted from machine-readable media. Now let us imagine that the information contained in one record is arbitrarily divided into two sets, and that each of these subsets retains the original identifier (see Figure 8-1). The information must be presented to the computer as two distinct sets of records. Conceptually, no difficulty exists in sorting both sets of records on the identifier and matching the identifiers to reconstruct the original record. However, this reconstruction can be achieved in one of two ways: sequentially, and by linking pointers. The sequential approach requires an algorithm that begins with the first record in each set, interrogates the identifier of each, and takes a predetermined action depending on whether the identifier in the second set of records

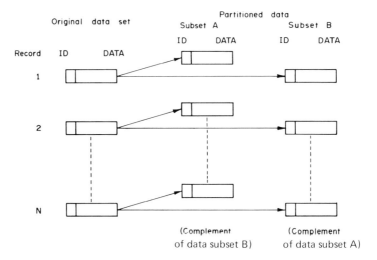

Figure 8-1. Partition of a Data Set into Subfiles

is smaller, equal to, or greater than the identifier in the first set of records. The sequential approach may fail if records are not adequately sorted by identifiers, or if an identifier can not be adequately interpreted because of parity errors.

The alternative of linking the files by pointers requires advance planning at the time the data are arbitrarily divided. The records of the first subset of data must be tagged with the *address* (or physical location) at which records for an individual can be found in the second set of data. Similarly, records of the second set of data must be tagged with the address at which the corresponding record in the first set can be found. Subsequent manipulation of the two data sets must assure that each datum is always located in the same physical location it occupied at the time the data subsets were generated. [2] In fact, this bit of *legerdemain* is easily accomplished by utility programs for dumping the contents of specified areas of memory and reinstating those contents in the memory. Such programs are standard in every computer system and are extremely efficient.

The pointers embedded in each subrecord instruct the computer to visit the location of the matching complement. The full set of data can be assembled from an initial visit at either subset and the pointers establish and assert the existence of both subsets of information for an individual. (See Figure 8.2a). In contrast to the algorithm for matching data by sequentially interrogating identifiers, the algorithm for creating the pointers must be used only once; thereafter the computer program can directly use the information embedded in a record to assemble an entire data set. The sequential approach must repeat the algorithm for visiting data sets, and for handling records that are out of

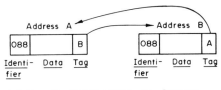

(a) Records Doubly-Linked by Pointers

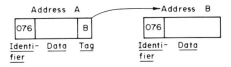

(b) Records Singly-Linked by Pointers

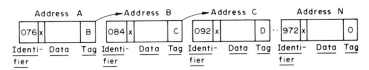

(c) A Chain of Records With Common Characteristics x (Singly-Linked)

Figure 8-2. Use of Pointers to Link Records

sequence, in each instance where elements of both data subsets are required.

This discussion of pointers created at the time when a basic data set is decomposed into subsets establishes the logic required to create and use pointers in any situation:

Creation—An algorithm that specifies the address of the record to be linked to that first visited must be used to create pointers.

Maintenance—The algorithm must document the first and last records in the chain and the number of records in the chain. This information simplifies maintenance and future access to the chain.

Use—Subsequent use of the linked data sets require an algorithm that interprets the pointer on the data set first visited.

Other applications of pointers are simple variants of the algorithms above. For example, it is quite possible that pointers reside only in the first of the data subsets (see Figure 8.2b). Then it becomes impossible to find the complement of the second data subset. Such a file is singly- rather than doubly-linked.

Pointers and Missing Data

Pointers have a distinct advantage over sequential linking of data in the handling of missing records. A null pointer can be used to assert the absence of any record to complement the one at hand.

The sequential method may resolve the missing record problem in one of three ways: 1) link indicators, 2) dummy record creation, or 3) sequential search.

Sequential search is the only method that does not require amending the original data structure. The search technique relies on the sorting order of the two sub-files to provide the clues concerning lacunae. For example, records may be ordered in ascending sequence of identifiers. When no matching record is found in the complementary file additional records are read from that file until an identifier is found that exceeds the value of the identifier on the original file. Logically that condition can only occur when the complementary record is missing. However, the condition can and does arise in practice when parity errors or sorting errors exist in the file. In that instance a matching record is ignored.

Both dummy record creation and link indicators require a preliminary reading of both files and the creation of a record of the matches completed. Link indicators are present on the file to be matched and are in reality an amputated pointer—they assert the existence of a match but do not direct the user of the file to the location of the matching record. Dummy records entail an enlargement of the complementary file to include a cipher that is interpreted as missing data and completes a rectangular data matrix. When sorting errors exist dummy records are as prone to failure as the sequential search procedure.

This discussion makes clear that a fail-safe procedure for identifying missing data with sequential matching requires as much effort as the creation of pointers. Pointers can automatically deal with missing data, and create the same positive information on linkage that is preserved in a record indicator, while expediting the retrieval of information from the linked files.

Pointers Used to Define Commonalities

Pointers may also be used to establish commonalities among the records originally generated, rather than assembling the components of the original data. (Compare Figure 8-2c and Figure 5-7.)

We give a simple example of the latter use of pointers. For the sake of concreteness we suppose that the original data set can be partitioned into five classes on the basis of current and former marital status (single, married, widowed, separated, divorced). Individuals with a common marital status can be linked in two ways: (A) Each record can identify the address of the next record

Table 8-1
Algorithm to Create Pointers that Partition a Data Set

Requirements

1. Working-vector with k cells—one cell for each partition to be established for the particular variable
2. Relative record addresses
3. Provision for the pointer within each record
4. File to be located on direct access media (for efficiency)
5. Pointer value of zero signifies end-of-list

Procedure

0. $N \Rightarrow n$, where N is the number of records in the file.
1. Read the nth record on the file.
2. Retrieve the value of the variable and convert this to a cell address in the working-vector.
3. Retrieve the contents of the cell in the working-vector and store this in the storage area for the pointer on the record.
4. Store the relative address of this record in the working-vector-cell indexed by the value of the variable generating the pointer.
5. $n - 1 \Rightarrow n$.
6. If $n = 0$ *stop*, else go to step 1.

with that marital status; or, alternatively, (B) each record can identify the previous record with that marital status. The use of pointers of both types causes the class of individuals with a common marital status to be doubly-linked. All persons in that class can be found whichever individual is first visited. With the singly-linked file of type A the entire class can be located only if the computer visits the first individual with that characteristic. [3]

The generation of pointers of type A is achieved by a simple algorithm that requires reading of the entire list of data only once. The algorithm is a simple extension of the creation algorithm alluded to earlier. The algorithm should document the first and last records in the chain and the number of records in the chain. That information simplifies maintenance and future access to the chain, (see Table 8-1). The results of this algorithm are illustrated by Figure 8-3. This figure shows 10 records in a set of 100 and the pointers that have been generated for each. A zero value for the pointer indicates that no more records occur in that chain. The generation of the pointers is made clear by examining the working vector as each record is read. Initially the working vector is null. After one record in each class has been read, each cell of the vector will contain the address of the next record with a particular marital status. The components of the vector refer to addresses of widowed, divorced, separated, married, and single persons (in that order). After the first iteration of the algorithm the last record has been identified as single and the working vector appears as

Relative Address	1	2	...93	94	95	96	97	98	99	100
Martial Status*	S	S	...S	E	D	W	S	D	M	S
Data Available										
Marital Status Pointer	2	5	...97	0	98	0	100	0	0	0

*W = Widowed; D = Divorced;   E = Separated;   M = Married;   S = Single.

Figure 8-3. A Data Array Partitioned by Pointers

(, , , 100). Subsequent iterations of the algorithm produce the following changes in the working vector:

After reading record	Record whose pointer is derived from the working vector	
99	(, , ,99,100)	98
98	(,98, ,99,100)	97
97	(,98, ,99, 97)	96
96	(96,98, ,99, 97)	95
95	(96,95, ,99, 97)	94
94	(96,95,94,99, 97)	93
93	(96,95,94,99, 93)	92

The pointers assigned in Figure 8-3 were obtained by reading the address in the cell of the vector indexed by the marital-status information in the "current" record.

The working vector may include a cell for illegal characters. The pointers created for those records will expedite error correction, and will segregate errors from legitimate data in subsequent use. (See Section 6.3.)

It is also clear from this simple example of how the housekeeping and documentation required for the creation of pointers reveals important characteristics of the data set. The first nonzero element in each component position of the working vector is the last record in the *chain*, (and file) when reading the *file* "backwards." The final values of the vector are the initial records in the chain. Length of the chains can be obtained by a simple tally or the number of times each component of the vector is altered. This desirable housekeeping for documenting pointers thus automatically gives frequency distributions on the characteristics defining the classes.

Use of Pointers in Programming

It is now clear that a pointer may either include a null value or the actual location of a datum needed in connection with information at hand. If the problem is to reconstruct a large vector from components stored in several different subsets, null values indicate missing data and refer the program to missing data algorithms. Positive values give the program what is required to assemble the desired information in the form of an array in the immediate access memory for computation and other processing.

Sometimes a large number of records of the same type are chained together by the pointers (the classes of marital status given as our example). In this situation, the program may proceed to extract desired information from each subrecord as it becomes available without creating an array corresponding to the entire class of records. Null pointers indicate the end of each chain; positive pointers locate the next case of interest.

For the case in which the data of interest are structured as in Figure 5–8, combinations of these alternative treatments may be appropriate. For example, it may be of interest to retain income in a particular year or the smallest value of income over a period of years to be studied in relationship to income variance and marital status. The latter quantities would be values that pertain to classes of the basic records; the first quantity is a unique part of the array of income information.

Parity Errors and Pointers

Discussion of sequential matching procedures indicated that parity errors could result in the failure to match appropriate records. While the same problem arises with pointers, it is not nearly so serious. First, parity errors are generally encountered in reading tapes and infrequently encountered in retrieving data from disc or drum storage. The analyst using pointers must use direct access media and has a smaller probability of encountering a failure. This observation may appear to be question begging since information in direct access files was probably loaded from tapes at an earlier point in time. However, it is precisely the fact that loading a file occurs before the file is interrorgated for analytical purposes that makes it possible for the user to recover from errors in reading the tape. For example, records omitted in reading the tape can be regenerated in the disc file by the EDIT program or a similar procedure. (See Section 6.3.)

If a pointer is not identified because of machine failures, the user can continue his analysis by using the logic in the algorithm that created the pointer as a substitute for the missing information. Alternatively, the analyst can reverse the sequence of visiting the data to use B-type pointers rather than A-type pointers. (See Figure 8–2c for an illustration of the A-type pointer.) The latter procedure requires doubly-linked chains partitioning the file.

Logical Functions of Pointers

If several pointers have been generated to describe different dimensions of linkage, then it becomes an easy matter to generate logical functions of the pointers. For example, suppose that pointers have been generated to define both age and income classes. To extract data for old or poverty-stricken persons requires that the two pointers for those classes be logically combined. If we assume that records were stored in sequence by identifiers when pointers were created, then logic requires that we always visit the *lesser* address indicated by the two pointers for age and income class (j, k). The algorithm would proceed in the following fashion:

Algorithm: Class j in partition 1   OR   Class k in partition 2

(L_{jn} indicates the pointer on the nth record in the class j, and L_{kn} indicates the pointer on the nth record in the class k. W_1 and W_2 are "working" storage that record the value of the next relevant address in partitions 1 and 2 respectively.)

INITIALIZE   1.   Obtain the address L_{j1} of the first member of class j and the address L_{k1} of the first member of k. $L_{j1} \Rightarrow W_1, L_{k1} \Rightarrow W_2$.

ENTER   2.   If $W_1 < W_2$, retrieve record at W_1; store its pointer for class j ($L_{jn} \Rightarrow W_1$); EXIT. Otherwise go to step 3.

             3.   If $W_1 \geq W_2$, retrieve record at W_2; store its pointer for class k ($L_{kn} \Rightarrow W_2$); EXIT.

The intersection of two classes can be obtained by slightly more complex logic.

Class j in partition 1   AND   Class k in partition 2

INITIALIZE   1.   Obtain the address of the first member of class j (L_{j1}) and the first member of class k (L_{k1}). $L_{j1} \Rightarrow W_1, L_{k1} \Rightarrow W_2$.

ENTER   2.   If $W_1 = W_2$, the individual is in the intersection; retrieve the record for output. Store $L_{jn} \Rightarrow W_1$ and $L_{kn} \Rightarrow W_2$. EXIT. Otherwise go to step 3.

             3.   If $W_1 < W_2$, retrieve record at W_1; $L_{jn} \Rightarrow W_1$; go to step 2. Otherwise go to 4.

4.   If $W_1 > W_2$, retrieve record at $W_2; L_{kn} \Rightarrow W_2$; go to step 2.

It may appear wasteful to visit each record in the union, when the intersection of two classes is desired. However this algorithm has the advantage that no information other than pointers is required.

An alternative approach is to visit the address indicated by the larger pointer. This alternative requires that the *content* of that record be interrogated to determine whether the individual falls in the appropriate class on the second dimension. For example, if $L_{jn} > L_{kn}$, the record at L_{jn} is retrieved. However, the next member of the class $k \in 2$ cannot be ascertained from the pointer $L_{k' n + i}$ which may refer to a class other than the desired class k. Additional information and program logic similar to that used in the creation of the pointers is required to determine whether the record is in the class k.

The approach indicated for the OR and AND functions allows us to use housekeeping data to compute the cost of retrieving data. If N_j and N_k are the total number of records in the chain j and the chain k, then no more than $N_j + N_k$ records will be visited. In addition the approach can easily be generalized in several ways.

Combinations of AND and OR can be used to find $j \cap -k$, $-j \cap k$ and $j \cup k - j \cap k$. The algorithms can easily be extended to deal with the union and intersection of three or more classes. Indeed all that is required is repeated application of these functions.

File Segmentation, Sampling, and Pointers

The previous discussion needs to be amplified in the case in which the file has been segmented (Section 7.6). The same principles apply in creating pointers and their use, except that the pointers must be developed within each sample or file segment. Otherwise the pointers may refer to records not included in the file segment.

Concatenation or other merging of samples or file segments can easily be accomplished using the housekeeping data generated for each segment. As the first and last record in a particular chain is known for both segments, the loading of several segments requires a simple program to enter pointers that cross-reference the two files. A dictionary of the location of the first record in the second file segment can be used for this purpose. Indeed the whole process can be made entirely automatic if the first and last record addresses and chain length are encoded in a special dictionary record at the beginning of each file segment. The dictionary is simply an array consisting of first record address, last record address, and length of record chain for each class in each set of pointers. The concatenation of two file segments then requires that the

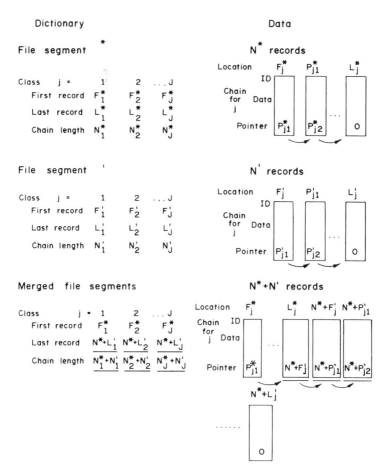

Figure 8–4. Concatenation of Pointers on Two File Segments

two dictionaries be merged to describe the combined set of records. The process is illustrated in Figure 8–4. Record addresses in the second file segment will automatically be incremented to allow for the storage of the first file segment. The underlined numbers indicate adjustments that must be made by the concatenation algorithm.

The figure shows that enlargement of a data set and its associated system of pointers can be easily accomplished if adequate documentation has been planned.

The selection of random samples from a larger set is not so economical. While no problems exist in defining pointers on the basis of random numbers to generate random subsets, the use of the subset would generally entail the

AND algorithm that we have just discussed. That algorithm, in turn, requires visiting all records in the union of the sets defined by the randomly generated pointers and some substantive characteristic of interest. Much of the economy of subsampling is thereby lost. For example, if the random subsample is 20% and the class of interest is also 20% of the sample, 36% of the sample must be retrieved although only 4% of the intersection needs to be retrieved. The desired economy can be achieved if the subsample is planned as a file segment.

8.2 Pointers, Statistical Analysis, and Program Simplification

The use of pointers decomposes the problem of analyzing complex data sets into two manageable pieces: the creation of pointers and links that define the data structure and useful partitions, and the development of data reduction techniques using the logic embedded in the pointers to determine the units of analysis and the population under study. Confusion about the number of replications that should appear in the statistics (as when multiple observations are generated from a single input record), the level at which transformations are to be executed (Is a mean of ratios or a ratio of means desired?), and the handling of missing data is greatly reduced. In addition, pointers permanently record a number of housekeeping details that would have to be repeated in multiple applications of the same logic in programs attempting similar analyses on the archive. For example, number of records in a population subset, the identifiers of the first and last records of that set, and the logic of relationship between records of different types (e.g., observations on tax records versus observations on individuals) are all available from interrogation of pointers or scanning the algorithm creating the pointers. The information is more easily retrieved and checked than in sequentially ordered files.

The chaining together of like records makes it possible to deal economically with subsets of the data archive, while offering the power to extend any analysis on a subpopulation to the entire population—either by iterating the analysis on all possible chains in a partition or by eliminating the logic by which the program is directed to a particular chain.

For many types of statistical analysis the desired objective is a set of parameter estimates replicated for a mutually exclusive and exhaustive classification of the underlying data set. Handling the entire classification may become prohibitive in terms of the demands on the immediate access memory of the computer. Failure to handle the entire classification may commit the analyst to numerous passes of the entire data set, or complex file handling prior to the analysis, both of which are prone to error and needless cost.

Fortunately the existence of pointers and the storage of the data on direct access media obviates the need for either procedure. One subgroup can be designated as the subject for a particular analysis run. The logic that must be incorporated in the driver is elementary. Subsequent runs produce the required statistics on the remaining classes of the data subset with virtually no change in the program. Each record needs to be found only once; it is used at the time that substantive information in the record is interrogated by the analysis program.

One may carry this point of view one step further. While a set of descriptive statistics developed on a partition may be the objective of the analysis, it is often desired to estimate a relationship in the same dimensions that define the partition. (For example, age may define a partition that distinguishes those eligible for social security benefits from the remaining population. Age continues to be a variable of importance for explaining lifetime income distributions within each group.) Standard statistical approaches call for regression in the case of variables containing an underlying cardinal scale, and for analysis of variance in cases in which the scale is nominal. Interactions and nonlinearities in the relationship give rise to difficulties, as it is often difficult to specify in advance from what universe a hypothesis that is to be tested is drawn (Light and Margolin, 1971, and Goodman, 1970, are exceptions). Moreover, the range of hypotheses that can be tested is often empirically limited by the distribution of the sample population over the dimensions that define the relationship.

It would appear, therefore, that these difficulties could be usefully overcome by employing pointers to achieve step-by-step reduction of data. A first reading of the data would generate frequency counts on the explanatory array. The same reading of the data creates new records described by array position (i.e., the definition of pointers generating the array element) which contain the summary statistics on the dependent variables that are desired for the analysis. Armed with knowledge of the frequency distribution of his sample, the analyst may then determine what nonlinearities and interactions can be fruitfully investigated. Once that information is available, the statistics of each cell of the array can be linked by an algorithm that generates appropriate information for either regression or analysis of variance.

We mention this concept of data analysis because our experience has been almost exclusively with statistical routines that are oriented toward using each logical record as the basic determinant of frequency. The concept of partially aggregated data that can be reinterpreted and further aggregated for study appears extremely useful in avoiding repeated access to records for individuals—access that may be extremely expensive in an archive as large as WAIS. [4]

The full value of linkage in the analysis of data can only be obtained when statistical routines make the aggregation of intermediate statistical information, such as correlation matrices, frequency counts, and variance components, convenient, automatic, and error free.

8.3 Random or Hashed Storage of Records

The value of storing data on direct access media should now be clear. Data on a disk or drum are available to the computer in milliseconds while a portion of magnetic tape or a card may take minutes to find. Such accessibility makes it possible to link and retrieve items of information by pointers in a small amount of time. However, the reader may have already wondered whether the cost of finding an address that is arbitrary relative to the portion of the disk or drum that is physically available is not prohibitive in relation to the cost of advancing a magnetic tape by one physical record.

This question is best answered by considering the concept of efficient storage of information on sequential media. Investigation of that problem reveals that storage of the records on direct access media is not nearly as critical as storing records on tape for the same application. For example, the most efficient analysis of mean income for each of the marital classes defined in Section 8.1 would require that all the records for a given class of marital status be grouped sequentially on tape. Other sequences of the data either require more machine memory or multiple passes of the tape file. (The programmer using serial media or unlinked files, even if on direct access media, would solve the problem by accumulating one sum at a time. This procedure is reasonable if memory on the computer is very limited or very expensive to use.) In any case, it is clear that a failure to use the optimum order of the file generates expense, in reading the file or using the computer core memory, that is a direct function of the size of the problem to be solved.

On the other hand, the worst organization of a direct access file entails the cost of waiting for the drum or disc to revolve once as each item of information is assembled. In practice this is a short span of time compared with the time required to read a record from tape. In all but pathological cases it would be virtually impossible to achieve such a poor organization of the file in relation to the drum or disc storage medium. One could expect that if the address of one datum is chosen at random with respect to the address to which it points, then no more than half a revolution of the drum or disk would be required on average to complete access to the complement of an item of information that is already available in the computer's core memory.

Fortunately it is possible to achieve even greater efficiency in the retrieval of linked records. We need only to observe that both elements in a link have the same identifier. Hence the storage location of both elements can be optimized by making the storage address a function of the identifier. The function can be chosen so that the second file bears that physical relation to the first which corresponds to the time it takes for the computer to interpret the address location and dispatch a command to retrieve the linked datum.

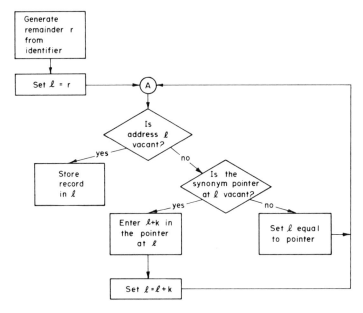

Figure 8–5. Algorithm to Store Data when Addresses Generated from Identifiers are not Unique

Clearly the only problem that remains is to choose a function that will translate the identifier into an appropriate relative address. If the identifier is a compact set without gaps, the problem is trivial. If the identifier is given by x, relative addresses for the first datum can be chosen as x and addresses for the second datum can be chosen as $x + c$ (c can be chosen to give an optimum response time). The WAIS identifier and SSN are not compact sets and some way must be found to store information in a manner that allocates data to all of the physical parts of the memory medium in a uniform manner. At the same time, data pertaining to the same identifier should be stored in an optimum relation to one another.

One technique, or trick, for converting the identifiers into a reasonably compact set is to divide the identifier by the smallest prime number exceeding the number of records in the set. Clearly, the remainders from that division must be a set of numbers smaller than the divisor. If the remainder r is unique, we can use its value as the relative address for storing a record. Then $r + c$ can be used to store the record to be linked. However, the remainders are not necessarily unique. (For example, four records might be identified with 06, 16, 23, 33; division by 5 produces only two remainders, 1 and 3.) Fortunately that problem can be overcome by a simple algorithm using pointers (see Figure 8-5). [5] Even though this method suggests an added burden to retrieval of data, the burden is small relative to other systems for storing information. The number of records that must be interrogated to obtain a random record according to the algorithm being used for retrieval are as follows:

	Number of Records in File			
	2	16	1024	262,144
Serial	1.0	8.0	512.0	131,072.0
Binary	1.0	4.0	10.0	18.0
Hashed [6]	1.5	1.5	1.5	1.5

The storage of records on magnetic tape gives the retrieval characteristics shown under serial. The binary algorithm for locating a record was discussed in Section 6.1. *Hashed* refers to a file stored randomly and compactly in a given area of direct access medium. The number of retrievals will be even smaller (and the costs of retrieving the data much less) if the data are not stored compactly. For example, if a prime number twice as large as the number of records to be stored is used to generate the storage addresses, the probability of generating two identical addresses is clearly smaller than if the smallest prime larger than the number of records is used. At the same time, more direct access memory must be reserved and more than half will be vacant. Clearly a trade-off exists between the time required to follow a chain of pointers entailing charges for the central processing unit and the cost of additional disc or drum storage.

8.4 Applications of Linkage and Hashed Files—The Merging of Identifiers from the First and Second Tax Record Collections

The discussion in Chapter 4 made clear that birth-date information for individuals represented in the first batch of tax records collected was obtained from earnings records, beneficiary records, and a supplementary search of Wisconsin vital and other administrative records. When the second batch of tax records were collected, additional information on birth data became available as the Department of Revenue included birth data on the tax form beginning in 1964. Clearly it was desirable to merge the newly acquired information with that already integrated in the ID file.

Merging information in the first and second collections of tax records posed an even more serious problem—how could tax records inadvertently included under two different identifiers in the process of collecting both sets of data be properly integrated? Although considerable efforts had been taken to assure that coders searched lists of existing identifiers to determine whether tax records for 1959–1964 corresponded to persons for whom identifiers had already been assigned, this operation was inherently difficult and liable to human error. The coders were being asked to scan a list to verify that an individual was *not* represented prior to assigning a new identifier. Failure to find an existing identifier was not an event that gave the coder a cause for alarm and triple-checking of his work.

The two problems mentioned were resolved by using the SSN and manual examination of records with identical addresses to determine whether an identifier in the series assigned to the second tax record collection was in fact assigned to a new entrant to the sample. If not, data under the two identifiers were integrated under the legitimate, original identifier. The process involved can be sketched briefly:

a. Match the ID file created for the second tax record collection against that created for the first.

b. Compare records with identical names and addresses to determine whether the same individual is involved. (At this point the fact that the 1959 tax record was collected with both sets of data proved invaluable in establishing unique matching of individual data.)

c. Designate identifiers as primary or secondary. Primary identifiers designate an adult. Secondary identifiers may designate an individual originally described as a dependent or an individual inadvertently assigned more than one identifier.

d. Transfer information on the secondary identifier to the primary identification record. Reconcile any discrepancies in age that result.

The last step of this process poses a difficult retrieval and data storage problem. Since new identifiers were assigned seriatum within name groups, the secondary identifier might have a value distant, and randomly removed from the value originally assigned. The problem was solved by storing the secondary ID record according to an address determined by the value of the primary identifier encoded on the record. Thus the process for matching primary and secondary ID data developed in the following way.

The matching process sketched in steps b and c above allowed us to encode an indicator that specified the existence of several identifiers for one individual. The indicator appears on both the primary and secondary ID records. It also designates ID records as primary or secondary. The ID file containing all records (both primary and secondary) was read. All records designated as secondaries were extracted into a subfile. The subfile was stored on direct access media by the prime number algorithm described in Section 8.3. The ID file was then read a second time and each primary record for which secondary records existed generated a computer address at which the secondary record could be found.

That address was used as a pointer. The pointer directed the computer to the information on age which could only be obtained from the secondary record.

The efficiency of the process is recorded in Table 8-2. The table indicates

Table 8-2
Hashed File Performance

File Segment ICFSEC	(1) Record Count[a]	(2) Density of Non-Zero Information[b] Col. (1)/503	(3) Average Accesses for Retrieval
6	177	.4-	1.18
7	192	.4-	1.19
2	195	.4-	1.16
1	211	.4+	1.28
3	229	.4+	1.27
8	249	.5-	1.38
5	259	.5+	1.30
9	267	.5+	1.35
4	395	.8-	1.47

[a]The files are ordered in ascending magnitude of record count.

[b]The records were written into a storage area that could contain 513 records. The storage locations were obtained by dividing 503 into the identifier so that only 503 records could be compactly stored by the algorithm without generating at least one synonym.

that in most cases the desired records were located on the first or second iteration of the algorithm in Figure 8-5. An average of 1.3 accesses to the disk file were required to find the desired secondary record.

Once the secondary record corresponding to the primary had been located, it was an easy matter to transcribe birth data into the primary, where none had been available.

The final step in the processing of the second collection of tax data required that invalid identifiers on the MF and other records be replaced by the valid identifier. The offending identifier was retained in the ID so that any record can be traced to its correct primary identifier, even if the invalid identifier has not been altered on some document or working file.

8.5 File Organization Using Indicators and Pointers

The structure of the summary record mentioned in Section 5.5 provides a useful example for discussing the use that can be made of record indicators and pointers in the context of a difficult data reduction problem. The process whereby a format was developed for the summary record, and the alternatives selected from the options available also help to understand some of the problems that must be solved when handling a large data archive.

Four major sets of decisions had to be made in the process of developing the summary record. The first pertained to the number of records to be summarized. A single record could be created for each individual or for each marital unit, or for an entire household. Two considerations led us to choose the first alternative: (1) a file based on individuals was far more compact than a file based on households; (2) the identifier had already been designed to minimize the problems of assembling marital units and households from sequential media. Whenever the file is ordered by identifier all persons in the same household will be ordered sequentially in the file. Hence it is relatively easy to locate records for a spouse once a single record for the marriage partner is available.

Choice of the individual as the basis for the summary record forced a two-stage development of the summary record. The first stage summarized the information that is available for a given individual. The second stage reconciled summaries for several individuals to resolve questions of marital status at a given point in time and the number of tax returns available for the husband and wife at that point in time.

In fact, this staging of the development of the summary record proved useful for another reason. A second decision that had to be made in creating the summary record pertained to the years for which no tax return was available. How was information from the several years of available data to be used to assign a meaning to the absence of a tax return? Was the return missing, or out of the sample? Both deaths and marriages imply that persons can disappear abruptly from the sample universe.

To assign missing data codes to years in which no tax returns were filed proved to be a complex problem. The tax form elicited information on the filing of returns in the prior year. Hence the most common source of information about gaps in the tax returns filed by an individual is in the year following the gap. However, during the second collection of tax records WAIS also coded an indicator of information available in the file for the year following the present year as a double check on the completeness of the process of transcribing information from the original records. Thus, for 1959–1964, the year prior to the gap in a series of tax returns could also be consulted to determine whether a return was missing or out of the sample. In addition, in all sample years the spouse's return prior to a gap could contain an indication that the spouse died during the year.

It became clear that the assignment of a code interpreting gaps in the sequence of tax records available would require information from the year prior to the gap and the year following the gap. In addition, the information was contained in three variables for the years prior to 1959 and four variables following 1958. Depending on the analysis to be undertaken, the significance attached to these various sources of information about missing returns might vary. Hence the second decision, which was strongly influenced by the decision to use individual records, was to extract all the data pertaining to the filing of tax returns in the first stage and relegate the creation of codes interpreting missing data to the second stage of development of the summary file, when an array of pertinent information for both husband and wife could be easily obtained from the initial extract.

A similar problem pertained to the consistency of marital status reported by the husband and wife. Two variables refer to the marital status of the taxpayer. However, those variables were not always completed by the taxpayer, so that they are subject to substantial reporting errors. Ideally a taxpayer should report the event of marriage during the year, his current marital status, and whether his spouse filed a tax return. When there are gaps in this information, or when the information reported by both marriage partners is different, some difficult problems of interpretation arise. It is clear from the large number of women who report a spouse when their husbands fail to do so that the number of married persons would be badly understated by the decision to treat as married only couples who *both* report a spouse in the current year. Fortunately, information on the filing of tax returns also elicits information on marriages so that both an interpersonal consistency and an intertemporal examination of information related to marital status can be undertaken.

Again, the two-stage development of the summary record permitted assembly of all the relevant information in an initial extract followed by an interpretive coding of consistency in the second stage.

The third major decision concerning the summary record pertained to the nature of the pointers. Pointers in binary coded decimal form (BCD) would be compact and easily transferred between computers. Binary equivalents would be restricted to the computer on which the pointers were created (the UNIVAC 1108) but would be far more efficient when used in analysis programs on that machine. In the end BCD pointers were retained in the summary record to maintain flexibility. In that fashion, the master file could be transported to other machines with direct access memory and loaded according to relative addresses specified by the BCD pointers without having to recreate the pointers themselves.

The fourth major decision pertaining to the summary record concerned the choice of links describing demographic groups of interest in analysis. This decision, even more than the choice of interpretations of marital status and missing data, was governed by the particular analysis being undertaken by WAIS. We mention the specifics of the links established primarily to illustrate how useful classifications of explanatory variables can be defined on a dynamically changing set of variables (cf. Section 3.3), and how the choice of such groups simplified the problem of simulating averaging for tax purposes on the file.

Consider the following candidates for the demographic classifying variables used in an analysis of income averaging for tax purposes from 1951–1964 (Miller and David, 1971): [7]

Sex (M = Male, F = Female)
Marital Status (N = Never married, A = Always married, P = Sometimes

married, or partially married in the filing time span)

Current Filing Status (J = Joint, I = Single, not relevant for $MS = N$ or A since we necessarily assume joint filing by married couples)

Age

Labor Force Status

Principal Occupation

(a) Ever change? (Never, Once, More than once)

(b) "Independent" (Farm, Professional, Proprietorship, Rent) or "Dependent (Managerial, Supervisory, Other "White Collar," Other "Blue Collar")

Source of Income

(a) *Major* source in period (Wages and Salaries, Non-W-S sources)

(b) Significant investment source (average annual capital gains, dividends and interest above some threshold level?)

(c) If married, spouse ever had separate income while married?

(d) Number of distinct Wage and Salary Sources

To illustrate our approach, consider the categories of age and labor force status. One classification which captures the joint effect of both for most persons is:

a. Achieved age 65 before 1951

b. Left labor force or reached 65 in 1951–1958

c. Left labor force or reached 65 in 1959–1964

d. Was between 21 and 65 and in labor force, entire period 1951–1964

e. Entered labor force or achieved age 21 during 1951–1958

f. Entered labor force or achieved age 21 after 1958

g. Never in labor force, entire period 1951–1965, but not in (a) above

These brief descriptions do not do justice to the classification, but are suggestive only (ambiguous cases such as those who entered *and* left the labor force exist in the scheme as it is). More detailed description will eliminate ambiguities, but two points should be clear from this description: (1) The obvious correlation between age and labor force participation has been exploited to keep the distinct categories down to seven in number; and (2) the combined significance of age and *length* of labor force participation has been emphasized as being of significance for income variation through time.

Further discussion of the pointers generated on the summary file requires a brief introduction to the simulation analysis which motivated the creation of a summary file in the first place. (See Miller and David, 1971, for a more complete discussion.) The problem was to extract information from the MF to permit the simulation of a variety of tax averaging schemes. The data required involved a number of tax records for each individual and the reconstruction

of a joint income for husband and wife on the basis of the collection of tax
returns for both individuals in years in which they were married. Thus marital
status is not only an important variable to describe the results of the simulation, it is a key variable for determining the algorithm that assembles the information from several tax records for one or two persons to produce a measure of
tax savings under averaging.

The latter aspect of marital status caused us to develop a pointer based
on marital status (MSTAT), spouse separate income (SEPINC) and sex. Six
categories were defined:

    a.   Male, always single 1947–1964
    b.   Female, always single
    c.   Always married, spouse had separate income sometime
    d.   Always married, spouse never had separate income
    e.   Married at some time, spouse had income at some time
    f.   Married at some time, spouse never had separate income

Groups a and b represent the simplest situation for computing the effect of tax
averaging. Simulation requires assembly of information from several years of
tax returns for one individual and no more. Group d in fact requires no more
information, but entails a somewhat different computation of exemptions and
tax rates. Group c requires the assembly of information from two persons, but
raises no questions concerning the treatment of years prior to a marriage or
subsequent to the dissolution of a marriage. Groups e and f create the most complex programming problems since they must include rules for the treatment of
individuals for whom a change in income is related to a change in the number
of earners and dependency status of individuals. Group e also requires assembly
of tax records for husband and wife during years that they are married.

The pointer based on sex and marital status thus neatly segregates mean-
ingful demographic groups in such a way that the algorithm for simulating the
impact of tax-averaging rules can be developed on cases that are both conceptually and computationally straightforward. The algorithm can then be extended to handle those instances which require more difficult assembly of data from
the archive and conceptually more debatable rules concerning the underlying
tax policy on which the simulation is based.

The decisions made concerning the summary record enabled us to convert
a relatively intractable data-handling problem into a series of smaller problems
that could be solved simultaneously by different people without endangering
the meaning of the results. Thus, one programmer was delegated to develop
the first-stage extract for the summary record; a second programmer was given
the task of developing an algorithm to deal with tax averaging for cases a and b
above; a third and independent effort was undertaken to develop the logic for
creating pointers; and the chief researchers on the project struggled with diffi-

cult substantive questions raised by the inconsistency of marital status and the absence of tax records.

8.6 Conclusions

In this chapter we have described concepts recently used by WAIS in handling its data archive. These concepts require the use of direct access storage media, and thrive in an environment in which interactive control of files is feasible. However, the concepts are fundamental, and have been anticipated in the theoretical discussions of data in Chapter 5. In Figure 5–5 relationships between data elements were described by lines. In this chapter we have shown how those lines can be translated into machine-readable pointers that capture structural relationships among records.

The fact that it is possible to scan a body of data with a large number of functions and create different partitions of data implies that it is possible to develop an equally large number of different types of pointers. For some specialized uses of the data there may be no merit in storing such pointers in a permanent archive. However, pointers that describe basic demographic data, pointers that link records including rare and interesting events (loss of a job, beginning of self-employment activities) or pointers that group replications of observations for particular individuals, will receive general and continuing use.

The pointer makes it possible for each analyst to place useful traces in the data that reveal its structure. Work done at a later point in time can then proceed without rediscovering the algorithms of earlier workers, and with a considerable body of information that comes with the documentation for a set of pointers.

Pointers appear to be useful in at least four ways:

a. They can establish links between records of different types and facilitate the easy recovery of information that might otherwise be inaccessible. (For example, pointers appear essential to the retrieval of stock-price data; see Section 5.5. They greatly simplified the matching of age data to valid ID's.)

b. Pointers can facilitate the partition of data sets into subfiles in a fashion that conserves storage space by eliminating null and irrelevant records.

c. Pointers can provide classification of records into mutually exclusive sets that are particularly useful for simplifying programming functions. (The problems involved in computing averageable income discussed in Section 8.5 are a good example.)

    d.   Pointers establish useful subgroups for analysis and minimize the costs of accessing data on pertinent subgroups.

Pointers are not a substitute for good planning of file organization, adequate segmentation, and subsampling.

The use of pointers and hashed files proved to be enormously effective in dealing with the complex problems of merging the first and second collections of tax-record information. It appears that the use of pointers would be highly desirable in expediting error correction and reducing the cost of access to inconsistent or illegal cases. Finally, it appears that pointers will provide an economical way of restructuring the analysis of data from a process of repeated references to a fixed record to a process that continuously updates and restructures aggregates of the underlying data set. This latter view of the problem is particularly useful when the opportunity of linking alternative data sources to those at hand depends on being able to quickly alter the level of aggregation and the unit of analysis.

9

The Data Archive, A Management Information System

Much of the foregoing discussion can be integrated by pointing to the similarities between the problems faced by the manager in compiling data for making decisions and the problems of the researcher with a complex data archive. Indeed, hints of the similarities between the two sets of data-handling problems were already set forth in the summaries to Chapters 1 and 2. In the sections that follow we will discuss the requirements of a management information system, procedures that are required to implement such a system, and the manner in which requirements and procedures apply to the WAIS archive.

9.1 Requirements of a Management Information System (MIS)

Ideally, a management information system (hereafter MIS) provides quick responses, based on observations of real phenomena, to questions posed by its creators. The research scientist seeks to confirm hypotheses derived from a theoretical structure. The manager seeks to exercise an optimizing choice among alternative processes. Information derived from a management information system can show an hypothesis or proposed process to be untenable or inferior. However, the existence of a tenable hypothesis or an optimal process at one point in time does not imply that it will continue to remain optimal as more information is added to the system. It is the nature of both the search for scientific knowledge and optimizing solutions to management problems that the details of answers vary as knowledge increases.

Hence one of the first requirements of a MIS is to be able to add new information and deal with it using procedures that were developed for a preexisting data base. New information may take the form of additional observations or replications of past measures; it may also take the form of totally new types of measures. The latter form of data needs to be linked to existing information with appropriate relations and cross-references.

A second feature of an MIS is that it must be sufficiently flexible to deal with several levels of aggregation—Questions may concern individuals, activities of individuals, events (such as job changes), or groups of individuals (the beneficiaries of a social security account).

The key motivation behind the MIS is to provide the scientist or decision maker with a technique for rapidly juxtaposing data collected from a variety of sources in order to test an hypothesis or derive a necessary measure.

9.2 Procedures to Implement MIS Concepts

Data collected and stored in machine-readable form do not suffice to provide the rapid access that is required for either a data archive or an MIS. What is needed is to embed those data in a system for handling information that is sufficiently general that the manager or scientist does not need to find a new language and a new set of concepts for each new question.

Basic to the creation of such a data system is a technique for documentation that clearly lays out the parallels and differences between classes of information on the same subject collected at different points in time. The database document in Appendix E is one approach. (See also section 5.4). Work done by the Inter-University Consortium for Political Research (1973) is another.

After the commonalities of different observations have been adequately described, linkage of those observations must be created to allow rapid access to samples of time series and cross-sections of data pertaining to individuals. Access to random samples of events and decisions made by individuals are also valuable. The importance of linkage lies in the fact that a complex data base cannot be stored or even conceptualized as a rectangular array. (The facts of birth and death alone create a logical nonrectangularity in a sample of tax documents over time.) However, statistical analyses that are addressed to the data are defined for rectangular arrays. The task of linkage is to economize on storage and ease of access by translating implicit structure in the data into a particular array that is necessary to answer the question at hand. The discussions in Section 5.5 and Chapter 8 indicate some concepts that are useful for economizing in the cost of storage and data retrieval.

An equally important problem and one that has received considerable attention in file-management systems (Godsen, 1972), is the problem of data entry. Here the problem is to screen each new observation for consistency and logical errors prior to entering the data in the MIS. WAIS experience with error correction and data entry indicates the value of direct entry techniques and the importance of rapid retrieval of observations from an archive to economize on the cost of error correction (see Chapter 6).

9.3 The Evolution of WAIS as a Data
Archive and an MIS

Discussion of several features of WAIS experience indicates that the solutions to complex processing problems lay in conceptualizing the archiving problem as the problem of rapid retrieval in an MIS. Data correction and entry only became economical when interactive on-line retrieval made it possible for coding staff to manipulate records in the computer. Processing the large file was achieved economically only after control, through file segmentation, was placed on the size of problems presented to the computer. That same segmentation made it economic to conceive of pointers as the mechanism of linkage and dispense with cumbersome sequential algorithms for matching portions of the data structure.

The need for systematic planning in developing a complex data archive is obvious and, as we know from experience, underestimated. We hope that the modest ideas laid out in this monograph will be of help to others in the future.

Appendixes

Appendix A
WAIS Bibliography—Major Items
and Thesis Efforts

Publications

Bauman, R., David, M., and Miller, R.F. [1967].
David, M. [1969].
David, M. [1971a].
David M. [1971b].
David, M., Groves, H., Miller, R.F., and Wiegner, E.A. [1970].
David, M. and Miller, R.F. [1969].
David, M. and Miller, R.F. [1970].
David, M. and Miller, R.F. [1972].
Geffert, J. [1966].
Miller, R.F. [1969].
Miller, R.F. [1971].
Miller, R.F. and David, M. [1971].
Miller, R.F., David, M., Wiegner, E. and Groves, H. [1969].
Moyer, M.E. [1966a].
Moyer, M.E. [1966b].
Schroeder, L., and David, M. [1970].

Theses

Brown, E. (pending)
Bussman, W.V. (1972)
Durant, R.O. (1965)
Schroeder, L. (1971)
Wiegner, E. (1968)

Working Memoranda

Files of working documents prepared by the WAIS staff are indexed and available for inspection at the Social Systems Research Institute in Madison. Each document is referenced by a six-digit number, e.g. 689–030. A list of papers referred to follows:

Number	Author	Title
645–020	Geffert	Proposal for Consistency Check
645–060	Geffert	Consistency Check Program Edits
656–037	Geffert	Logical Construction of the 400 Character Master File

667–002	Moyer, Geffert, Bauman, deVries, Hinckley	Processing 1959–1964 Wisconsin Tax Filing Coding Manual
689–013	Gates	The Present and Potential Use of Data Descriptors
689–024	Schroeder	Some New Master File Field Definition Problems
689–027	Schilberg	SUPPFMT Documentation
689–028	Schilberg	SCHILB/NEWFMT Series of Programs
689–030	Whitaker	Directions for Evaluating Form 4 Edits
690–012	Schroeder	Detecting Inconsistencies in the Master File
690–016	Schroeder	Using Amount Fields on the New Master File
690–033	Schroeder	A Comparison of Federal and State Treatments of Business Loss Carryover and Deductible Medical Expenses
701–006	Gates	Interest Expenses: Chronology
701–022	Tam	Demographic Codes for the Merged 1946–64 Data File
712–004	Gates	Format: Identification Control File
712–016	Aldrich	The Validity of Indicators on the 46–60 Master File

Appendix B
Assignment of Identifiers to
Taxpayers and Beneficiaries

Tax Record Identifiers

The identifiers of individuals in the tax sample were assigned according to the rules which follow. The first two digits of the identifier encode the alphabetic name group cluster to which this household belongs. Persons living together at the same address were originally assigned a common four-digit household number seriatim within each name group cluster. Individuals within the household were then identified by sex and relationship to the head of the household:

Code	Males	Code	Females
00	Head of household	10	First spouse of the household head
01	Dependent son (eldest)	11	Dependent daughter (eldest)
02	Dependent son	12	Dependent daughter
	·		·
	·		·
	·		·
		20	Second spouse of the household head
		30	Third spouse of the household head

Finally, each record was identified according to the calendar year to which encoded data pertained.

In connection with the survey taken in 1964, some additional individuals were sampled by extending the alphabetic clusters of the original name groups. Such names were given a household number beginning with 1001. Identifiers assigned to the second collection of tax data were given a serial beginning with 4001.

The benefit data clearly showed that some persons originally in households became institutionalized. In order to avoid complicating the assignment of identifiers still further, the same household numbers were used for individuals both before and after they entered institutions. As a consequence, the individuals grouped under a single household include:

1. The household head and his spouse

165

2. Unmarried children who continue to live at the same address up to the end
    of the sample period
3. Institutionalized persons who are beneficiaries of an account which pays
    benefits to the person.

Checking identifying information for beneficiaries required the assignment
of new identifiers whenever the individual was not included in the original
sample of tax records. The rules for the assignment of identifiers described
above applied whenever the individual was part of the original name group
samples. Two other groups of beneficiaries existed:

a. Persons with names outside the original sample frame
b. Lump-sum death benefits paid to institutions and unknown relatives outside
    the original sample frame

Data for these groups were preserved by treating *a* as a separate name group
(70) and *b* as a separate individual within the original household.

Beneficiary Identifiers

The ID's, name, age, and address for all persons in the households of the
benefit account holders were listed prior to assigning beneficiary identifiers.
Identifiers were assigned according to the following rules:

1. If the beneficiary is in the same family unit as shown on the printout of
    ID's, use the previous ID, if any. If no previous ID was previously assigned,
    give the beneficiary a new ID within his family unit.
2. If the beneficiary is not in the same family unit as shown on the printout,
    give him a new ID in a different unit. The new ID should be assigned as
    follows:
    a. If the new head is in the WAIS name groups, assign an eight-digit ID
        as follows:

Digits	Content
1-2	same as appropriate name group
3	2–designates assigned ID from SS benefit data
4-6	consecutive number beginning with 001
7-8	sex-family status

    b. If the new head is not in the WAIS name group assign an eight-digit ID
        as follows:

Digits	Content
1-2	70
3-6	consecutive number beginning with 0001
7-8	sex-family status

Note that the rules above do not depend on such things as: (*i*) the beneficiary being in the tax sample at any time; (*ii*) the beneficiary's residence in or outside of Wisconsin; or (*iii*) dependency as defined by the Social Security Administration. These conditions are purposely ignored for several reasons: Taxpayer status (item *i*) is not obvious from the benefit data and ID's alone, and hence is not easily coded. Taxpayer status also varies according to the years included and possible future supplements to the tax sample. Item *ii* is easily determined by the county code in our ID. No purpose appeared to be served by introducing a geographic code into the identifier. Item *iii* is still available, if desired, through matching on benefit account number and the beneficiary identifying code.

One other advantage of the rules is that the new ID's will be compatible with previously assigned ID's. Hence, integrating, updating, and other operations may be applied to the entire ID File. Beneficiaries not identified by tax record identifiers posed a problem to management of the identifier system. The rules above resolve that problem while making it possible to recapture the manner in which individuals enter the sample.

The only other problem in assigning identifiers was posed by lump-sum death payments (LSDP). These payments are sometimes made to unknown beneficiaries. In such cases, the ID created was vacuous since no name, address, or birth date was available. The WAIS ID number that was assigned for the purpose of recording the data is:

1-6	First six digits of account holder's ID
7-8	71 for LSDP to unknown male relative
	72 for LSDP to unknown female relative
	73 for LSDP to a funeral home
	74 for LSDP to the estate
	79 for all other unidentified LSDP

All new numbers assigned as well as tax record ID's associated with a beneficiary's former household were recorded on the ID. Some examples of assignments are shown in Figures B-1 and B-2.

In Figure B-1, the SSN of a Wisconsin taxpayer is linked to the beneficiaries of the SSN. The taxpayer and one of his children already have ID's since they filed Wisconsin tax returns during the years included in our sample. Their benefit history is recorded under their original ID's. In Figure B-2, the wife and two other children have not filed (so far), so ID's are created, and their

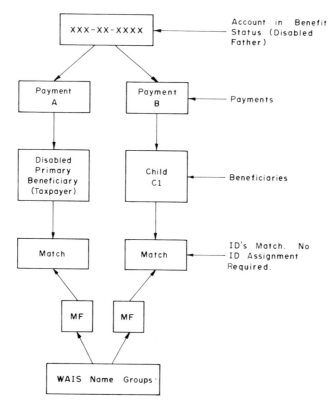

Figure B-1. Assignment of ID Numbers to Beneficiaries—ID Pre-assigned to Taxpayers

benefit history is recorded under the new ID's. (The law may require separate payments to different beneficiaries, depending on who is to endorse the checks issued. That distinction creates the two "payment" boxes shown.)

In Figure B-2, the primary beneficiary, already has an ID; he is divorced. The mother, remarried, has custody of the children. ID's must be assigned to her and two of the three children. The ID to be assigned will depend on the surname. If the surname of a child is in WAIS name groups, then he should be given an ID in the relevant name group, but not in the same household as his father. Otherwise the child's identifier falls in name group 70.

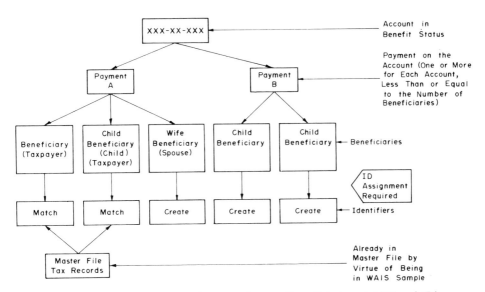

Figure B-2. Assignment of ID Numbers to Beneficiaries—Additional ID's
Generated

Appendix C
Beneficiary Record Structure

Three digits are used to specify card types. These are the one-digit card number (col. 3) and the two-digit sequence number (cols. 79–80). Card 1 is used for benefit *account* information. (The sequence number for Card 1 is always blank.) The account ties in with the wage earnings record of a person who became "insured" under the provisions of the Social Security law. If he receives retirement benefits, he becomes a beneficiary. Otherwise the beneficiaries are legally related to or dependents of the insured, but need never have made a contribution in payroll taxes and do not necessarily have tax records or ER records.

Cards 2 and 3 are used for *beneficiary* information. These cards always have a numeric sequence number. Card 2 is used when the source document is an SSA Form 9249. Card 3 is used when the source document is an SSA computer printout. An individual's data may be on cards numbered 2 only, cards numbered 3 only, or cards numbered 2 and 3—depending upon the *form* of the source document(s). (The processing of the tax return data also depended upon the *form* used. In the first collection it was necessary to allow for six types of tax forms.)

Card 4 is a special card used only where there is a representative payee who receives the payment in trust for the beneficiary.

If Card 3 or Card 2 is used and there is no change in the beneficiary identifying code (BIC), the 00 sequence card containing basic demographic data on the individual is always used. If any transactions information is also present, this is recorded chronologically on cards with sequence numbers 01, 02, etc. Each sequence card has space for four transactions entries. Each entry represents an amount that the Treasury is instructed to pay on this account.

If Card 2 is used and there is more than one BIC, data related to the first BIC is recorded first in chronological order. Data from the second BIC is recorded as follows: demographic data is recorded on a card identified by a sequence number of 10. Monthly payment information is recorded on cards with sequence numbers 11, 12, etc.

When a person has data on both Cards 2 and 3, Card 3–01 is a chronological continuation of the Card 2 with the highest sequence number.

For example, suppose a woman starts receiving benefits on her husband's account. After five changes in the monthly payment amount, i.e., five transactions, her husband dies and she is entitled to benefits as a widow (new BIC). After three more transactions, her benefit payment history is continued on the SSA computer printout which shows two additional transactions. All data for the woman is recorded on eight cards as shown in Table C-1.

Table C-1

Record Structure Used to Encode Beneficiary Payment Data

Card No. Col. 3	Seq. No. Col. 79–80	BIC Col. 21	Summary of Data Included
1	blank	–	Basic account information–primary beneficiary ID, # of beneficiaries, etc.
2	00	B	Basic data for wife–ID, date of benefit, date of entitlement, etc.
2	01	–	First four transactions for wife
2	02	–	Fifth transaction for wife
2	10	D	Basic data for widow since BIC and date of entitlement change
2	11	–	Sixth to eighth transaction entries
3	00	D	Basic data for widow repeated, since format differs
3	01	–	Ninth and tenth transaction entries

$B \sim$ beneficiary identifying code for wife's benefits
$D \sim$ beneficiary identifying code for widow's benefits

Input Card Descriptions for UPDATEAL

All input cards are made up of three selections:

a. The identification section   (cols. 1–18)
b. The action section   (cols. 19–20)
c. The data section   (cols. 21–80)

The record identification—the sortfield(s)—can be numeric, alphabetic, or both. If it is less than 18 positions long, justify to the left. The program treats everything to the left and including the first nonblank character in the identification section as the record identifier. If a blank is a legal character in a sortfield of the file, code the "stand-for-blank" character in its field in the identification section. If there is more than on sortfield on the file, arrange these in decreasing order of precedence without interrupting spaces from left to right in the identification section.

The action section contains a symbol defining the action to be taken in the first position (col. 19). The meaning of symbols appearing in col. 20 depends on the card type, as described below. Five types of cards are defined by the action symbols described below.

D-Card: Specifies which record(s) should be deleted from the file.

Cols. 1–18   Identification.
Col. 19   *D*
Col. 20   Blank, or *J* if the record should be listed when deleted from the file.
Cols. 21–24 Blank.
Cols. 25–80 Comments (optional).

M-Card: Modifies existing records. Any field except the sortfield(s) can be modified.

Cols. 1–18   Identification.
Col. 19   *M*
Col. 20   Blank or *J* if the record should be listed before and after the change.
Cols. 21–35 A field designator with data.
Cols. 36–50 A field designator with data or blank.
Cols. 51–65 A field designator with data or blank.
Cols. 66–80 A field designator with data or blank.

C-Card: Modifies existing records. Any field can be modified, but at least some part of a sortfield *must* be modified using field designator(s) with data (contrary to M-cards where this is not allowable). The record will be resequenced. Otherwise the C-card is the same as the M-card excepting that col. 19 contains a C.

A-Card: Specifies a new record which is composed from the field designators with data. The identification must be of the same length as the sortfield(s). The record will be inserted only if a record with identical sortfield(s) does not yet exist. Do not omit the sortfield(s) in the data section.

Col. 19   *A*

Col. 20   Blank, or *J* if the record should be listed at the time it is inserted into the file.

Cols. 21-80 Same as type M-card.

Numbered Cards: Do the same as an A-Card, but in a different way. Field designators with data are not used. Instead, the first 60 characters of the record to be established are entered on card 1, the second 60 characters on card 2, etc. Whatever remains to be put on the last card is left-justified to col. 21. Do not omit the sortfield in the data section. The record will be inserted only if there is yet no other record with the same sortfield(s) on the file.

Cols. 1-18   Identification.

Cols 19-20   Card number beginning with 01 and with a maximum of 17, depending on the record length. If the record should be printed out in the form it has been put on the updated file, then code the first card only as 0*J* instead of 01. Leading zeros must always be coded.

Cols. 21-80 Information to be put in record in blocks of 60 characters.

Any number of A or M cards for the same identification may be specified. However, change of identifier is incompatible with retaining that identifier, so that both should not reference the same record on the input file. The data section of A, C, or M cards contains up to four field designators each fifteen positions long. If less than four such field designators are used on a card, use up the leftmost parts of the data section first.

The sequence of fields specified is irrelevant. Comments may be entered in unused field designators, if at least the first four positions of the first unused field designator are left blank. The format of a *field designator* is as follows:

1   *The field length:* Numbers 1, 2, . . . , 9, 0, where 0 stands for 10. This designates the length of the data and correspondingly the length of the field on the record into which the data must be moved.

2-4   *The field address:* Numbers 001, 002, . . . , *nnn*. This designates the high order or leftmost position of the affected field on the record.

nnn is the record length (a record mark cannot be specified on the cards).

5-14   *The data:* Data to be put on the record, i.e., either to overlay existing data in a record or to specify new data for a new record. Left-justify the data if the field is less than ten positions long.

15   Blank.

Appendix E
Database Document for Merged
Master File 1946-1964

This data-base document represents WAIS documentation of variables which appear on the WAIS 1946-1964 MF. The material from Moyer (1966b), the 1960-1964 codebook, various WAIS papers, and our own experience were combined and put in this form for easy retrievability. (Titles and authors of WAIS working papers are shown in Appendix A; each paper is designated by a six-digit number, e.g. 701-001.)

Each variable is listed in the order in which it appears on the merged master file. The document is divided into sections. The format for the variables in each section accompanies the documentation. Forms from which data were extracted are shown in Table E-1.

E.1 FORMAT: Master 46-64 and Contents of Appendix

Section	Fields	Size	Beginning Page
Control variables	6	28	179
Variables related to income	16	128	185
Variables related to deductions	15	105	196
Tax liability and miscellaneous variables	15	120	206
Indicators related to household and filing status	19	23	215
Indicators related to labor force and employment	9	13	234
Indicators of geographic location	4	9	244
Miscellaneous indicators	13	14	250
Transformation variables	6	42	260
Deduction indicators (total or deductible 46-60 only)	3	3	263
	106	485	
Padding		19	
		504	

The padding permits division of the record size by 6 and 8 and is optimal for 1108 drum storage.

Table E-1
Individual Tax Forms in Use for 1946-1964[a]

	Long Form		Short Form	
Year	Husband	Wife	Husband	Wife
1946	X	X	X	
1947	X	X	X	X
1948	X	X	X	X
1949	X	X	X	X
1950	X	X	X	X
1951	X	X	X	X
1952	X	X	X	X
1953	X	X		
1954	X	X		
1955	X	X		
1956	X	X		
1957	X	X	X	X
1958	X	X	X	X
	Combined		Combined	
1959	1			
1960	1			
1961	1			
1962	2		4	
1963	3		4	
1964	3		4	

[a]The numbers identify form numbers used in Appendix F.

E.2 Format for the Documentation

Each module of documentation includes four types of information mentioned in Section 5.4: I. Variable description, II. Content qualification, III. File definition, and IV. Narrative description. The content of each of these sections is explicated using *YR* as an example:

				YR
I.	Full name and description of variable Location of items in source document, by year and type of form Predecessor list, variable classification (defined on p. 84), successor list	*I.*	*Year* *All forms* *[1]*	
II.	Content qualification (C.Q.) Restriction(s) on valid data entered	*II.*	*C.Q.* *46 ≤ YR ≤ 64*	

III. Physical file definition for perma-
      nent files (F.D.)
      Years [Type, position]
      Type is character (C) or word (W).
      Position gives the first and last
      positions occupied by the datum.
IV.   Narrative description comments and
      references used in interpreting the
      datum

III. F.D.

46-59 [C, 2-9]
60-64 [C, 2-9]
46-64 [C, 2-9]

IV.   N.D.

*Records for the years 59-
60 may have had their
origin in either the first
or second collection of
tax records. The source
code indicates in which
file the record originated.*

Table E-2
Control Variables

Control Variables (Merged)	Descriptors	Old (1946-1960)	New (1959-1964)	Size
1	SC	–	–	1
2-3	UPDATE	–	1	2
4-11	IDNUM	2-9	2-9	8
12-13	YR	10-11	10-11	2
14-22	SS	Obtained from ID for 46-59	395-403	9
23-28	TBIRTH	from ID	from ID	6
6 Fields				28

SC

I.   Source Code (all forms)
     [4]
II. C.Q.
     SC = 0, 2, 3
III. F.D.
     46-59 [C, 1]
     60-64 [not present]
     46-64 [C, 1]

IV.   N.D.

The source code is 0 if the record was originally part of the 46–59 master
file. Records originally in the 1960–1964 master file received a source
code of 2. However, records which originated in the 60–64 MF but were
blank except for certain demographic fields, received a source code of 3.
(These records are usually wives who are in-and-out of the labor force, and
thus have blank records in the amount fields for the years in which they
do not work). The code 1 was not used because it was thought that we
might want to expand the zero code at some later date. The test performed
by the program which created the source codes for the 60–64 file was
simply a presence of income delineating a 2 while no income indicated a 3.

UPDATE

I.   Update Code
      64, 63, 62, 61, 60, 59, 58, 57, 56, 55, 54, 53, 52, 51, 50, 49, 48, 47, 46—
      all forms
      [4]
II.   C.Q.
      $00 \leqslant \text{UPDATE} \leqslant 07$
III. F.D.
      46–59 [not available]
      60–64 [C, 1]
      46–64 [C, 2-3]
IV.   N.D.

The update code was set at 0 for all records which had originally been on
the 46–59 master file by WAIS/OUTFD4 just prior to the creation of
the merged file. It was then expanded to a two-digit code by the merge
program. Those records which originally were a part of the 59–64 master
file have an update code of 02; those in which an error was detected the
EDIT program were subsequently either corrected by teletype or determined to be an uncorrectable error are coded 03 in the update field. These
are the codes available on MASTER1.

The codes on MF are as follows:

04 = Used to indicate that social security number wasn't the same on both
     the ID file and the master file, the social security number from the
     ID was moved to the master.
05 = The original master file record was under the secondary IDNUM.
     The IDNUM has now been changed to the primary IDNUM and
     the record has been put in the proper sequence.
06 = Code for a standard master file record. There was a match between
     ID and master file records and, if SS number and birth year was
     available on the ID, it was added to the master file record.
07 = Any master file record which doesn't match an ID record.

On the 2nd pass, when matching was attempted after IDNUM had been changed, 05 and 07 were left as they were. If the records which had not matched the first time matched on the second pass, the original 05 or 07 was changed to an 04.

IDNUM

I.   WAIS ID Number
     All forms
     [1]
II. C.Q.
     $01000100 \leqslant IDNUM \leqslant 51999999$
III. F.D.
     46-59 [C, 2-9]
     60-64 [C, 2-9]
     46-64 [C, 4-11]
IV. N.D.
     The WAIS ID number is an eight-digit number which can be divided into three segments, the name group identifier, the household identifier, and the sex and household position identifier.

Name Group Identifier.   The first 2 digits of the IDNUM represents the name cluster of which the taxpayer is a part. There were originally to be fifty of these name clusters, but a part of the Nielsen group was discovered after the integration process had been (it was thought) completed.

Household Identifier.   The next four digits of the identification number represent the household number of which the individual is a part. These groups were filed in alphabetical order and were numbered consecutively beginning with 0001. Errors in the integration process discovered after numbers had been assigned caused some numbers to be discarded. Household numbers with 4XXX indicate that there was no *adult* number for the household in the 46–59 master so an adult number was assigned in the 60–64 master. (However, often there was a child identification number in the 46–59 master, which presents us with a legitimate IDNUM.)

Sex and Household Position Identifier.   Digits 7 and 8 represent the position of the individual taxpayer in the family unit. The male head of the family was given 00. The wife or female head of a family was given 10. If a male married again after his first wife's death or divorce, his second wife was given a 20. Wives in the 60–64 file for whom there was no real indication of their position in the household regarding first wife, second wife, etc. were assigned a 99 in positions 7 and 8 of the IDNUM.
     In the 46–59 file, children within a household who filed returns were

assigned dependent or "child" IDNUM's within the household. The first single male filer in the household was 01, the second filer was 02, etc. The first single female filer was given 11, the second was given 12, etc. Because of the difficulties involved in properly identifying dependents within a household, the procedure was not continued in assigning IDNUM's in the 59–64 file. Instead the rule was followed that any dependent single individual who filed a return was entitled to a separate household number which was assigned from the 4XXX series.

YR

I.   Year (all forms)
     [1]
II. C.Q.
     $46 \leqslant YR \leqslant 64$
III. F.D.
     46–59 [C, 2-9]
     60–64 [C, 2-9]
     46–64 [C, 12-13)
IV. N.D.
     Records for the years 59 and 60 may have had their origins in either the 46–59 master file or the 60–64 master file. The source code indicates which of the files supplied the record.

SS

I.   Social Security Number
     64, 63, 62, 61, 60, 59, 58, 57, 56, 55, 54, 53, 52, 51, 50, 49—all forms, p. 1
     48—Form 1 (SS# not available)
       —Form 1a, Form 1W, Form 1Wa, p. 1
     47—Form 1, 1W, and 1Wa (SS# not available)
       —Form 1a, p. 1
     46—All forms (SS# not available)
II. C.Q.
     Any nine-digit code
III. F.D.
     46–59 ID file [C, 10-18]
     60–64 MF [C, 395-403]
     46–64 MF [C, 14-22]
IV. N.D.
     The Social Security number was not added to the 400-character master file record but rather put on the ID file at the time of the creation of the 46–59 master file. When the 60–64 file was developed, the social

security number was included as part of the MF. The instructions
to the coders for the 59–64 file regarding this field are as follows:

> *Social Security Number*
> *Source:* written at the top of the folder or on the gummed
> address label on the top of the folder.
> This number must agree with that on the returns themselves.
> If it is not identical to the number on any of the returns, see the
> supervisor.
> If it is identical to the number on some returns but not all,
> and you are confident that all these returns were filed by the same
> person or married couple, turn the code sheet over on its back
> and record all the social security numbers given on the tax returns
> for the various years.
> The first one should be the number written at the top of the
> folder or printed on the gummed label.
> Another case where you might have to take action is that
> where neither the folder nor the gummed label on the folder
> indicates any social security number. If the returns also do not
> have a social security number, leave the field blank and continue
> coding. If, however, you find a social security number on any of
> the returns and you are reasonably certain that this pertains to
> the individual whose returns you are coding, take this as his social
> security number.

Those records which were originally NO8bbbbbb in the SS field
were later machine recoded to 999999999.

If a taxpayer consistently left the social security field blank, he was
sometimes assigned a "social security number" by the tax department.
In early years this was a four-digit number which was never copied by
the coder. Later a nine-digit number beginning with a 9 was used and the
coder did put this number on the codesheet. (No number issued by the
social security administration begins with a 9.)

TBIRTH

I.   Birth Date
     64–p. 3
     [3]
     64s–p. 2
     [3]
     63–p. 3
     [3]
     63s–p. 2
     [3]
     62–p. 3

[3]
62s–p.2
[3]
46–61–All forms (not present)
[3]

II. C.Q.
Digits 1 & 2 (month) = 1–12, 99
Digits 3 & 4 (century) = 18–19, 99
Digits 5 & 6 (year) = 00–99

III. F.D.
ID [C, 122–127]
46–64 [C, 23–28]

IV. N.D.
Birth date was derived from the tax form from the question "age?" on the table where the taxpayer indicated his exemptions and their ages. The coder calculated "age in 1964" on the code sheet and the birth year was calculated from this information. For taxpayers who filed only in years in which the age question was not included on the form, our source of information is the 805 file or the supplementary age data file which was placed in EBIRTH field on the ID.

In cases where there was a discrepancy between TBIRTH and EBIRTH, or only one was present, certain conventions were followed so the most precise information could be put in the TBIRTH field. A BIRDIS indicator was also put on the file. The algorithm followed in each situation and the proper discrepancy code is documented in WAIS 712-004, p. 3 in the explanation of BIRDIS codes.

It should be noted that when the second phase of ID work was begun it was observed by looking at data dumps that there were no incorrect matches of age information from 805 with ID but there were occasionally some matches that could have been made that were not.

The additional codes are as follows:

990000 unknown age
980000 person was born before 1899 but date unknown
970000 person was born before 1867

WAGE1

I. Largest Wage
64, 63, 62, 58, 57, 56, 55, 54, 53, 52, 51, 50, 49, 48, 47, 46–p. 2, line 1
[2, TOTINC]
64s, 63s–front, line 4
[2, TOTINC]
62s–back, line 6

Table E–3
Variables Related to Income

Merged	Descriptor	Old	New	Size
29–36	WAGE1	28–36	57–64	8
37–44	WAGE2	37–45	65–72	8
45–52	OTHWGE	46–54	73–80	8
53–60	UNEMP	–	369–376	8
61–68	INT	55–63	81–88	8
69–76	DIVI	64–72	89–96	8
77–84	RENT	73–81	97–104	8
85–92	CPGAIN	82–90	105–112	8
93–100	BUSFAR	91–99	113–120	8
101–108	PSHIP	109–117	129–136	8
109–116	TRUST	100–108	121–128	8
117–124	OTHERY	118–126	137–144	8
125–132	PREFND	–	377–384	8
133–140	TOTINC	127–135	145–152	8
141–148	AUTBUS	136–144	153–160	8
149–156	AGI	145–153	161–168	8
16 Fields				128

[2, TOTINC]
61, 60, 59, 58s, 57s, 52s, 51s, 50s, 49s, 48s, 47s, 46s–p. 1, line 1
[2, TOTINC]

II. C.Q.
$0 \leqslant WAGE1 \leqslant 99999999$; SOURWG, TERR

III. F.D.
46–59 [C, 28–36]
60–64 [C, 57–64]
46–64 [C, 29–36]

IV. N.D.
This field is to contain the largest source of wages or the only source of wages.

If the taxpayer recorded his wages without giving the source and if the coder was unable to determine the source [s] , SOURWG = 9 was coded and the amount placed in WAGE1.

TERR = 1, 13 may affect this field. (690–016)

WAGE2

I. Second Largest Wage
64, 63, 62, 58, 57, 56, 55, 54, 53, 52, 51, 50, 49, 48, 47, 46–p. 2, line 1
[2, TOTINC]
64s, 63s–front, line 4
[2, TOTINC]

62s–back, line 6
[2, TOTINC]
61, 60, 59, 58s, 57s, 52s, 51s, 50s, 49s, 48s, 47s, 46s–p. 1, line 1
[2, TOTINC]

II. C.Q.
    0 ≤ WAGE2 ≤ 99999999; SOURWG, TERR

III. F.D.
    46-59 [C, 37–45]
    60-64 [C, 65-72]
    46-64 [C, 37–44]

IV. N.D.
The contents of this field should be the second largest source of wages.
    TERR = 1, 13 may affect this field. (690–016)

OTHWGE

I. Other Wage
64, 63, 62, 58, 57, 56, 55, 54, 53, 52, 51, 50, 49, 48, 47, 46–p. 2, line 1
[2, TOTINC]
64s, 63s–front, line 4
[2, TOTINC]
62s–back, line 6
[2, TOTINC]
61, 60, 59, 58s, 57s, 52s, 51s, 50s, 49s, 48s, 47s, 46s–p. 1, line 1
[2, TOTINC]

II. C.Q.
    0 ≤ OTHWGE ≤ 99999999; SOURWG, TERR, WAGEX

III. F.D.
    46-59 [C, 46-54]
    60-64 [C, 73-80]
    46-64 [C, 45-52]

IV. N.D.
If there were more than two OTHWGE this field reflects the coder-determined sum.
    WAGEX, the supplementary Unemployment Benefits paid to workers, especially by American Motors, General Motors, and International Harvester were added to OTHWGE when they appeared on the ALK file. (689–027, 689–028)
    TERR = 1, 13 may affect this field. (690–016)

UNEMP

I. Unemployment Compensation
64–p. 2, line 1

[2, TOTINC]
64s, 63, 63s, 62, 62s, 61, 60, 59—ALK file
[2, TOTINC]
58, 58s, 57, 57s, 56, 55, 54, 53, 52, 52s, 51, 51s, 50, 50s, 49, 49s, 48, 48s, 47, 47s, 46, 46s
[5]

II.   C.Q.
      $0 \leqslant$ UNEMP $\leqslant 99999999$; TERR

III. F.D.
      46-59 [not available]
      60-64 [C, 369-376]
      46-64 [C, 53-60]

IV.   N.D.
      On 1964 forms the tax department has a special line for unemployment compensation as a source of income. In our processing an effort was made to detect unemployment and include it on the A card of the ALK file. If an amount existed on the Master record and on the ALK the ALK amount was used. If there was no amount on the ALK file the Master record was left as is. (689-027, 689-028)
          TERR = 1, 13 may affect this field.

INT

I.   Interest Received
      64, 63, 62—p. 2, line 5
      [1, TOTINC]
      64s, 63s, 62s
      [5]
      61, 60, 59—p. 3, Schedule C, line 1
      [1, TOTINC]
      58, 57, 56, 55, 54, 53, 52, 51, 50, 49, 48, 47, 46, 46s—p. 2, line 2
      [2, TOTINC]
      58s, 51s, 52s, 51s, 50s, 49s, 48s, 47s—p. 1, line 3
      [2, TOTINC]

II.   C.Q.
      $0 \leqslant$ INT $\leqslant 99999999$; TERR

III. F.D.
      46-59 [C, 55-63]
      60-64 [C, 81-88]
      46-64 [C, 61-68]

IV.   N.D.
      If the testing program detected an error in TOTINC the coders would also use the INT amount from Schedule D. (690-012)

The short forms are coded as [5] above because INT and DIV could not be separated from OTHERY.

TERR = 1, 13 may affect this field.

I.   Dividends Received
     64, 63, 62–p. 2, line 4
     [1, TOTINC]
     64s, 63s, 62s
     [5]
     61, 60, 59–p. 3, Schedule C, line 2
     [1, TOTINC]
     58, 57, 56, 55, 54, 53, 52, 51, 50, 49, 48, 47, 46, 46s–p. 2, line 3
     [2, TOTINC]
     58s, 57s, 52s, 51s, 50s, 49s, 48s, 47s–p. 1, line 2
     [2, TOTINC]
II. C.Q.
     $0 \leqslant DIVI \leqslant 99999999$; TERR
III. F.D.
     46–59   [C, 64–72]
     60–64   [C, 89–96]
     46–64   [C, 69–76]
IV. N.D.
     The short forms are coded as [2] above because DIV and INT could not be separated from OTHERY.

     If the testing program detected an error in TOTINC the coders would also use the DIV amount from Schedule E. (690–012)

     On the short forms 46–52 no mention is made of the Wisconsin corporations that are not taxed (dividends).

     TERR = 1, 13 may affect this field. (690–016)

I.   Rent Income
     64, 63, 62–p. 2, line 6
     [1, TOTINC]
     64s, 63s, 62s
     [5]
     61, 60, 59–p. 3, Schedule C, line 3
     [INTPD, 1, TOTINC]
     58, 57, 56, 55, 54, 53, 52, 51, 50, 49, 48, 47, 46, 46s–p. 2, line 4
     [2, TOTINC]
     57s, 58s–p. 1, line 5

[2, TOTINC]
52s, 51s, 50s, 49s, 48s, 47s
[5]

II. C.Q.
     $0 \leqslant$ RENT $\leqslant 99999999$; TERR

III. F.D.
     46-59 [C, 73-81]
     60-64 [C, 97-104]
     46-64 [C, 77-84]

IV. N.D.
     The short forms are coded as [5] above because RENT is only defined in the case of the long form.

     If the testing program detected an error in TOTINC the coders would also use RENT as the taxpayer recorded it on either a separate schedule or in 59, 60, 61–p. 3, Schedule F (690–012).

     TERR = 1, 13 may affect this field. (690–016)

CPGAIN

I.   Gain or Loss (assets)
     64, 63, 62–p. 2, line 7
     [1, TOTINC]
     64s, 63s, 62s
     [5]
     61, 60, 59–p. 3, Schedule C, line 4
     [1, TOTINC]
     58, 57, 56, 55, 54, 53, 52, 51, 50, 49, 48, 47, 46–p. 2, line 5
     [1, TOTINC]
     58s, 57s, 52s, 51s, 50s, 49s, 48s, 47s, 46s
     [5]

II. C.Q.
     $-9999999 \leqslant$ CPGAIN $\leqslant 99999999$; TERR

III. F.D.
     46-59 [C, 82-90]
     60-64 [C, 105-112]
     46-64 [C, 85-92]

IV. N.D.
     The short forms are coded as [5] above because CPGAIN is only defined in the case of long forms.

     If the testing program detected an error in TOTINC the coders would also use CPGAIN as recorded by the taxpayer 59, 60, 61–p. 3, Schedule G; and 62, 63, 64–p. 4, Schedule C. (690–012)

     TERR = 1, 13 may affect this field. (690–016)

BUSFAR

I.   Profit or Loss, Business
    64, 63, 62–p. 2, line 8
    [1, TOTINC]
    64s, 63s, 62s
    [5]
    61, 60, 59–p. 3, Schedule C, line 5
    [1, TOTINC]
    58, 57, 56, 55, 54, 53, 52, 51, 50, 49, 48, 47, 46–p. 2, line 6
    [2, TOTINC]
    58s, 57s–p. 1, line 4
    [2, TOTINC]
    52s, 51s, 50s, 49s, 48s, 47s, 46s
    [5]

II. C.Q.
    $-9999999 \leqslant \text{BUSFAR} \leqslant 99999999$; TERR

III. F.D.
    46-59 [C, 91-99]
    60-64 [C, 113-120]
    46-64 [C, 93-100]

IV. N.D.
    The short forms are coded as [5] above because BUSFAR is only defined in the case of long forms.

      If the testing program detected an error in TOTINC the coders would also use BUSFAR recorded by the taxpayer in 59, 60, 61, 62, 63, 64, on the Farm or Business Schedules. (690-012)

      See Moyer (1966b, p. 39)–taxpayer duplication of loss carryover and WAIS 690-033–A comparison of federal and state treatments of business loss carryover and deductible medical expenses.

      TERR = 1, 13 may affect this field. (690-016)

PSHIP

I.   Partnership Income
    64, 63, 62–p. 2, line 9
    [1, TOTINC]
    64s, 63s, 62s
    [5]
    61, 60, 59–p. 3, Schedule C, line 6
    [1, TOTINC]
    58, 57, 56, 55, 54, 53, 52, 51, 50, 49, 48, 47, 46–p. 2, line 8
    [1, TOTINC]
    58s, 57s, 52s, 51s, 50s, 49s, 48s, 47s, 46s
    [5]

II.   C.Q.
      $-9999999 \leqslant$ PSHIP $\leqslant 99999999$; TERR
III. F.D.
      46-59 [C, 109-117]
      60-64 [C, 129-136]
      46-64 [C, 101-108]
IV.   N.D.
      The short forms are coded as [5] above because PSHIP is only defined in
      the case of long forms.
            TERR = 1, 13 may affect this field.

TRUST

I.   Trust and Estate Income
     64, 63, 62–p. 2, line 10
     [1, TOTINC]
     64s, 63s, 62s
     [5]
     61, 60, 59–p. 3, Schedule C, line 7
     [1, TOTINC]
     58, 57, 56, 55, 54, 53, 52, 51, 50, 49, 48, 47, 46–p. 2, line 7
     [1, TOTINC]
     58s, 57s, 52s, 51s, 50s, 49s, 48s, 47s, 46s
     [5]
II. C.Q.
     $-9999999 \leqslant$ TRUST $\leqslant 99999999$; TERR
III. F.D.
     46-59 [C, 100-108]
     60-64 [C, 121-128]
     46-64 [C, 109-116]
IV. N.D.
     The short forms are coded as [5] above because TRUST is only defined
     in the case of long forms.
           TERR = 1, 13 may affect this field. (690-016)

OTHERY

I.   Other Income
     64, 63–p. 2, line 12
     [1, TOTINC]
     64s, 63s–front, line 5
     [1, TOTINC]
     62–p. 2, line 11
     [1, TOTINC]
     62s–back, line 7

[1, TOTINC]
61, 60, 59–p. 3, line 8
[1, TOTINC]
58, 57, 56, 55, 54, 53, 52, 51, 50, 49, 48, 47, 46–p. 2, line 9
[1, TOTINC]
58s, 57s–p. 1, line 6
[2, TOTINC]
52s, 51s, 50s, 49s, 48s, 47s–p. 1, line 4
[2, TOTINC]
46s–p. 2, line 5
[2, TOTINC]

II.   C.Q.
      –9999999 ⩽ OTHERY ⩽ 99999999; TERR
III. F.D.
      46-59   [C, 118-126]
      60-64   [C, 137-144]
      46-64   [C, 117-124]
IV.   N.D.
      This field is to include any income not included in WAGE1, WAGE2, INT,
      DIV, BUS, CPGAIN, PSHIP, TRUST, or RENT, with the following
      exceptions:
          (1) In 59, 60, 61, if the taxpayer recorded an amount on p. 1, line 2,
      and the coder could not determine the source from p. 3 or from preceding
      and following years, then the amount was placed in OTHERY.
          (2) In 64s, 63s, and 62s, if there was no breakdown of income
      sources, except of wages, the other fields were coded in OTHERY.
          Other includes: jury duty, retirement pension, director's fees, strike
      pay, profit sharing trusts from employers, election booths, blood bank
      donations, bonuses, commissions, soil bank (if not on farm schedule), sale
      of crops (if not included on farm schedule), baked goods, winnings from a
      Florida race track, and a fox bounty.
          Moyer (1966b) states without explanation that this field may be
      negative.
          TERR = 1, 13 may affect this field.

                                                                    PREFND

I.   Refund of Wisconsin Income Taxes for Previous Year
      64, 63–p. 2, line 11
      [1, TOTINC]
      64s, 63s, 62, 62s, 61, 60, 59, 58, 58s, 57, 57s, 56, 55, 54, 53, 52, 51, 51s,
      50, 50s, 49, 49s, 48, 48s, 47, 47s, 46, 46s
      [5]

II. C.Q.
     $0 \leqslant$ PREFND $\leqslant 99999999$; TERR
III. F.D.
     46–59 [not coded]
     60–64 [C, 377–384]
     46–64 [C, 125–132]
IV. N.D.
     TERR = 1, 13 may affect this field. (690-016)

TOTINC

I.   Total Income
     64, 63–p. 2, line 13
     [WAGE1, WAGE2, OTHWGE, UNEMP, DIV, RENT, CPGAIN, BUSFAR,
     PSHIP, TRUST, PREFND, OTHERY, 1, AGI]
     64s, 63s–front, line 6
     [WAGE1, WAGE2, OTHWGE, OTHERY, 1, STNDED, NTI, AGI]
     62–p. 1, line 1
     [WAGE1, WAGE2, OTHWGE, UNEMP, DIV, RENT, CPGAIN, BUSFAR,
     PSHIP, TRUST, OTHERY, 1, AGI]
     62s–back, line 8
     [WAGE1, WAGE2, OTHWGE, OTHERY, 1, STNDED, NTI, AGI]
     61, 60, 59–p. 1, line 3
     [WAGE1, WAGE2, OTHWGE, INT, DIV, RENT, CPGAIN, BUSFAR,
     PSHIP, TRUST, OTHERY, 1, AGI]
     58, 57, 56, 52, 51, 50, 49, 48, 47, 46–p. 2, line 10
     [WAGE1, WAGE2, OTHWGE, INT, DIV, RENT, CPGAIN, BUSFAR,
     PSHIP, TRUST, OTHERY, 1, NTI, NETINC, AGI]
     58s, 57s–p. 1, line 6
     [WAGE1, WAGE2, OTHWGE, INT, DIV, BUSFAR, RENT, OTHERY, 1,
     TOTAX]
     55, 54, 53–p. 2, line 10 or 13
     [WAGE1, WAGE2, OTHWGE, INT, DIV, RENT, CPGAIN, BUSFAR,
     TRUST, OTHERY, 1, NTI, NETINC]
     52s, 51s, 50s, 49s, 48s, 47s–p. 1, line 5
     [WAGE1, WAGE2, OTHWGE, INT, DIV, OTHERY, 1, TOTAX]
     46s–p. 2, line 6
     [WAGE1, WAGE2, OTHWGE, INT, DIV, RENT, OTHERY, 1, NETINC]

II. C.Q.
     $-9999999 \leqslant$ TOTINC $\leqslant 99999999$; TERR
III. F.D.
     46–59 [C, 127–135]

60–64 [C, 145–152]
46–64 [C, 133–140]

IV. N.D.

On forms 1 and 3, TOTINC was added by machine correction (690–012).

"Adjusted Gross Income" does sometimes depend on TOTINC when it is AGI = TOTINC – AUTBUS. Prior to 1956 this adjustment is part of itemized deductions. On short forms (62–64) there is no field called AGI.

NTI (standard deduction basis) was not a field until 1949.

TERR = 1, 13, 15 affect this field.

AUTBUS

I. Auto or Business Expense
    64, 63–p. 2, line 14
    [1, AGI]
    64s, 63s, 62s, 58s, 57s, 52s, 51s, 50s, 49s, 48s, 47s
    [5]
    62–p. 1, line 2
    [1, AGI]
    62, 61, 59–p. 1, line 4
    [1, AGI]
    58, 57, 56–p. 2, line 11
    [1, AGI]
    55, 54, 53, 52–p. 2, line 18
    [1, AGI]
    48, 47, 46–p. 2, line 16
    [1, AGI]
    46s–p. 2, line 11
    [1, AGI]

II. C.Q.
    $0 \leqslant AUTBUS \leqslant 99999999$

III. F.D.
    46–59 [C, 136–144]
    60–64 [C, 153–160]
    46–64 [C, 141–158]

IV. N.D.

If the testing program detected an error, the coders would try to find AUTBUS as recorded on 59, 60, 61–p. 4, Schedule H; or 62, 63, 64–p. 4, Schedule A.

AUTBUS may include, besides auto expense–and in 1959, 60, 61 casualty losses–TAXPD, uniform or tool expenditure; these were in most cases left as recorded by the taxpayer using the principle of minimum intervention. (690–012)

There is a TERR = 9 for this field but was seldom used.

The 46s is excluded from grouping with the 58–56 because the forms are very different.

AUTBUS has always been primarily "Ordinary and Necessary Business Expenses," however in 1946–1951 this data was taken from a field called "Other Deductions." Beginning in 1952 through 1964 the "Ordinary and Necessary . . ." was the source of the data. It becomes confusing when in 1952–1958 the "Other Deductions" field is still present but is seemingly intended to contain and exclude data that might have been in this field before.

Furthermore the field AUTBUS was used to construct AGI for all years where it was undefined in 1946–1959.

AGI

I.   Adjusted Gross Income
     64, 63–p. 1, line 1
     [TOTINC, AUTBUS, 1, STNDED, NTI]
     64s, 63s, 62s
     [5]
     62–p. 1, line 3
     [TOTINC, AUTBUS, 1, STNDED, NTI]
     61, 60, 59–p. 1, line 5
     [TOTINC, AUTBUS, 1, NETINC]
     58, 57, 56–p. 2, line 12
     [TOTINC, AUTBUS, 1, IBFDON, NTI]
     58s, 57s, 52s, 51s, 50s, 49s, 48s, 47s–(AGI ← TOTINC)
     [TOTINC, 3]
     55, 54, 53, 52, 51, 50, 49, 48, 47, 46, 46s–(AGI ← TOTINC - AUTBUS)
     [TOTINC, AUTBUS, 3, IBFDON, NTI]
II. C.Q.
     $-9999999 \leqslant AGI \leqslant 99999999$; TERR
III. F.D.
     46–59 [C, 145–153]
     60–64 [C, 161–168]
     46–64 [C, 149–156]
IV. N.D.
     In years 61, 60, 59, the taxpayers' insistence of placing AGI in NTI caused slight coding problems. (690–012)
          If AGI is negative it may have been machine corrected. (690–012)
          64s . . . should have AGI constructed.
     TERR = 9 affects this field.

Table E-4
Variables Related to Deductions

Merged	Descriptor	Old	New	Size
157–163	MED	190–198	201–208	7
164–170	NBSINT	199–207	217–224	7
171–177	BUSINT	208–216	209–216	7
178–184	CASLS	–	361–368	7
185–191	YTXPD	172–180	185–192	7
192–198	UNION	181–189	193–200	7
199–205	ALMNY	235–243	233–240	7
206–212	CREXP	244–252	241–248	7
213–219	OTHDED	226–234	225–232	7
220–226	DIVDED	217–225	–	7
227–233	TOTDED	253–261	249–256	7
234–240	NETINC	262–270	257–264	7
241–247	FSSDED	271–279	265–272	7
248–254	IBFDON	280–288	273–280	7
255–261	DON	289–297	281–288	7
15 Fields				105

MED

I. Medical Dental Expenses
     64, 63, 62–p. 3, line 4
     [1, TOTDED]
     64s, 63s, 62s, 58s, 57s, 52s, 51s, 50s, 49s, 48s, 47s
     [5]
     61, 60, 59–p. 2, line 3
     [1, TOTDED]
     58, 57–p. 2, line 15
     [1, TOTDED]
     56–p. 2, line 18
     [1, TOTDED]
     55, 54, 53, 52, 51, 50, 49–p. 2, line 16
     [1, TOTDED]
     48, 47, 46–p. 2, line 13
     [1, TOTDED]
     46s–p. 2, line 10
     [1, TOTDED]
II. C.Q.
     $0 \leqslant MED \leqslant 9999999$; TERR, MEDIND
III. F.D.
     46–59 [C, 190–198]
     60–64 [C, 201–208]
     46–64 [C, 157–163]

IV.   N.D.
  If an error was detected by the testing program, the MED amount used by
  the coders may come from a separate schedule or in 61, 60, 59 from p. 2,
  Schedule A.
      Important: See Moyer (1966b, p. 42) special problem (MEDIND).
      In 1953 the amount not deductible changed from $50 to $75 and the
  maximum deductible from $500 to $1500. In 1963 the amount not
  deductible changed from $75 to $85 and the maximum deductible from
  $1500 to $2500.
      TERR = 10, 13, 15, 17 affect this field.

NBSINT (INTPD)

  I.   Non-Business Interest Paid
       64, 63, 62–p. 3, line 1
       [1, TOTDED]
       64s, 63s, 62s, 58s, 57s, 52s, 51s, 50s, 49s, 48s, 47s
       [5]
       61, 60, 59–p. 2, line 2
       [1, TOTDED]
       58, 57–p. 2, line 16
       [1, TOTDED]
       56–p. 2, line 19
       [1, TOTDED]
       55, 54, 53, 52, 51, 50, 49–p. 2, line 17
       [1, TOTDED]
       48, 47, 46–p. 2, line 14
       [1, TOTDED]
       46s–p. 2, line 8
       [1, TOTDED]
 II.   C.Q.
       $0 \leqslant TOTDED \leqslant 9999999$; TERR
III.   F.D.
       46-59 [C, 199-207]
       60-64 [C, 217-224]
       46-64 [C, 164-170]
IV.   N.D.
  If the testing program detected an error, the NBSINT amount used by the
  coders may be from a separate schedule.
      See WAIS 701-006.
      TERR = 10, 14, 15, 17 affect this field.

BUSINT

I. Business Interest Paid
    64, 64s, 63, 63s, 62, 62s, 58s, 57s, 52s, 51s, 50, 50s, 49, 49s, 48, 48s, 47,
    47s, 46, 46s
    [5]
    61, 60, 59—Schedule F, bottom
    [1, RENT]
    58, 57, 56, 55—p. 3, Schedule C, col. 1
    [1]
    54, 53, 52, 51—p. 2, Schedule B, col. 1
    [1]
II. C.Q.
    $0 \leqslant \text{BUSINT} \leqslant 9999999$
III. F.D.
    46-59   [C, 208-216]
    60-64   [C, 209-216]
    46-64   [C, 171-177]
IV. N.D.
    This is a subfield included in the sum of RENT.
    See WAIS 701-006 on the 1959-1961 returns.

CASLS

I. Casualty Losses
    64, 63, 62—p. 3, line 5
    [1, TOTDED]
    64s, 63s, 62s, 61, 60, 59, 58, 58s, 57, 57s, 56, 55, 54, 53, 52, 52s, 51, 51s,
    50, 50s, 49, 49s, 48, 48s, 46, 46s
    [5]
II. C.Q.
    $0 \leqslant \text{CASLS} \leqslant 9999999$; TERR, AUTOEX
III. F.D.
    46-59   [not available]
    60-64   [C, 361-368]
    46-64   [C, 178-184]
IV. N.D.
    Remember that in 61, 60, 59 CASLS is included explicitly in the AUTBUS
    schedule (p. 4, Schedule H), and does not enter into TOTDED but instead
    is included in the AUTBUS amount.
       In 1962 CASLS was explicitly moved to the itemized deduction
    schedule. Persons were probably including personal casualty losses in the
    AUTBUS schedule.
       TERR = 10, 14, 15 affect this field.

I. Wisconsin Income Tax Paid
64, 63–p. 3, line 6d
[1, TOTDED]
64s, 63s, 62s, 58s, 57s, 52s, 51s, 50s, 49s, 48s, 47s
[5]
62–p. 3, line 6
[1, TOTDED]
61, 60, 59–p. 2, line 4
[1, TOTDED]
58, 57–p. 2, line 13
[1, TOTDED]
56–p. 2, line 16
[1, TOTDED]
55, 54, 53, 52, 51, 50, 49–p. 2, line 14
[1, TOTDED]
48, 47, 46–p. 2, line 11
[1, TOTDED]
46s–p. 2, line 7
[1, TOTDED]

II. C.Q.
$0 \leqslant YTXPD \leqslant 9999999$; TERR

III. F.D.
46-59 [C, 172-180]
60-64 [C, 185-192]
46-64 [C, 185-191]

IV. N.D.
If the testing program detected an error, the YTXPD amount used by the coders may have come from a separate schedule.

Certain important conventions were adopted pertaining to this field's meaning in the 60-64 sample; WAIS 689-024 spells them out clearly. Generally this field is well defined.

TERR = 10, 14, 15, affect this field.

I. Union Dues Paid
64, 63, 62–p. 3, line 7
[1, TOTDED]
64s, 63s, 62s, 58s, 57s, 52s, 51s, 50s, 49s, 48s, 47s, 46s
[5]
61, 60, 59–p. 2, line 5
[1, TOTDED]

58, 57–p. 2, line 14
[1, TOTDED]
56–p. 2, line 17
[1, TOTDED]
55, 54, 53, 52, 51, 50, 49–p. 2, line 15
[1, TOTDED]
48, 47, 56–p. 2, line 12
[1, TOTDED]
II.   C.Q.
      $0 \leqslant UNION \leqslant 9999999$; TERR
III. F.D.
      46-59 [C, 181–189]
      60-64 [C, 193–200]
      46-64 [C, 192–198]
IV.   N.D.
      If the testing program detected an error in TOTDED, the union amount
      used by the coders may be from a separate schedule.
          TERR = 10, 14, 15 affect this field.

ALMNY

I.   Alimony Paid
      64, 63, 62–p. 3, line 8
      [1, TOTDED]
      64s, 63s, 62s, 58, 58s, 57, 57s, 56, 54, 53, 52, 52s, 51, 51s, 50, 50s, 49,
      49s, 48, 48s, 47, 47s, 46, 46s
      [5]
      61, 60, 59–p. 2, line 6
      [1, TOTDED]
II.   C.Q.
      $0 \leqslant ALMNY \leqslant 9999$; TERR
III. F.D.
      46-59 [C, 235–243]
      60-64 [C, 233–240]
      46-64 [C, 199–205]
IV.   N.D.
      ALMNY is a seldom used field.
          TERR = 10, 14, 15, 17 affect this field.

CREXP

I.   Forest Cropland
      64, 63, 62–p. 2, line 9
      [1, TOTDED]

64s, 63s, 62s, 58, 58s, 57, 57s, 56, 54, 53, 52, 52s, 51, 51s, 50, 50s, 49, 49s, 48, 48s, 47, 47s, 46, 46s
[5]
61, 60, 59–p. 2, line 7
[1, TOTDED]

II. C.Q.
$0 \leqslant CREXP \leqslant 9999999$; TERR

III. F.D.
46-59 [C, 244-252]
60-64 [C, 241-248]
46-64 [C, 206-212]

IV. N.D.
CREXP represents a seldom used field.
TERR = 10, 14, 15 affect this field.

OTHDED

I. Other Deductions
64, 63, 62, 61, 60, 59–taxpayer defined, ALK file
[2, TOTDED]
64s, 63s, 62s, 58s, 57s, 52s, 51s, 50s, 49s, 48s, 47s
[5]
58, 57–p. 2, line 17
[1, TOTDED]
56–p. 2, line 20
[1, TOTDED]
55, 54, 53, 52, 51, 50, 49–p. 2, line 19
[1, TOTDED]
48, 47, 46–p. 2, line 16
[1, TOTDED]
46s–p. 2, line 11
[1, TOTDED]

II. C.Q.
$0 \leqslant OTHDED \leqslant 9999999$; TERR

III. F.D.
46-59 [C, 226-234]
60-64 [C, 225-232]
46-64 [C, 213-219]

IV. N.D.
If the testing program detected an error, the OTHDED amount used by the coders may be from a separate schedule.
Sometimes = AUTBUS
From 1946 through 1951 "Other Deductions" was a mixture of

"Ordinary Business Expenses" and other things such as alimony and child support. *Taxes* establishes that this policy changed in 1950. Until 1950 child support was deductible but there seems to be a restriction that gross income must be less than $3000. For the entire period $800 alimony was deductible.

TERR = 10, 14, 15 affect this field.

DIVDED

I.   Dividends Deductible
     64, 64s, 63, 63s, 62, 62s, 61, 60, 59, 58, 58s, 57, 57s, 56, 55, 54, 53, 52, 51s, 50s, 49s, 48s, 47s
     [5]
     51, 50, 49–p. 2, line 18
     [DIV, 1, TOTDED]
     48, 47, 46–p. 2, line 15
     [DIV, 1, TOTDED]
     46s–p. 2, line 3
     [DIV, 1, TOTDED]
II. C.Q.
     0 ⩽ DIVDED ⩽ 9999999
III. F.D.
     46-59 [C, 217–225]
     60-64 [not available]
     46-64 [C, 220–226]
IV. N.D.
     None.

TOTDED

I.   Total Deduction Before Federal Tax and Donation
     64, 63–p. 1, line 3a
     [NBSINT, MED, CASLS, YTXPD, UNION, ALMNY, CREXP, 1, IBFDON]
     64s, 63s, 62s, 58s, 57s, 52s, 51s, 50s, 49s, 48s, 47s
     [5]
     62–p. 1, line 5a
     [NBSINT, MED, CASLS, YTXPD, UNION, ALMNY, CREXP, 1, IBFDON]
     61, 60, 59–p. 2, line 8
     [NBSINT, MED, YTXPD, UNION, ALMNY, CREXP, 1, NETINC]
     58, 57–p. 2, line 18
     [YTXPD, UNION, MED, NBSINT, OTHDED, 1, NETINC]
     56–p. 2, line 21

[YTXPD, UNION, MED, NBSINT, OTHDED, 1, NETINC]
55, 54, 53, 52, 51, 50, 49—p. 2, line 20
[YTXPD, UNION, MED, NBSINT, AUTBUS, OTHDED, 1, NETINC]
48, 47, 46—p. 2, line 17
[YTXPD, UNION, MED, NBSINT, DIVDED, OTHDED, 1, NETINC]
46s—p. 2, line 12
[YTXPD, DIVDED, MED, OTHDED, 1, NETINC]

II. C.Q.
     $0 \leqslant$ TOTDED $\leqslant$ 9999999; TERR

III. F.D.
     46-59 [C, 253-261]
     60-64 [C, 249-256]
     46-64 [C, 227-233]

IV. N.D.
     If there was an error detected by the testing program then the coders may
     have arrived at the TOTDED amount by using a separate schedule.
         TERR = 10, 14, 15 affect this field.

NETINC

I.   Net Income Before Federal Tax and Donation
     64, 64s, 63, 63s, 62, 62s, 58s, 57s, 52s, 51s, 50s, 49s, 48s, 47s
     [5]
     61, 60, 59—p. 2, line 9
     [AGI, TOTDED, 1, IBFDON]
     58, 57—p. 2, line 19
     [AGI, TOTDED, 1, IBFDON]
     56—p. 2, line 22
     [AGI, TOTDED, 1, IBFDON]
     55, 54, 53, 52, 51, 50, 49—p. 2, line 21
     [TOTINC, TOTDED, 1, IBFDON]
     48, 47, 46—p. 2, line 18
     [TOTINC, TOTDED, 1, IBFDON]
     46s—p. 2, line 18
     [TOTINC, TOTDED, 1, IBFDON]

II. C.Q.
     $-999999 \leqslant$ NETINC $\leqslant$ 9999999; TERR

III. F.D.
     46-59 [C, 262-270]
     60-64 [C, 257-264]
     46-64 [C, 234-240]

IV. N.D.
     This field often affected by the taxpayer's incorrect transferral of the AGI
     amount from page 1 to page 2.

If NETINC is negative it may have been machine corrected. (690–012)

TERR = 18 affects this field.

FSSDED

I. Federal Tax and Social Security Deductions
    64, 64s, 63, 63s, 62, 62s, 58s, 57s, 52s, 51s, 50s, 49s, 48s, 47s
    [5]
    61, 60, 59–p. 2, line 10
    [NETINC, 1, IBFDON]
    58, 57–p. 2, line 20
    [NETINC, 1, IBFDON]
    56–p. 2, line 23
    [NETINC, 1, IBFDON]
    55, 54, 53, 52, 51, 50, 49–p. 2, line 22
    [NETINC, 1, IBFDON]
    48, 47, 46–p. 2, line 19
    [NETINC, 1, IBFDON]
    46s–p. 2, line 14
    [NETINC, 1, IBFDON]
II. C.Q.
    $0 \leqslant FSSDED \leqslant 9999999$
III. F.D.
    46-59 [C, 271-279]
    60-64 [C, 265-272]
    46-64 [C, 241-247]
IV. N.D.
    If the testing program detected an error, the coders may have used the
    FSSDED from a separate schedule.
    One problem found by the coders was that in most cases this amount
    could not be checked with other schedules or sources.
    This amount is always limited to 3% of NETINC.
    Starting in 1962 FSSDED is no longer deductible.

IBFDON

I. Net Income Before Donations
    64, 63–p. 1, line 3b
    [AGI, TOTDED, 1, NTI]
    64s, 63s, 62s, 58s, 57s, 52s, 51s, 50s, 49s, 48s, 47s
    [5]
    62–p. 1, line 5b
    [AGI, TOTDED, 1, NTI]

       61, 60, 59–p. 2, line 11
       [NETINC, FSSDED, 1, NTI]
       58, 57–p. 2, line 21
       [NETINC, FSSDED, 1, NTIITE]
       55, 54, 53, 52, 51, 50, 49–p. 2, line 24
       [1, NTIITE]
       48, 47, 46–p. 2, line 21
       [1, NTIITE]
       46s–p. 2, line 16
       [1, NTIITE]

II.   C.Q.
       $-999999 \leqslant$ IBFDON $\leqslant 9999999$; TERR

III. F.D.
       46-59 [C, 280-288]
       60-64 [C, 273-280]
       46-64 [C, 248-254]

IV. N.D.
       If IBFDON is negative, it may have been machine corrected. (690–012)
          TERR = 11 affects this field.

DON

I.   Donations
       64, 63–p. 1, line 3c
       [1, NTI]
       64s, 63s, 62s, 58s, 57s, 52s, 51s, 50s, 49s, 48s, 47s
       [5]
       62–p. 1, line 5c
       [1, NTI]
       61, 60, 59–p. 2, line 12
       [1, NTI]
       58, 57–p. 2, line 22
       [1, NTIITE]
       56–p. 2, line 25
       [1, NTIITE]
       56–p. 2, line 24
       [NETINC, FSSDED, 1, NTIITE]
       55, 54, 53, 52, 51, 50, 49–p. 2, line 23
       [NETINC, FSSDED, 1, NTIITE]
       48, 47, 46–p. 2, line 20
       [NETINC, FSSDED, 1, NTIITE]
       46s–p. 2, line 15
       [NETINC, FSSDED, 1, NTIITE]

II.   C.Q.
      -999999 ≤ DON ≤ 9999999; TERR
III. F.D.
      46-59 [C, 289-297]
      60-64 [C, 281-288]
      46-64 [C, 255-261]
IV.   N.D.
      If an error was detected by the testing program the DON recorded by the
      coders may have come from a separate schedule, or in 61, 60, 59–p. 2,
      Schedule B, or in 62, 63, 64–p. 3, part III.
          TERR = 12 affects this field.
      This amount is always limited to 10% of IBFDON.

Table E-5
Tax Liability and Miscellaneous Variables

Merged	Descriptor	Old	New	Size
262-269	STNDED	154-162	169-176	8
270-277	EXEMP	307-315	289-296	8
278-285	NTI	–	177-184	8
286-293	NTISTN (old)	163-171	–	8
294-301	NTIITE	298-306	–	8
302-309	TOTAX	316-324	297-304	8
310-317	TAXOUT	–	345-352	8
318-325	TXWH	–	385-392	8
326-333	TPMCR	–	353-360	8
334-341	INST1	325-333	305-312	8
342-349	NOTXIN	334-342	313-319	8
350-357	ADJTI	352-360	329-336	8
358-365	TOADTX	361-369	337-344	8
366-373	SSREC	343-351	321-328	8
374-381	INCTXY	370-378	–	8
15 Fields				120

STNDED

I.   Standard Deduction
      64, 63–p. 1, line 2
      [1, NTI]
      64s, 63s–p. 1, line 7
      [1, NTI]
      62–p. 1, line 4
      [1, NTI]
      62s–p. 2, line 9
      [1, NTI]

61, 60–p. 1, line 6
[1, NTI]
59, 58, 57, 56, 55, 54, 53, 52, 51, 50, 49, 48, 47, 46–p. 2, line 11
[4, NTISTN]

II. C.Q.
1947-1954 STNDED ≤ 9% of AGI if TOTINC is less than $5,000, else
STNDED = $450
1955-1965 STNDED ≤ 10% of AGI

III. F.D.
46-60 [C, 154-162]
60-64 [C, 169-176]
46-64 [C, 262-269]

IV. N.D.
In the file for 46-59, all cases, whether deductions were standard or itemized, standard deductions were calculated using the rule of 10% of adjusted gross income for the years 1955-1960. In the years 1947-1954 the rule was 9% of adjusted gross income, if TOTINC was less than $5000 or else $450 was entered in the standard deduction field. WAIS 645-020 gives documentation on the consistency check program which calculated these fields.

In the records which originated with the 60-64 master the standard deduction field contains zeros when the itemized deduction option is taken.

This field is affected when TERR = 2.

EXEMP

I. Exemptions
63, 64–p. 1, line 6
[1]
63s, 64s–p. 2, line 12
[1]
62–p. 1, line 8
[1]
62s–p. 2, line 14
[1]
61, 60, 59–p. 1, line B
[1]
58, 57–Form 1a and 1Wa, p. 1, line B
[1]
58, 57–Form 1 and 1W, block 2, line B
[1]
56–Form 1 and 1W, line 2, block 2 or tax table used
[1]

55, 54, 53–Form 1 and 1W, line 2, block 2 or tax table used
[1]
52, 51, 50, 49, 48, 47, 46–p. 1, line 2
[1]

II.   C.Q.
      $0 \leqslant EXEMP \leqslant 9999$
III. F.D.
      46-59 [C, 307-315]
      60-64 [C, 289-296]
      46-64 [C, 270-277]
IV.   N.D.
      In 1946 through 1961 the individual exemption was $7. In 1962 through
      1964 it was $10. Usually the amount in this field should be divisible by 7
      or 10, depending on the year, but occasionally the exemption is divided
      awkwardly between husband and wife to remove the wife's tax liability.
          TERR = 5 may affect this field.

                                                                          NTI

I.   Net Taxable Income
      64s, 63s–p. 1, line 8
      [1]
      62s–p. 2, line 10
      [1]
      64, 63–p. 1, line 4
      [1]
      62–p. 1, line 6
      [1]
      61, 60–p. 1, line 7
      [1]
      59, 58, 57, 56, 55, 54, 53, 52, 51, 50, 49, 48, 47, 46–all forms
      [5]
II.   C.Q.
      $-9999999 \leqslant NTI \leqslant 9999999$; TERR
III. F.D.
      46-59 [not available]
      60-64 [C, 177-184]
      46-64 [C, 278-285]
IV.   N.D.
      TERR = 2, 3 may affect this field. (690–016)

                                                                        NTISTN

I.   Net Taxable Income (Standard Deduction Basis)

64, 63, 62, 61, 60, 59—all forms
[5]
58, 57—Form 1 and 1W, p. 2, line 26
[1]
56—Form 1 and 1W, p. 2, line 14
[1]
55, 54, 53, 52, 51, 50, 49—Form 1 and 1W, p. 2, line 12
[1]
58, 57, 56, 55, 54, 53, 52, 51, 50, 49—Form 1a and 1Wa (not available—tax table used)
48, 47, 46—all forms
[5]

  II. C.Q.
-9999999 ⩽ NTISTN ⩽ 9999999

 III. F.D.
46-59 [C, 163-171]
60-64 [not available]
46-64 [C, 286-293]

 IV. N.D.
None.

NTIITE

   I. Net Taxable Income (Itemized Deduction Basis)
64, 63, 62, 61, 60—all forms
[5]
59—Form 1, p. 2, line 13
[1]
58, 57—Form 1a and 1Wa (not available)
[5]
58, 57—Form 1 and 1W, p. 2, line 23
[1]
56—Form 1 and 1W, p. 2, line 26
[1]
55, 54, 53, 52, 51, 50, 49—Form 1 and 1W, p. 2, line 25
[1]
48, 47, 46—Form 1 and 1W
[1]

  II. C.Q.
-9999999 ⩽ NTIITE ⩽ 9999999

 III. F.D.
46-59 [C, 298-306]
60-64 [not present]
46-64 [C, 294-301]

IV. N.D.
     None.

TOTAX

I.   Total Tax
     64, 63–p. 1, line 7
     [1]
     64s, 63s–p. 2, line 13
     [1]
     62–p. 1, line 9
     [1]
     62s–p. 2, line 15
     [1]
     61, 60, 59–p. 1, line E
     [1]
     58, 57–Form 1a and 1Wa, p. 1, line E
     [1]
     58, 57–Form 1 and 1W, block 2, line E
     [1]
     56–Form 1 and 1W, block 2, line 5
     [5]
     52, 51, 50, 49, 48, 47, 46–Form 1a and 1Wa, p. 1, line 8 (or line 6 if the
     taxpayer did not take the 2% discount, line 9 if he paid in installments)
     [1]
     55, 54, 53, 52, 51–Form 1 and 1W, p. 1, line 12
     (including Teacher's Surtax; this was preferred) or p. 1, line 5 (when no
     Teacher's Surtax was due) or field for "total installments" box at the
     bottom of p. 1.
     [1]
     50–Form 1 and 1W, p. 1, line 14
     (including Teacher's Surtax) or p. 1, line 7 (when no Teacher's Surtax
     was due)
     [1]
     49, 48, 47, 46–Form 1 and 1W, p. 1, line 12
     (including Teacher's Surtax; this was preferred) or p. 1, line 5 (when no
     Teacher's Surtax was due) or field for "total installments" box at the
     bottom of p. 1.
     [1]

II. C.Q.
     $-9999999 \leqslant \text{TOTAX} \leqslant 99999999$
III. F.D.
     46-59 [C, 316-324]

        60-64 [C, 297-304]
        46-64 [C, 302-309]

IV.   N.D.
        This conceivably could be a negative field if the taxpayer had more money withheld than his tax liability was calculated to be but filed a return to get his refund.
           TERR = 4, 6, 20 may affect this variable.

TAXOUT

I.   Tax to Other States
        64, 63–p. 1, line 8
        [1]
        64s, 63s–p. 2, line 14
        [1]
        62–p. 1, line 10
        [1]
        62s–p. 2, line 16
        [1]
        61–p. 1, line H
        [1]
        60, 59, 58, 57, 56, 55, 54, 53, 52, 51, 50, 49, 48, 47, 46–all forms
        [5]

II.   C.Q.
        $0 \leqslant \text{TAXOUT} \leqslant 9999999$

III.   F.D.
        46-59 [not present]
        59-64 [C, 345-352]
        46-64 [C, 310-317]

IV.   N.D.
        None.

TXWH

I.   Tax Withheld
        63, 64–p. 3, line 6d
        [1]
        63s, 64s–not available
        [1]
        62, 61, 60, 59, 58, 57, 56, 55, 54, 53, 52, 51, 50, 49, 48, 47, 46–all forms
        (not available)
        [5]

II.   C.Q.
        $0 \leqslant \text{TXWH} \leqslant 9999999$

III.   F.D.
    46–59 [not present]
    60–64 [C, 385–392]
    46–64 [C, 318–325]
IV.   N.D.
    None.

TPMCR

  I.   Total Payments and Credits
    64, 63–p. 1, line 12
    [1]
    64s, 63s, 62s–not available
    [5]
    62- p. 1, line 14
    [1]
    61, 60, 59, 58, 57, 56, 55, 54, 53, 52, 51, 50, 49, 48, 47, 46–all forms
    (not available)
    [5]
 II.   C.Q.
    $0 \leqslant TMPCR \leqslant 9999999$
III.   F.D.
    46–59 [not available]
    60–64 [C, 353–360]
    46–64 [C, 326–333]
IV.   N.D.
    None.

INST1

  I.   First Installment
    64, 63, 62–all forms (not available)
    [5]
    61, 60, 59–p. 1, line 2
    [1]
    58, 57–Forms 1a and 1Wa, p. 1, line II
    [1]
    58, 57, 56–Forms 1 and 1W, p. 1, line II
    [1]
    52, 51, 50, 49, 48, 47, 46–Forms 1a and 1Wa, p. 1, line 10
    [1]
    55, 54, 53, 52, 51, 50, 49, 48, 47, 46–Forms 1 and 1W, from the middle
    column of the "For Installment Payment" box (The field was skipped
    if this was blank.)
    [1]

II.   C.Q.
      $0 \leqslant$ INST1 $\leqslant 9999999$
III. F.D.
      46-59 [C, 325-333]
      60-64 [C, 305-312]
      46-64 [C, 334-341]
IV.   N.D.
      None.

NOTXIN

I.   Non-Taxable Income
      64, 63, 62, 61, 60, 59, 58, 57, 56, 55, 54, 53, 52, 51, 50, 49, 48, 47, 46—
      all forms, anywhere on return
      [1]
II.   C.Q.
      $0 \leqslant$ NOTXIN $\leqslant 9999999$
III. F.D.
      46-59 [C, 334-342]
      60-64 [C, 313-319]
      46-64 [C, 342-349]
IV.   N.D.
      The field TYPNON indicates what type of non-taxable income such as
      military deduction, student income, retirement income or combination.
      Since the taxpayer was never specifically asked to include it, it may not
      have been included with the information on the tax form by the taxpayer.

ADJTI

I.   Adjusted Taxable Income
      64, 63, 62, 61, 60—all forms, anywhere on tax department assessment
      notice.
      [1]
      59, 58, 57, 56, 55, 54, 53, 52, 51, 50, 49, 48, 47, 46—all forms, Adjusted
      Taxable Income (on Tax Department Form) minus NTIITE or NTISTN,
      whichever applied
      [3]
II.   C.Q.
      $-9999999 \leqslant$ ADJTI $\leqslant 9999999$
III. F.D.
      46-59 [C, 352-360]
      60-64 [C, 329-336]
      46-64 [C, 350-357]
IV.   N.D.
      None.

I.   Total Additional Tax
     64, 63, 62, 61, 60—all forms, anywhere on tax department assessment
     sheet
     [1]
     59, 58, 57, 56, 55, 54, 53, 52, 51, 50, 49, 48, 47, 46—all forms, last line
     of assessment form
     [1]

II. C.Q.
     $-9999999 \leqslant \text{TOADTX} \leqslant 9999999$

III. F.D.
     46-59 [C, 361-369]
     60-64 [C, 337-344]
     46-64 [C, 358-365]

IV. N.D.
     When there was a refund a "-" was punched preceding the field.

I.   Social Security Received
     64, 63, 62, 61, 60—all forms, usually written on p. 1 of the tax form
     [1]
     59—Form 1 p. 1, line 1
     [1]
     58, 57, 56—Form 1 and 1W (not available)
     [5]
     58, 57—Form 1a and 1Wa (not available)
     [5]
     55, 54, 53, 52, 51, 50, 49, 48, 47, 46—Form 1 and 1W, keypuncher
     punched it if it was found anywhere on the return
     [1]
     52, 51, 50, 49, 48, 47, 46—Forms 1a and 1W (not available)
     [5]

II. C.Q.
     $0 \leqslant \text{SSREC} \leqslant 9999999$

III. F.D.
     46-59 [C, 343-351]
     60-64 [C, 321-328]
     46-64 [C, 366-373]

IV. N.D.
     Since there was no specific spot on the tax form where the keypuncher
     looked to find the amount and no specific questioning of the taxpayer
     regarding Social Security Received, skepticism regarding the completeness
     of the data in this field is probably deserved.

I. Taxable Income Incomplete Form
    64, 63, 62, 61, 60 (not available)
    [5]
    59, 58, 57, 56, 55, 54, 53, 52, 51, 50, 49, 48, 47, 46—all forms, taken
    from taxable income (by whatever basis)
    [1]
II. C.Q.
    $-9999999 \leqslant INCTXY \leqslant 9999999$
III. F.D.
    46–59 [C, 370–378]
    60–64 [not available]
    46–64 [C, 374–381]
IV. N.D.
    WAIS 656-037, p. 2 indicates that when FORM = 6 INCTXY is created.
    Form 6 contains no source of deduction items but does have Taxable
    Income (by whatever basis) and exemption and tax liability figures.

Table E–6
Indicators Related to Household and Filing Status

Merged	Descriptor	Old	New	Size
382	MARR	24	39	1
383	MSTAT	–	35	1
384	SY5960	386	–	1
385	SEPINC	23	37	1
386	INCRL	–	38	1
387	MSCON	–	36	1
388	DISMAR	–	40	1
389	HEADFM	25	51	1
390–391	DEP	26–27	41–42	2
392–395	DEPAGE	–	43–46	4
396	DEPADR	–	47	1
397	STU	–	48	1
398	RETPR	21	33	1
399	FILED	–	14	1
400	NXTYR	–	56	1
401	CONS	–	15	1
402	ENCL	385	54	1
403	SUPSCH	382	53	1
404	NORES	–	25	1
19 Fields				23

I. Taxpayer Newly Married
    64, 63, 62, 61, 60—top of p. 1
    [4]
    62s—front of the return
    [4]

63s–not available
[5]
64s–available only if wife's maiden name is asked (top, front of return)
[4]
59, 58, 57, 56, 55, 54, 53, 52, 51, 50, 49, 48, 47, 46–coded according to
answer given on the tax return
[4]

II. C.Q.
    MARR = 0, 1, 2, 3, 4, 5, 9
III. F.D.
    46-59 [C, 24]
    60-64 [C, 39]
    46-64 [C, 382]
IV. N.D.
    The coders for the 1946-1959 file were given the following instructions:

Marriage During Tax Year? Marriage Details Given?
Code: 0 No marriage
         1 Marriage, no details
         2 Marriage, with details
Notes: 1. No answer is to be considered a negative answer.
       2. For men, "details" consists of giving wife's former
           name and address. For women, "details" consists of
           giving wife's former name and address and husband's
           former address.
       3. Do not use a priori information; use only the infor-
           mation given by the taxpayer on the return under
           consideration.

The codebook for the 60-64 master file gave the following instructions:

Information re recent marriage
    Source: answer to question "If marriage took place in 19 . .
(tax year) give full name and address of wife before marriage."
This question is at the top of page 1 for all "long" forms; for
1962 short forms on the front of the return; for *1963 short
forms* totally absent; for *1964 short forms* only the wife's maiden
name is asked (top, front of return).
Use the following codes:
0 No marriage took place during the tax year
1 Marriage took place during the tax year; complete information
2 Marriage took place during the tax year; incomplete information
3 Marriage took place; no information
9 Not ascertained; no answer.

Code 3 can be derived from the codes you assigned in the previous
year and the current year: if this year was coded as 1 *and* if the

previous year was *not* coded as 1, you may assume that a marriage did take place, although no information was supplied.

Information is "complete" if the wife's maiden name and former address are given, "incomplete" if only the maiden name or only her former address is given. *1963 short forms* should be coded 9, *1964 short forms* 0 if no marriage took place, 2 if marriage did take place and wife's maiden name is given.

On the merged 46-64 tax file the codes were transformed and the following set of codes were adopted (see WAIS 701-022, revised version) for complete documentation of all demographic transformations):

Combined 1946-1964 File

0   No marriage during tax year
1   Marriage took place, no information (60-64)
2   Marriage took place, no details (46-59)
3   Marriage took place, incomplete information (60-64)
4   Marriage took place, complete information (60-64)
5   Marriage with details (46-59)
9   Not ascertained, no answer

MSTAT

I. Marital Status
    64, 63, 62, 61, 60
    [3]
    59, 58, 57, 56, 55, 54, 53, 52, 51, 50, 49, 48, 47, 46—(not available)
    [5]
II. C.Q.
     MSTAT = 0, 1, 2, 3, 4, 5, 6, 9
III. F.D.
     46-59 [not available]
     60-64 [C, 35]
     46-64 [C, 383]
IV. N.D.
     In the 46-59 file there was no actual code for MSTAT but it could be derived from the SEPINC (Does wife have separate income?). This was developed into a marital status code and transformed into a combined code in the merged file.
     The coders for the 1960-1964 file were given the following instructions:

Marital status code
   Source: 1° the answers at the top of page 1 (front on short forms) will give some indication about the filer's marital status (we will assume that if a husband and wife file a combined return, they are married, unless there is clear evidence to the con-

trary). If no indication exists from these answers, check the following:

2° the answers to the questions "for persons claiming head of family exemption", which are *absent* on the *1962–1964 short forms*, can be found on page 4 of the *1959–1961* forms and on page 3 of the *1962–1964* long forms;

3° other returns and/or documents in the folder which may indicate the existence of a spouse.

4° check the personal exemptions claimed by the taxpayer.

Codes to be used:

0 Single
1 Married
2 Widowed
3 Divorced
4 Separated
9 Not ascertained

In the merged file the following codes were transformed:

Marital Status Code— *MSTAT 1946–1959* *File (from SEPINC)*	*1960–1964 File*	*Combined* *1946–1964 File*
	0 Single	0 Single (60–64)
0 No spouse		1 No spouse (46–59)
	1 Married ⎱	
1 Spouse, no separate income	⎰	2 Married
2 Spouse, separate income		
3 Spouse died during year		3 Spouse died during year (46–59)
	2 Widowed	4 Widowed ⎱
	3 Divorced	5 Divorced ⎬ (60–64)
	4 Separated	6 Separated ⎰
	9 Not ascertained	9 Not ascertained

SY5960

I. Spouse Separate Income 59–60
    64, 63, 62, 61–not coded
    [5]
    60, 59–p. i, second column
    [4]
    58, 57, 56, 55, 54, 53, 52, 51, 50, 49, 48, 47, 46–not coded
    [5]

II. C.Q.
    SY5960 = blank, 0, 1

III. F.D.
    46–59 [C, 386]

60-64 [not coded]
46-64 [C, 384]

IV. N.D.

The SY5960 code will only appear on 1960 records which had their origin in the 46–59 file with a source code of 0. In checking dumps of the 46–59 film, a blank is often found in fields for 1959 and 1960 which should be set specifically at 0 or 1. In years other than 59 and 60 the field is blank. Spouse has income in tax year record [either 59 or 60] = 1, otherwise = 0

SEPINC

I. Spouse Separate Income

64, 63, 62, 61, 60–p. 1, top of page
[4]
64s, 63s–determined by examining returns
[4]
59, 58, 57, 56, 55, 54, 53, 52, 51, 50, 49, 48, 47, 46–p. 1
[4]

II. C.Q.

SEPINC = 0, 1, 2, 3, 9

III. F.D.

46-59 [C, 23]
60-64 [C, 37]
46-64 [C, 385]

IV. N.D.

The codebook for the 1946-1959 file gives the following instructions:

Spouse's Name Given? Does Spouse Have Separate Income?
Code: 0 No spouse
       1 Spouse, no separate income
       2 Spouse, with separate income
       3 Spouse died during year
Notes: 1. If the questions are not answered by the taxpayer, the answer is to be assumed to be negative.
       2. Do not use a priori information; use only the information given by the taxpayer on the return under consideration.

Moyer (1966b, p. 24) gives the following additional information:

"If the taxpayer did not answer the questions, *the answers were assumed to be negative even if a return for the spouse was in the folder.* The only deviation from this rule was for the year 1957 when the question about separate income was not asked of the taxpayer. Then the response was coded according to whether the spouse's return was in the folder or not. This deviation was not consistently followed, however, so 1957 data are very poor."

The code book for the 60–64 data gives the following instructions to coders:

Spouse separate income
    Source: answer to the question "Do husband and wife each have income?", at the top of page 1 (1959–1964). Note that on the *1963 and 1964 short forms* the question is not asked. In these cases you will have to examine the returns and determine whether only one spouse declared income or both of them did.

Codes to be used:
0   Not applicable (taxpayer not married; therefore no spouse)
1   Yes
2   No
3   Spouse died during the year
9   Not ascertained

An additional note was added after the codebook was typed "The main criteria for judgment is what is found by examining the returns." In the merged 46–64 file the codes were transformed to the following:

Combined 1946–1964 File
0   Not applicable
1   Spouse, no separate income
2   Spouse, separate income
3   Spouse died during year
9   Not ascertained

INCRL

I.   Income Reliability Indicator
     64, 63, 62, 61, 60—see coder instructions
     [4]
     59, 58, 57, 56, 55, 54, 53, 52, 51, 50, 49, 48, 47 46—not coded
     [5]
II. C.Q.
     INCRL = 0, 1
III. F.D.
     46–59 [not available]
     60–64 [C, 38]
     46–64 [C, 386]
IV. N.D.
     On records where SC = 0, this field is not coded—the 0 in the field is merely to fill the field.
     The instructions for the coders from 1960–64 codebook are as follows:

     Spouse's income reliability indicator

Source: the code you assigned to SEPINC, combined with the actual presence or absence of a return.

Codes to be used:

0   No inconsistency; not applicable (SEPINC coded "0")

1   Inconsistency

MSCON

I.   Marital Status Consistency Code

64, 63, 62, 61, 60

[4]

59, 58, 57, 56, 55, 54, 53, 52, 51, 50, 49, 48, 47, 46—all forms

[5]

II.   C.Q.

MSCON = 0, 1

III.   F.D.

46-59   [not coded]

60-64   [C, 36]

46-64   [C, 387]

IV.   N.D.

On records where SC = 0, this field is not coded—the 0 in the field is merely to fill the field.

The instructions to coders for the 60-64 file are as follows:

Consistency indicator

Source: the code you assigned in MARR, combined with the answer given by the taxpayer's spouse (if any) or the absence of a spouse's return. From these sources you can determine whether the answer you coded in MARR is consistent with other information or whether it is not.

Codes to be used:

0   Consistency (e.g., spouses agree)

1   Inconsistency (spouses do not agree)

"The code will usually be 0. An example of a case in which 1 should be coded is: the husband says he is single; the wife says she is divorced."

DISMAR

I.   Dissolution of Marriage

64, 63, 62, 61, 60

[4]

59, 58, 57, 56, 55, 54, 53, 52, 51, 50, 49, 48, 47, 46—all forms

[5]

II.   C.Q.

DISMAR = 0, 1, 2, 9

III.   F.D.
       46-59 [not coded]
       60-64 [C, 40]
       46-64 [C, 388]
IV.   N.D.
       On records where SC = 0, this field is not coded—the 0 in the field is to
       fill the field.
       The following are the instructions to the coders in the 1960-1964 code-
       book:

> *Dissolution of marriage:*
>   *Source:* compare the codes you assigned to MSTAT for this
> year and for next year, as well as any indication on the forms
> (e.g., "alimony paid") of a dissolved marriage.
> *Codes to be used:*
> 0 Not applicable; no indication of dissolution of marriage
> 1 Divorce took place during the tax year
> 2 Separation took place during the tax year
> 9 Not certain whether dissolution of marriage took place
>   during tax year (e.g., although no indications of death or
>   divorce, a formerly married male begins to file separate
>   returns).

HEADFM

I.   Head of Family
      64, 63, 62, 61, 60, 59, 58, 57, 56, 55, 54, 53, 52, 51, 50, 49, 48, 47, 46
      [4]
II.   C.Q.
      HEADFM = 0, 1, 2, 3, 9
III. F.D.
      46-59 [C, 25]
      60-64 [C, 51]
      46-64 [C, 389]
IV.   N.D.
      The coders instructions in coding the 1946-1959 data are as follows:

> "Head of Family" Exemption Claimed?
> Code: 0 No
>   1 Yes
> Notes: 1. This information is not requested on forms 1W and
>   1Wa; the recorder will enter an automatic "0" when
>   those forms are being considered.
>   2. In addition, on form 1a for the years 1957-1958,
>   "Head of Family" information is located on page 2.

If page 2 was not microfilmed, enter a "0".
3. From 1959 on, information on page 4.

The 1960–64 coders were instructed as follows in coding this variable:

"Head of Family" Exemption Claimed?

Source: compare the exemptions claimed (Item B, page 1 on 1959–1961; line 8, page 1 on 1962 "long"; line 6, page 1 on 1963–1964 "long"; line 11, back on 1962 "short"; line 10a, back, on 1963–1964 "short") with the answers to the questions "For persons claiming head of family exemption" (*1959–1961* page 4, *1962–1964* page 3; no information on *1962–1964 short forms*).

For the coding of this field, two questions have to be answered:

1. Did the taxpayer claim "Head of family" exemption? This can be determined by comparing the number of dependents with the amount of exemptions claimed e.g. for a married couple with two children the amount of exemptions claimed should equal four times the "unit exemption" for that year, except if one or both parents were over 65. If the amount of exemptions is larger than the expected amount by one "unit exemption" it is likely that the Head of Family exemption was claimed.
2. Did the taxpayer have a right to claim "Head of Family" exemption? This is so if the taxpayer was not married (but single, widowed, divorced, separated) *and* supported one or more dependents.

A combination of the answers to the two above questions will then tell you whether the action taken by the taxpayer was the correct one.

The codes to be used are:
0 No (correctly *not* claimed)
1 Yes (validly claimed)
2 No (but should have claimed)
3 Yes (but did not have the right to claim)
9 Not ascertained (e.g. short forms where insufficient information is available)

On the merged 1946–1964 master file the following transformations were made:

"Head of Family" Exemption Claimed – HEADFM

1946–	*1960–*	*Combined*
1959 File	*1964 File*	*1946–1964 File*

0 No	0 No	0 No
1 Yes	1 Yes	1 Yes
	2 No, but should have claimed	2 No, but should have claimed
	3 Yes, but did not have the right to claim	3 Yes, but did not have the right to claim } (60–64)
	9 Not ascertained	9 Not ascertained

DEP

I. Dependents
   64, 63, 62, 61, 60, 59, 58, 57, 56, 55, 54, 53, 52, 51, 50, 49, 48, 47, 46 – all forms
   [4]

II. C.Q.
   $00 \leqslant DEP \leqslant 99$

III. F.D.
   46-59 [C, 26-27]
   60-64 [C, 41-42]
   46-64 [C, 390-391]

IV. N.D.
   The instructions to coders in the 1946-1959 codebook are as follows:

   Number of dependents
      Code: Actual number by count, using two digits.
      Notes: Do *not* include a spouse as a dependent; if listed as such
            omit when counting the number of dependents.
   In the 60-64 codebook the coding instructions were as follows:
   Number of dependents:
   Source: Count the number of names written under the heading "Dependents" (*1959-1961*–page 1) or under the heading "Exemptions" (*1962-1964*, page 3, *1962-1964 short forms* on the back of the return).
      In several cases a husband will list his wife as a dependent (on the 1962-1964 forms, husband and wife will usually be found on the designated line); neither the wife nor the taxpayer himself should be counted as dependents.
      If all the lines are filled, make sure that you check for enclosures where additional dependents may be listed (the returns allow for only five dependents). Allot *all* dependents to the husband if they "belong" to a married couple.

In the case of divorced or separated couples: if both parents claim all of the children (or if, in general, any dependent is claimed more than once), all dependents should be allotted to the ex-husband; if the dependents are split up between the ex-spouses (but no duplication of claims took place), each taxpayer will be allotted the number of dependents he (or she) claimed.

The number is always written in a 2-digit code–for example, 01. When you are unable to tell the number of dependents, code a 99.

On the merged file a coding scheme was adopted which was consistent with the 46–59 and the 60–64 coding.

Number of Dependents–DEP 1946-1959 File	1960-1964 File	Combined 1946-1964 File
2 digit code of dependents not including spouse	2 digit code of dependents not including spouse	2 digit code of dependents not including spouse

DEPAGE

I.   Dependents' Age

64, 63, 62, 61, 60

[4]

59, 58, 57, 56, 55, 54, 53, 52, 51, 50, 49, 48, 47, 46–not coded

[5]

II.   C.Q.

$000000 \leqslant DEPAGE \leqslant 999999$

III.   F.D.

46-59 [not coded]

60-64 [C, 43-46]

46-64 [C, 392-395]

IV.   N.D.

The information given to coders in the 1960-1964 codebook is as follows:

Dependents' age code:

Source: age(s) given with the dependents' information; for *1960-1961*: under the heading "dependents" on page 1; for *1962-1964*: under the heading "exemptions" on page 3. The 1959 returns do not ask for information on the ages of dependents; in many cases, working back from later returns will allow you to deduce the dependent's age for 1959. Dependents will be classified into six groups depending on their age:

a)   those under 10 years of age (0–9)

b)   those under 18, but not under 10 (10–17)

c)   those under 22, but not under 18 (18–21)

d) all other under 65 (22–64)

e) all dependents 65 or over (65+)

f) those with ages not ascertained.

This field is a six-digit code, where each digit is coded as the number of dependents in the corresponding age-groups;

digit 1   ages 0–9

digit 2   ages 10–17

digit 3   ages 18–21

digit 4   ages 22–64

digit 5   ages 65 and over

digit 6   ages not ascertained

Codes "0" for each digit where you find no dependents.

for example: Gerald Pfeifer has 7 dependents listed, aged 1, 7, 12, 15, 17, 68, and one for whom no age is given. This would be coded:

digit 1   2

digit 2   3

digit 3   0

digit 4   0

digit 5   1

digit 6   1

If there are more than 9 children in a single age group, the code should be 9. The code for uncertainty about the number of dependents and their age group is 9999.

DEPADR

I.   Dependents' Address

64, 63, 62, 61, 60

[4]

59, 58, 57, 56, 55, 54, 53, 52, 51, 50, 49, 48, 47, 46—all forms; not coded

[5]

II. C.Q.

0 ≤ DEPADR ≤ 9

III. F.D.

46–59 [not coded]

60–64 [C, 47]

46–64 [C, 396]

IV. N.D.

The instructions to coders on the 1960–1964 master file are as follows:

Dependent's address (if living elsewhere)

Source: answers given to question "complete address if different from yours", *1959–1961* under heading "dependents" on page 1; 1962–1964 under heading "exemptions" on page 3 ("long" forms). *1962–1964 short forms* do not supply the required information (use code "9", see below).

0   Not applicable
1   Some dependent(s) at different address—other household
2   Some dependent(s) at different address—college or university
3   Some dependent(s) at different address—hospital or other
    institution
4   Some dependent(s) at different address—type not ascertained,
    misc.
5   All dependent(s) at different address—other household
6   All dependent(s) at different address—college or university
7   All dependent(s) at different address—hospital or other institu-
    tion
8   All dependent(s) at different address—type not ascertained,
    misc.
9   No information about dependent's address.

N.B. Codes 1–4 are only to be used if at least one of the dependents is living at the same address of the taxpayer; codes 5–8 are
only to be used if no dependents are living at the same address as
the taxpayer. Code 9 is only to be used if no address indication is
given for one or more dependents, but you nevertheless have
valid reasons to assume that they are *not* living at the same
address as the taxpayer. If there are several dependents, each
living at a different type of address (e.g. one in college, one in
other household), use codes "4" or "8".

STU

I.   Students Over 18 in College
     64, 63, 62, 61, 60
     [4]
     59, 58, 57, 56, 55, 54, 53, 52, 51, 50, 49, 48, 47, 46—not coded
     [5]

II. C.Q.
     $0 \leqslant STU \leqslant 9$

III. F.D.
     46–59   [not available]
     60–64   [C, 48]
     46–64   [C, 397]

IV. N.D.
     Since the taxpayer was never specifically asked to differentiate between
     dependents living in his household and those away attending college, the
     information was available only if it was volunteered by the taxpayer.
     The instructions for the coders of the 1960–1964 file were as follows:

     Students over 18 in college
         Source: the address code as used in DEPADR supplemented
     by whatever other information is available on the returns.

Code to be used: count the number of dependents who are identified as students over 18 in college or university; code the number you counted.

RETPR

I.   Return Filed Previous Year
     64, 63, 62, 61, 60
     [4]
     59, 58, 57, 56, 55, 54, 53, 52, 51, 50, 49, 48, 47, 46
     [4]
II. C.Q.
     $0 \leqslant \text{RETPR} \leqslant 9$
III. F.D.
     46-59 [C, 21]
     60-64 [C, 33]
     46-64 [C, 398]
IV. N.D.
     The instructions to the coders of the 1946-1959 file were as follows:

     Return filed previous year? If not, reason why not.
     Code: 1 yes
            2 no, insufficient income
            3 no, student
            4 no, lack of knowledge
            5 no, in military service
            6 no, not Wisconsin resident
            7 no, unemployed
            8 no, reason unknown
            9 unknown (item not completed by taxpayer)
     Notes: This information is to be recorded in accordance with
            the taxpayer's reply to the relevant question on the
            return for the year under consideration; not with
            regard to the returns actually in the folder.

     The instructions in the 60-64 codebook regarding the location
     and coding of this information are as follows:
     Source: the taxpayer's answer to the questions: "Did you file
     a 19 . . (previous year) return?" and "If you did not file a 19 . .
     (previous year) return, why did you not file?" Both questions are
     on page 1 for all long forms front for short forms.

     Codes to be used:
     0 Yes
     1 No; non-resident
     2 No; less income than the filing requirements
     3 No; reasons other than those above (make out "Form S")
     8 No; reason not ascertained

9   Not ascertained

N.B. Code "8" is used if the first question was answered (indicating that *no* return was filed for the previous year) but the second one was not; code "9" is used if both questions were not answered.

The merge of the 1946–1959 file with 1960–1964 file produced the codes below on the merged master file.

Combined 1946–1964 File

0   Yes
1   No, non-resident
2   Absent, insufficient income
3   No, unemployed (as coded in 1946–1959 file)
4   No, student (46–59 File)
5   No, lack of knowledge (46–59 File)
6   No, in military service (46–59 File)
7   Absent, other (as coded in 1960–1964 file)
8   No, reason unknown
9   Unknown, item not completed or both questions not answered

FILED

I.   Return Filed
    64, 63, 62, 61, 60
    [4]
    59, 58, 57, 56, 55, 54, 53, 52, 51, 50, 49, 48, 47, 46–all forms
    [5]

II. C.Q.
    FILED = 0, 1, 2, 3

III. F.D.
    46–59   [not coded]
    60–64   [C, 14]
    46–64   [C, 399]

IV. N.D.
    Codes of the 1960–1964 file were instructed as follows:

    Return filed
       Source: the presence or absence of the return in the folder.

    Codes to be used:
    0   Return present
    1   Part of return present
    2   Return missing
    3   Return missing because of field audit
    If a return was out for field audit, the folder shot will indicate this. If you find such cases, do not continue the coding of these returns. Write "out for field audit" in the "Remarks" column of the filing-coding sheet log and give the folder to the supervisor.

I. Next Tax Year
    64, 63, 62, 61, 60
    [4]
    59, 58, 57, 56, 55, 54, 53, 52, 51, 50, 49, 48, 47, 46—all forms
    [5]
II. C.Q.
    NXTYR = 0, 1, 2, 3, 4, 8, 9
III. F.D.
    46-59 [not coded]
    60-64 [C, 56]
    46-64 [C, 400]
IV. N.D.
    The instructions to the 1960-1964 coders concerning this variable were
    as follows:

    Next year filed indicator
    Source: for all except the most recent return, you can check
    the actual presence or absence of the next return in the folder; if
    it is absent, check the indication on the microfilm record to make
    sure that it is legitimately missing (if not, see the coding supervisor).
    If the next year's return is legitimately missing, try to find the
    reason why it is absent.
    For the most recent return you can, of course, not go by the
    microfilm record or the returns themselves (although in some
    cases 1965 returns were filmed). In some cases, however, there
    will be an indication that chances for further returns have
    decreased (e.g. if there is conclusive evidence that the taxpayer
    moved out of state or died during the tax year).

    Codes to be used:
    0 Yes, next year's return present
    1 Taxpayer moved out of state
    2 Taxpayer changed name (therefore not part of sample any
       more)
    3 Taxpayer died during the taxation year or any previous year
    4 Taxpayer's income for subsequent year lower than filing
       requirements
    8 Return absent, reason not known (do *not* use this code on
       1964 returns)
    9 Not known whether next year's return will be present (this
       code only to be used on 1964 returns)

CONS

I. Consistency Indicator for FILED
    64, 63, 62, 61, 60
    [4]
    59, 58, 57, 56, 55, 54, 53, 52, 51, 50, 49, 48, 47, 46–all forms
    [5]
II. C.Q.
    CONS = 0, 1
III. F.D.
    46-59 [not coded]
    60-64 [C, 15]
    46-64 [C, 401]
IV. N.D.
    The following instructions were given to the coders of the 1960-1964
    file regarding this variable:

    Consistency indicator
    Source: the presence or absence of the return, as compared
    with the indication on the "folder shot". If the two indications
    agree, use code "0"; if they disagree (e.g. the "folder shot" indi-
    cates that a return should be present, but you cannot find the
    return in the folder), use code "1".
    The "folder shot" was taken just previous to the microfilms
    of each return which indicated which year returns, if any, were
    missing.

ENCL

I. Enclosures
    64, 63, 62, 61, 60, 59, 58, 57, 56, 55, 54, 53, 52, 51, 50, 49, 48, 47, 46
    [4]
II. C.Q.
    $0 \leqslant ENCL \leqslant 9$
III. F.D.
    46-59 [C, 385]
    60-64 [C, 54]
    46-64 [C, 402]
IV. N.D.
    WT9 is the withholding statement sent to taxpayers; the "informational"
    usually is a statement of interest or dividends received.

The sequence of the codes was as follows:

Enclosures—ENCL

1946–1959 File	*1960–1964 File*	*Combined 1946–1964 File*	
0 No	0 No enclosures	0 No enclosures	
	1 WT9 only	1 WT9 only	
	2 "informational" only	2 "informational" only	
	3 WT9 and "infor-mational"	3 WT9 and "informa-tional"	
	4 "other" only	4 "other" only	
	5 WT9 and "other"	5 WT9 and "other" (60–64)	
	6 "informational" and "other"	6 "informational and "other"	
	7 WT9, "informa-tional" and "other"	7 WT9, "informational" and "other"	
	8 Enclosure, type not identified	8 Enclosure, type not identified	
1 Yes		9 Yes, coded in 1946–1959 file	

SUPSCH

I.   Supplementary Schedules
     64, 63, 62, 61, 60, 59, 58, 57, 56, 55, 54, 53, 52, 51, 50, 49, 48, 47, 46—
     all forms—see C.Q. section
     [4]
II. C.Q.
     SUPSCH = 0, 1, 2, 3, 4, 5
III. F.D.
     46–59 [C, 382]
     60–64 [C, 53]
     46–64 [C, 403]
IV. N.D.
     The historical and present codes for this field are as follows:

Supplementary Schedule Indicator–SUPSCH

1946–1959 File	1960–1964 File	Combined 1946–1964 File
0 No	0 No	0 No
	1 Farm Schedule	1 Farm Schedule (60–64 file)
	2 Business Schedule	2 Business Schedule (60–64)
	3 Farm & Business Schedule	3 Farm and Business Schedule (60–64)
	4 Supplementary Schedule but don't know what kind	4 Supplementary Schedule but don't know what kind (60–64)
1 Yes		5 Yes coded in 1946–1959 File

NORES

I.   Non-resident Indicator
     64, 63, 62, 61, 60
     [4]
     59, 58, 57, 56, 55, 54, 53, 52, 51, 50, 49, 48, 47, 46
     [5]

II. C.Q.
     NORES = 0, 1, 9

III. F.D.
     46–59 [not coded]
     60–64 [C, 25]
     46–64 [C, 404]

IV. N.D.
     The instructions in the 1960–1964 codebook regarding this program are as follows:

> *Non-resident indicator*
>   *Source:* In some cases you will find an indication that this return was filed by someone who was not a Wisconsin resident. Indications can be of the following kinds:
>   –the taxpayer may have used a "Non-resident Form" (Form 1N) to file his return;
>   –the taxpayer may have used a Form from another State to file his return;
>   –he may indicate by means of his address (top section of page 1 of the return) that he is not a Wisconsin resident.
>
> *Code to be used:*
>   0 Resident
>   9 Resident status not ascertained

Table E-7
Indicators Related to Labor Force and Employment

Merged	Descriptor	Old	New	Size
405–408	IND	–	28–31	4
409–410	OCC	18–19	26–27	2
411	OCCH	20	32	1
412	LABPR	–	34	1
413	REL	–	55	1
414	NWAGE	381	49	1
415	SDIV	383	50	1
416	PTNR	22	–	1
417	AUTOEX	384	52	1
9 Fields				13

IND

I.   Industry Code
     64, 63, 62, 61, 60
     [4]
     59, 58, 57, 56, 55, 54, 53, 52, 51, 50, 49, 48, 47, 46
     [5]
II. C.Q.
     $0000 \leq IND \leq 9999$
III. F.D.
     46–59 [not coded]
     60–64 [C, 28–31]
     46–64 [C, 405–408]
IV. N.D.
     Coders assigned a general industry code from the list in Appendix A of
     667-002. Certain corporations which employed large numbers of Wisconsin
     residents had a specific code which applied only to their corporation but
     had the first 2 digits representing the basic industry in which they were
     employed. For example, the code for Food and Kindred Products is 2000
     while the specific industry code for Oscar Mayer and Company is 2003.
        The Wisconsin Manufacturers' Association Directory and the Mil-
     waukee Yellow Pages were used as guides when there was uncertainty
     concerning what products were manufactured by a particular company.
     The instructions to the 1960-1964 coders regarding this variable were as
     follows:

        Industry code: a 4-digit numeric code
           Source: in many cases, you will be able to code this from the
        answer regarding occupation (OCC). In other cases, evidence
        regarding the taxpayer's employer will be available (Source of

income—page 1, *1959–1961*, page 2, *1962–1964*, back, *1962 short form*, front, *1963–1964 short forms*). In other cases, withholding forms with the employer's name will be available; in still other cases, correspondence might carry the employer's letterhead, etc.

Codes to be assigned: if you can identify the taxpayer's employer, check the list of main Wisconsin and U.S. corporations in Appendix D of 667–002. If you find the employer on this list, use the four-digit code as indicated on the list. If the employer is not on the list of Appendix D of 667–002, or cannot be identified, determine the industry and find the *first two digits* of the industry code from Appendix C of 667–002; the last digits should be *00* for all these cases which were not identified on Appendix D of 667–002.

OCC

I.   Occupation Code
     64, 63—page 1
     [4]
     64s, 63s (not available)
     [5]
     62, 61, 60, 59, 58, 57, 56, 55, 54, 53, 52, 51, 50, 49, 48, 47, 46—all
     forms , p. 1
     [4]
II. C.Q.
     $01 \leqslant OCC \leqslant 38$ and 99
III. F.D.
     46–59 [C, 18–19]
     60–64 [C, 26–27]
     46–64 [C, 409–410]
IV. N.D.
     The instructions for the coding of occupation code in the 46–59 codebook
     are as follows:

     Occupation
     Code: 2 digits (the occupation index and code numbers are
            listed below).
     Notes: 1. The index given below is an abbreviated version of
               the "Three-Digit Occupational Groups," Dictionary
               of Occupational Titles, U.S. Government Printing
               Office. A copy of the D.O.T. will be made available
               to the recorders for assistance in clarifying
               doubtful cases.
            2. The recorder must exercise considerable discretion
               when completing this item. For example, the tax-

payer's occupation may remain the same over a period of years while his description of that occupation may vary; thus the return for a particular year cannot be considered completely in isolation from those for other years.

3. Note that within some of the major categories there is a code number for persons believed to belong in that category but not specifically identifiable, e.g., 17 Professional and Semiprofessional Occupations—n.e.c. If however, the occupation is not given and/or it is impossible to make any other classification, enter the number 99.

The codes used for occupation in the 1946-1959 master are listed in Appendix C of 667-002.

Occupation code: a 2-digit numeric code—see Appendix D of 667-002.

Source: the answer written by the taxpayer on page 1 of the return, for his "occupation."

If you are in doubt about the specific code to be used, use the "Dictionary of Occupational Titles."

You will have to use your ingenuity in several cases: the taxpayer may give a new description of his occupation while in effect no change has taken place (e.g., undertaker—mortician; garbageman—garbologist; etc.).

Another case where your imagination will be helpful is that where the taxpayer is not explicit enough about his occupation. If necessary, look at the amount of income to determine whether the proper classification is skilled, semiskilled, or unskilled.

The number code adapted by the coders in the 60-64 file is not always consistent with the codes in the 46-59 file. Appendix D of 667-002 gives the codes used in the 60-64 file. Appendix E of 667-002 follows with the 46-59 codes and the 60-64 codes along with the codes which were transformed from them to create a consistent occupation code throughout this entire file. It is the codes in this document labeled "combined 1946-1964 file" which reflect the occupation codes on the present version of the merged master file.

OCCH

I.   Occupation Change
     64, 63, 62, 61, 60
     [4]

59, 58, 57, 56, 55, 54, 53, 52, 51, 50, 49, 48, 47, 46

[4]

II. C.Q.

$0 \leqslant OCCH \leqslant 9$

III. F.D.

46-59 [C, 20]

60-64 [C, 32]

46-64 [C, 411]

IV. N.D.

The instructions to the coders of the 1946-1959 file were as follows:

Occupation change
Code: 0 No change
 1 Change
 9 Unknown
Notes: 1. Code in accordance with Item 9, i.e., enter a 1 only if the entry for Item 9 has changed from that of the previous year.
 2. Enter a 9 if the taxpayer's return for the previous year is not available.

If work is not continuous in years but is continuous in occupation record, code a 0 (no change).

The coders for the 1960-1964 file had these instructions:

Occupation Change

Source: the occupation and employer as indicated on the return you are working on, compared with the same information for the year before the one you are working on. There are three factors which change; a change in any one of these does not necessarily imply that the other factors have to change too:

(a) change in employer
(b) change in industry
(c) change in occupation.

The way in which this code is constructed is to assign "values" to each of the separate elements: "0" for no change, "1" for "change in employer", "2" for "change in industry", "4" for "change in occupation". An easy way to find the code, then, is to decide which change (if any) occurred, find the values associated with these changes, and add them. You can check the value you find against the list of codes given below.

Code to be used:

0 No change
1 Change in employer *only*
2 Change in industry *only*
3 Change in industry *and* in employer

4 Change in occupation *only*
5 Change in occupation *and* employer (but not industry)
6 Change in occupation *and* industry (but *not* in employer)
7 Change in occupation *and* industry *and* employer
8 Entered labor force, retired, died
9 Not ascertained, unknown

In the combined 1946–1964 file no recoding was done. The source code of the record must be checked to determine which code set is to be used.

LABPR

I.   Labor Force Previous Year
     64, 63, 62, 61, 60
     [4]
     59, 58, 57, 56, 55, 54, 53, 52, 51, 50, 49, 48, 47, 46—all forms; not coded
     [5]
II. C.Q.
     $0 \leqslant \text{LABPR} \leqslant 9$
III. F.D.
     46–59 [not coded]
     60–64 [C, 34]
     46–64 [C, 412]
IV. N.D.
     Instructions to the coders for the 1960–1964 file concerning this variable are as follows:

> *Labor force indication for previous year*
>   *Source:* answers to the same two questions which you used to code OCC, supplemented (if necessary) by information on the previous year's return.
>
> *Code to be used:*
> 0 Employed
> 1 Unemployed (but seeking employment)
> 2 Student
> 3 Military service
> 4 Housewife (not employed!)
> 5 Retired
> 6 Underage
> 7 Other status (make out "Form S")
> 9 No indication of labor force status

Some of the same information can be gained by the variable RETPR for the years 1946–1959.

I.   Reliability Indicator
     64, 63, 62, 61, 60
     [4]
     59, 58, 57, 56, 55, 54, 53, 52, 51, 50, 49, 48, 47, 46
     [5]
II. C.Q.
     $0 \leqslant \text{REL} \leqslant 3$
III. F.D.
     46-59 [not coded]
     60-64 [C, 55]
     46-64 [C, 413]
IV. N.D.
     The instructions to the coders for the 1960-1964 file for this variable are
     as follows:

>   *Reliability indicator*
>   This indicator refers to the occupation code and the industry
>   code (fields 13 and 14) which you coded earlier. In the cases
>   where you had no problem in determining the correct industry
>   and occupation, the indicator will be 0. If, however, you had
>   trouble in determining the right occupation, or industry, or both,
>   use the following codes:
>
>   1   Occupation code not reliable (but industry code *is* reliable)
>   2   Industry code not reliable (but occupation code *is* reliable)
>   3   Occupation code as well as industry code are unreliable

I.   Number of Sources of Wages
     64, 63, 62, 61, 60—all forms
     [4]
     59, 58, 57, 56, 55, 54, 53, 52, 51, 50, 49, 48, 47, 46—all forms
     [4]
II. C.Q.
     $0 \leqslant \text{NWAGE} \leqslant 9$
III. F.D.
     46-59 [C, 381]
     60-64 [C, 49]
     46-64 [C, 414]
IV. N.D.
     In the 1946-1959 master file, this variable was the result of the key-
     puncher counting the number of sources of wages and salaries. If the

taxpayer worked for 9 or more employers during the year, a 9 was punched
in this field. In some cases this field was blank when it should be zero.

In the 1960-1964 master file, this information was provided by the
coders. Their instructions were as follows:

Total sources of wages (or salaries)
   Source: count the number of mentions of sources of wages.
1959-1961, page 1, question 1; *1962-1964* "long", page 2,
question 1; *1962 short*, question 6 (back); *1963-1964 short*,
question 4 (front).

   Do *not* include Unemployment Compensation as a source of
wages. Only payments from employers are to be counted; all payments from *one employer* are to be counted as coming from *one
source*.

   The case may occur where there are more WT 9's than
sources mentioned for a given year. If this happens, do the
following:

   1. Check the year on the WT 9's and make sure that every
one refers to the year you are working on; file any "misplaced"
WT 9 with the return it belongs to. If there are still more WT 9's
than sources mentioned.

   2. Compare the sum of the amounts indicated on the WT 9's
for that year with the sum of the total wages as indicated on that
year's return. If the two sums agree, take the number of sources
as you can identify them on the WT 9's. If the two sums do not
agree:

   3. See the supervisor.

Code to be used:
0   No income from wages on salaries
1   One source of income mentioned
2   Two sources of income mentioned
3-6   Three, four, five, six sources of income mentioned
7   Seven or more sources mentioned
9   Number of sources not ascertained

                                                                    SDIV

I.   Dividend Paid in Stock?
     64, 63, 62, 61, 60–all forms (not available)
     [5]
     58, 57, 56–Form 1 and 1W
     [4]
     58, 57–Form 1a and 1Wa (not available)
     55, 54, 53, 52, 51, 50, 49, 48, 47, 46–Forms 1 and 1W
     [4]
     52, 51, 50, 49, 48, 47, 46–Forms 1a and 1Wa (not available)

II.   C.Q.
      $0 \leqslant \text{SDIV} \leqslant 2$ and 9
III. F.D.
      46-59 [C, 383]
      60-64 [C, 50]
      46-64 [C, 415]
IV.   N.D.
      The question concerning stock dividends was asked of the taxpayer who
      filed a long form for every year through 1959. According to Moyer (1966b)
      the question was asked on page 3 or on page 4 for all years. In the 46-59
      master, the code was 1 if the taxpayer indicated that he had received a
      stock dividend and 0 for all other cases.
      In records for 59 which originated from the 1960-1964 tax file and
      have a source code of 2, the following were instructions to the coders:

      Dividend paid in stock?
      Source: answer to the question "Did you ever receive dividends
      paid in shares of stock from the corporation whose stock you
      sold in 1959?" at the bottom of page 3. This question was only
      asked on the 1959 returns; other years should not be coded.

      Codes to be used:
      1   Yes
      2   No
      9   Not ascertained; unknown (year 1959)

      In the records for 1960-1964 a 0 was punched in this field to indicate
      that it was inapplicable.

                                                                          PTNR

I.   Partnership Name Given?
      64, 63, 62, 61, 60—all forms (not available)
      [5]
      59, 58, 57, 56, 55, 54, 53, 52, 51, 50, 49, 48, 47, 46
      [4]
II.   C.Q.
      $0 \leqslant \text{PTNR} \leqslant 1$
III. F.D.
      46-59 [C, 22]
      60-64 [not available]
      46-64 [C, 416]
IV.   N.D.
      The instructions to the coders for the 1946-1959 tax file follow:

Partnership Name Given?
    Code: 0 No
            1 Yes
    Notes: 1. This information is to be found (on page 1) of all forms from 1947 through 1958 *except* forms 1a and 1Wa from 1947 through 1952. For the latter forms the recorder may automatically enter a 0.
            2. Beginning in 1959 the partnership information is to be found on page 3, Schedule C, line 6.

AUTOEX

I. Automobile Expense Itemized
64, 63, 62, 61, 60, 59
[4]
58, 57—Forms 1a and 1Wa (not available)
[5]
58, 57, 56—Forms 1 and 1W
[4]
55, 54, 53, 52, 51, 50, 49, 48, 47, 46—Forms 1 and 1W
[4]
52, 51, 50, 49, 48, 47—Forms 1a and 1Wa (not available)
[4]

II. C.Q.
$0 \leqslant$ AUTØEX $\leqslant 4$ and 9

III. F.D.
46-59 [C, 384]
60-64 [C, 52]
46-64 [C, 417]

IV. N.D.
Moyer (1966b) indicates "If the upper half of schedule F on page 3 were filled out or if an itemized list were included as 1 was punched, otherwise a 0 was punched in this field."

The instructions to the coders for the 1960-1964 master regarding this variable were as follows:

Automobile expense indicator
    Source: 1959-1961, answers to Schedule H, page 4; *1962-1964*, answers to Schedule A, page 4 and answer to line 5, page 3; *1962-1964 short forms*, no information on return itself, *plus* additional enclosures (all years) carrying information regarding casualty losses.
The method to determine the code you have to use goes in two steps:
    1. Check the answers to Schedule H (1959-1961) or Schedule

A (1962–1964) to find out whether the taxpayer had automobile expenses. If the answer was "yes," go to step (2a), if the answer was "no," go to Step (2b).

2a. Check for the presence or absence of casualty losses. If "yes," use code 3; if "no," use code 1.

2b. Check for the presence or absence of casualty losses. If "yes," use code 2; if "no," use code 0.

Codes to be used:
0 No (neither auto. expense nor casualty losses)
1 Auto. expenses indicated (but *no* casualty losses)
2 Casualty losses indicated (but *no* auto. expenses)
3 Casualty losses as well as auto. expenses indicated.
9 Not able to ascertain

If the automobile expenses are not shown on the actual return, do not code it as present. (If they are on the business sheet, disregard them!)

The merge programs for the 1946–1964 file did some recoding for the sake of consistency. The codes under the column "Combined 1946–1964 File" are those which have been adopted for the merged master.

Automobile Expense Indicator–AUTOEX

1946–1959 File	*1960–1964 File*	*Combined 1946–1964 File*
0 No	0 No	0 No
1 Yes	1 Auto exp but no casualty losses	1 Yes
	2 Casualty losses but no auto expense	2 Auto exp but no casualty losses (as coded in 60-64 file)
	3 Casualty losses and auto expense	3 Casualty losses but no auto expense (60-64)
	9 Not ascertained	4 Casualty losses and auto expense (60-64)
		9 Not ascertained (60-64)

Table E-8
Indicators of Geographic Location

Merged	Descriptor	Old	New	Size
418–419	CNTY	12–13	20–21	2
420–423	TAXDIS	14	16–19	4
424–425	CNTYPR	15–16	22–23	2
426	MOVED	17	24	1
4 Fields				9

CNTY

I. County of Residence
    64, 63, 62, 61, 60, 59, 58, 57, 56, 55, 54, 53, 52, 51, 50, 49, 48, 47, 46–
    all forms, p. 1
    [4]
II. C.Q.
    01 ≤ CNTY ≤ 72, 80, and 96 through 99
III. F.D.
    46-59 [C, 12-13]
    60-64 [C, 20-21]
    46-64 [C, 418–419]
IV. N.D.
    The 1946–1959 master file coders assigned a 3-digit code for county in
    which the third digit indicated sub-divisions within the county. The codes
    assigned are listed in Appendix D of 667–002 while the instructions to
    those coders follow:

    Residence Location
        Code: 3 digits (the residence location index and code
               numbers are given below).
        Notes: 1. This information is to be taken from the section
                   in which the taxpayer is requested to give the
                   name of the city, village or town and then the
                   county in which he resides; do not use the "Home
                   Address" response for coding.
               2. Note that the last item listed under each county
                   includes all villages *not specifically identified*; as
                   well as all towns (unincorporated villages and rural
                   areas). (NEC–Not Elsewhere Classified.)
               3. Note also that the County of Menominee is listed
                   at end as number 72.
               4. There are four special code numbers:
                   997 No fixed location
                   998 More than one location given

999   Residence location not given
980   Out of state

In assigning names to the variables the 3-digit code was divided into
2 separate variables: the first 2 digits became **CNTY** and the third digit
became **RESLOC** for the 1946–1959 master file.

In the 60–64 the county code was shortened to a 2-digit code which
corresponds exactly to the first 2 digits of the code used in the 46–59
master file. The 2-digit codes used are listed in Appendix D2 of 667–002.
The instructions to the coders in 1960–1964 are as follows:

County code
Source: page 1 on all forms; written after "TAX DISTRICT."
This is a 2-digit numeric code, according to the list in Appendix A
of 667–002; it should pertain to the taxpayer's *tax district*. In
most cases, the code will be identical to the one you wrote in
CNTY on ID but this is not necessarily so in all cases; especially if the taxpayer moved from one county to another, there
will be differences.
When the merged file was created the merged code was a 2-
digit code. Information on the codes is as follows.

County Code – CNTY

1946–1959 File	1960–1964 File	1946–1964 File
A 3-digit county code, the first 2 digits are county codes in the 1960–1964 file.	A 2-digit county code which exactly paral- lels the first two digits of the 1946– 1959 file.	A 2-digit county code which exactly parallels the first two digits of the 1946–1959 file.

Thus the codes for **CNTY** on the merged master are the same as those
listed in Appendix D2 of 667–002.

TAXDIS

I. Tax District
   64, 63, 62, 61, 60
   [4]
   59, 58, 57, 56, 55, 54, 53, 52, 51, 50, 49, 48, 47, 46
   [4]
II. C.Q.
   Both alphabetic and numeric codes.
III. F.D.
   46–59 [C, 14]

60-64 [C, 16-19]
46-64 [C, 420-423]

IV.   N.D.

The information was coded by the Wisconsin Department of Taxation coder and copied by the WAIS coder.

In the 1946-1959 file this was a 1-digit code following the county code which provided a further breakdown of location. (See Appendix D of 667-002 to see the precise codes.)

In the 1960-1964 file a 4-character alphabetic code was coded by the tax department coders and copied by the WAIS coders.

In the years 1960-1963 the code was usually the first 4 digits of the tax district name (e.g., MADI for Madison); however in 1964 the code was changed to reflect the type of governmental organization of the district and the first 3 letters of the district (e.g., CMAD for City of Madison and TMAD for Town of Madison). This code can only be used in conjunction with the county code because there are duplicate alphabetic codes (e.g., CMEN in County 67 is Menomonee Falls while CMEN in County 17 is Menomonee).

In the merged 1946-1964 file the records with a source code of 0 (record) originated in the 1946-1960 master file) the first digit is the number coded for the breakdown of each county, the next 3 numbers will always be zero.

CNTYPR

I.   County Previous Year
      64, 63, 62, 61, 60
      [4]
      59, 58, 57, 56, 55, 54, 53, 52, 51, 50, 49, 48, 47, 46
      [4]
II.   C.Q.
      $01 \leqslant CNTYPR \leqslant 72$ and 98
III. F.D.
      46-59 [C, 15-16]
      60-64 [C, 22-23]
      46-64 [C, 424-425]
IV.   N.D.

The instructions to the 1946-1959 master file coders were as follows:

> *County Prior Year*
>   Code: 2 digits (the counties and their code numbers are
>   listed below).
>   Notes: 1. This information is to be taken, whenever possible,
>   from the answer to the question, "In what county
>   did you reside in 19–?"

2. If the question was not answered by the taxpayer, enter the first two digits of the residence location code number (Item 6) for the year prior to the one under consideration.
3. If the taxpayer did not answer the question or did not file a return the previous year, then enter the number 99.

The codes listed for the coders are in Appendix D of 667-002.

The coders for the 1960-1964 master file were given the following instructions:

County prior year: again a 2-digit numeric code (Appendix D of 667-002).

Source: the response to the question "In what county did you reside in 19 . . (the previous year)?" on page 1 of the return. If the taxpayer did not answer the question but the previous year's return is in the folder, take the information from that source. If the question was not answered and the previous year's return is not present, use code 99 (not ascertained).

In the merged file no changes were made in the coding scheme since it was consistent throughout the entire file.

County Prior Year Code—CNTYPR

1946-1959 File	1960-1964 File	1946-1964 File
2-digit county code which follows codes for first 2 digits of county field.	Same 2-digit county code as in 1946-1959 file.	Same 2-digit county code as in 1946-1959 file.

MOVED

I. Address Change
   64, 63, 62, 61, 60
   [4]
   59, 58, 57, 56, 55, 54, 53, 52, 51, 50, 49, 48, 47
   [4]
II. C.Q.
   $0 \leqslant$ MOVED $\leqslant 7$ and 9
III. F.D.
   46-59 [C, 17]
   60-64 [C, 24]
   46-64 [C, 426]
IV. N.D.

The instructions to the coders for the 1946–1959 file concerning the coding of this variable were as follows:

Address Change
        Code: 0 No
               1 Yes
               9 Unknown
        Notes: 1. *Any* changes of address is to be recorded. Thus, items 6 and 7 are not by themselves sufficient indicators but may be used as preliminary guides. The procedure will be:
               a. If for the current year Item 7 differs from the first two digits of Item 6, the taxpayer has obviously moved.
               b. If Item 6 for the current year differs from Item 6 for the previous year, the taxpayer has moved.
               c. If neither a nor b indicate the taxpayer has moved, then the forms for the current year and the previous year must be compared to determine whether there has been a change in the taxpayer's mailing address.
               2. If there is no return for the taxpayer for the previous year, enter the number 9.

The coders for the 1960–1964 had a further breakdown on address change:

Address change
        Source: the address as indicated at the top of page 1 of the return you are currently working on, as compared with the address on the return for the year before the current one.

The codes to be used are:
        0 No change
        1 Change, within tax district
        2 Change, within county
        3 Change, within state
        4 Change, interstate
        7 Possible change, but coder cannot be sure
        8 Change, extent not known
        9 Not ascertained, unknown
            Codes 1–4 indicate an increasing "extent" of change, so you have to select the code which is most applicable to the change—for example, if a person changes address within the same county, but into a different tax district, code 2 is the most applicable (even though code 3 could also be applied).

Code 4 includes all address changes where the *state* of residence changed; it also includes those cases where the taxpayer moved into or out of the country.

The program which merged the 2 files used the following formula for converting the data.

Address change–MOVED

1946–1959 File	*1960–1964 File*	*1946–1964 File*	
0 No change	0 No change	0 No change	
	1 Change, within tax district	1 Change, within tax district	
	2 Change, within county	2 Change, within county	
	3 Change, within state	3 Change, within state	As coded in
	4 Change, inter-state	4 Change, inter-state	1960–1964
	8 Change, extent not known	5 Change, extent not known	file
		6 Change (as coded in 1946–1959 file)	
1 Change	7 Possible change, coder cannot be sure	7 Possible change, coder cannot be sure (as coded in 1960–1964 file)	
9 Not ascertained	9 Not ascertained, unknown	9 Not ascercertained, unknown	

Table E-9
Miscellaneous Indicators

Merged	Descriptor	Old	New	Size
427	FORM	387	393	1
428	COMP	388	394, 408	1
429	YADKY	392	–	1
430	ATOKY	393	–	1
431	SDEDKY	394	–	1
432	DED1KY	395	–	1
433	NBTKY	396	–	1
434	NBDKY	397	–	1
435	NIBKY	398	–	1
436	BLKCOL	379	–	1
437	TYPNON	380	320	1
438	PERC	–	404	1
439–440	TERR	–	405–406	2
13 Fields				14

FORM

I.   Type of Form
     64, 63, 62, 61, 60, 59, 58, 57, 56, 55, 54, 53, 52, 51, 50, 49, 48, 47, 46
     [4]
II. C.Q.
     $1 \leqslant FORM \leqslant 6$
III. F.D.
     46–59 [C, 387]
     60–64 [C, 393]
     46–64 [C, 427]
IV. N.D.
     This code indicates the type of tax department form which the taxpayer
     used that year. The form numbers have to be evaluated in conjunction
     with the source code.

If SC = 0	1	Forms 1 and 1W (1946–1955)
	2	Forms 1a and 1WA (1947–1952)
	3	Forms 1 and 1W (1956–1958)
	4	Form 1a and 1Wa (1957–1958)
	5	Form 1 (1959–1960)
	6	Forms 1 and 1W which are incomplete in some way (1946–1958)
If SC = 2, 3	1	Form 1 (1959–1961)
	2	Form 1 (1962)
	3	Form 1 (1963–1964)
	4	Form 1a (1962–1964)

In cases where dummy returns are filed, this code is blank.

In records where FORM = 6, the net income amount is found in the code INCTXY. These records will usually show only taxable income, exemptions, and tax liability figures.

COMP

   I. Completeness Indicator
      64, 63, 62, 61, 60, 59, 58, 57, 56, 55, 54, 53, 52, 51, 50, 49, 48, 47, 46
      [4]
  II. C.Q.
      $0 \leqslant COMP \leqslant 1$
 III. F.D.
      46-59 [C, 388]
      60-64 [C, 394 and 408]
      46-64 [C, 428]
 IV. N.D.
      Moyer (1966b) indicates that 0 was the code to indicate completeness of the record and 1 was the code to indicate incompleteness. The indication on the format of the source field as "From form type 6" seems to imply that this code is only an interpretation when FORM = 6. However, we have reason to suspect (although this is undocumented) that this indicator may apply to the whole file.

In the 1960-1964 master file the program WAIS/DMT(#1044) adopted the same coding scheme to indicate completeness or incompleteness. If COMP on the input file = 0 and the continuation indicator = Z, the COMP code for the merged file is 0 (to indicate completeness), else it is a 1 to indicate incompleteness.

YADKY

   I. Income Addition Key
      64, 63, 62, 61, 60
      [5]
      59, 58, 57, 56, 55, 54, 53, 52, 51, 50, 49, 48, 47, 46
      [4]
  II. C.Q.
      $0 \leqslant YADKY \leqslant 9$
 III. F.D.
      46-59 [C, 392]
      60-64 [not available]
      46-64 [C, 429]
 IV. N.D.
      WAIS 656-037 gives additional information about this variable.

If the largest wage + other income is not equal to other sources of income, this key indicates the size of the discrepancy according to the following scale:

Discrepancy Scale Code	Amount (absolute value)
0	$ 0.00-$ 4.99
1	5.00- 20.00
2	20.01- 40.00
3	40.01- 60.00
4	60.01- 80.00
5	80.01- 100.00
6	100.01- 200.00
7	200.01- 300.00
8	300.01- 400.00
9	400.01- or over

Blank is also used as a code to reflect no discrepancy.

ATOKY

I.   Compute Auto Key
     64, 63, 62, 61, 60
     [5]
     59, 58, 57, 56, 55, 54, 53, 52, 51, 50, 49, 48, 47, 46
     [4]
II. C.Q.
     $0 \leqslant ATOKY \leqslant 9$
III. F.D.
     46-59 [C, 393]
     60-64 [not available]
     46-64 [C, 430]
IV. N.D.
     WAIS 656-037 gives additional information about this variable. If total of TOTINC minus AUTBUS is not equal to AGI the size of the discrepancy is indicated in the **ATOKY** field according to the following scale.

Discrepancy Scale Code	Amount (absolute value)
0	$ 0.00-$ 4.99
1	5.00- 20.00
2	20.01- 40.00
3	40.01- 60.00

4	60.01– 80.00
5	80.01– 100.00
6	100.01– 200.00
7	200.01– 300.00
8	300.01– 400.00
9	400.01– or over

Blank is used as a code when there was no discrepancy.

SDEDKY

I. Standard Deduction Incomplete Key
    64, 63, 62, 61, 60
    [5]
    59, 58, 57, 56, 55, 54, 53, 52, 51, 50, 49, 48, 47, 46
    [4]
II. C.Q.
    $0 \leqslant SDEDKY \leqslant 9$
III. F.D.
    46-59 [C, 394]
    60-64 [not available]
    46-64 [C, 431]
IV. N.D.
    The method for calculating this variable varies with the particular year
    involved. From 1946-1955 the algorithm if TOTINC minus STNDED is
    not equal to NTISTN then SDEDKY is set according to the discrepancy
    scale below. In the years 1956-1960 the algorithm if AGI minus STNDED
    is not equal to NTISTN then SDEDKY is set according to the scale below.

Discrepancy Scale Code	Amount (absolute value)
0	$ 0.00–$ 4.99
1	5.00– 20.00
2	20.01– 40.00
3	40.01– 60.00
4	60.01– 80.00
5	80.01– 100.00
6	100.01– 200.00
7	200.01– 300.00
8	300.01– 400.00
9	400.01– or over

Blank is also used as a code in cases where Standard Deduction is not
taken.

WAIS 656–037 outlines the procedures used in coding this variable.

I.   First Phase Deductions Key
     64, 63, 62, 61, 60
     [5]
     59, 58, 57, 56, 55, 54, 53, 52, 51, 50, 49, 48, 47, 46
     [4]
II. C.Q.
     $0 \leqslant DED1KY \leqslant 9$
III. F.D.
     46-59 [C, 395]
     60-64 [not available]
     46-64 [C, 432]
IV. N.D.
     The method of coding this variable is outlined in WAIS 656-037. The
     algorithm is if YTXPD + UNION + MED + NBSINT + DINDED + OTHDED
     + ALMNY + CREXP is not equal to TOTDED then the DED1KY reflects
     the amount of the discrepancy according to the following table:

Discrepancy Scale Code	*Amount (absolute value)*
0	$ 0.00-$ 4.99
1	5.00- 20.00
2	20.01- 40.00
3	40.01- 60.00
4	60.01- 80.00
5	80.01- 100.00
6	100.01- 200.00
7	200.01- 300.00
8	300.01- 400.00
9	400.01- or over

Blank is also used as a code in cases when the itemized deduction is taken.
     The formula implies that neither the total portion or deductible
portion of the variables yield the proper result.

Discrepancy Scale Code	*Amount (absolute value)*
0	$ 0.00-$ 4.99
1	5.00- 20.00
2	20.01- 40.00
3	40.01- 60.00
4	60.01- 80.00

5	80.01– 100.00
6	100.01– 200.00
7	200.01– 300.00
8	300.01– 400.00
9	400.01– or over

NBTKY

I. Net Income Before Federal Tax Key
    64, 63, 62, 61, 60
    [5]
    59, 58, 57, 56, 55, 54, 53, 52, 51, 50, 49, 48, 47, 46
    [4]

II. C.Q.
     $0 \leqslant NBTKY \leqslant 9$

III. F.D.
      46–59 [C, 396]
      60–64 [not available]
      46–64 [C, 433]

IV. N.D.
     The outline for the code of this variable can be found in WAIS 656-037.
     The algorithm applied for the years 1946-1955 is that if TOTINC minus
     TOTDED is not equal to NETINC then NBTKY reflects the amount of the
     difference. For 1956-1959 if AGI minus TOTDED is not equal to
     NETINC then NBTKY reflects the amount of the difference. In both cases
     the discrepancy scale is as follows:

Discrepancy Scale Code	Amount (absolute value)
0	$ 0.00–$ 4.99
1	5.00– 20.00
2	20.01– 40.00
3	40.01– 60.00
4	60.01– 80.00
5	80.01– 100.00
6	100.01– 200.00
7	200.01– 300.00
8	300.01– 400.00
9	400.01– or over

NBDKY

I.   Net Income Before Donations Key
     64, 63, 62, 61, 60
     [5]
     59, 58, 57, 56, 55, 54, 53, 52, 51, 50, 49, 48, 47, 46
II. C.Q.
     $0 \leqslant \text{NBDKY} \leqslant 9$
III. F.D.
     46-59 [C, 397]
     60-64 [not available]
     46-64 [C, 434]
IV. N.D.
     The outline for the coding of this variable is provided in WAIS 656-037.
     The algorithm used was: if NETINC minus FSSDED is not equal to
     IBFDON, the size of the discrepancy is indicated in NBDKY and FIXIND
     is blank. This formula implies that neither the total portion nor the
     deductible portion yields the proper result. The codes for the amount of
     the discrepancy are as follows:

IV. N.D.
     In 1953-1956 a taxpayer filing on Forms 1 and 1W had the option of
     choosing whether to simply use a tax table to determine his taxes or to
     use the tax rate schedule. This variable is an indicator of which route the
     taxpayer chose. The codes are as follows:
     1 taxpayer used tax table and used col. 1 on page 1
     2 taxpayer used tax rate schedule.

NIBKY

I.   Net Income Itemized Basis Key
     64, 63, 62, 61, 60
     [5]
     59, 58, 57, 56, 55, 54, 53, 52, 51, 50, 49, 48, 47, 46
     [4]
II. C.Q.
     $0 \leqslant \text{NIBKY} \leqslant 9$
III. F.D.
     46-59 [C, 398]
     60-64 [not available]
     46-64 [C, 435]
IV. N.D.
     WAIS 656-037 gives the scheme for coding of this variable. "If IBFDON
     minus DON is not equal to NTIITE the size of the discrepancy is indicated
     in NIBKY and DONIND is blank." This formula implies that neither the
     total portion or deductible portion of DON yields the proper result.

Discrepancy Scale Code	*Amount (absolute value)*
0	$ 0.00-$ 4.99
1	5.00- 20.00
2	20.01- 40.00
3	40.01- 60.00
4	60.01- 80.00
5	80.01- 100.00
6	100.01- 200.00
7	200.01- 300.00
8	300.01- 400.00
9	400.01- or over

BLKCOL

I. Block or Column (tax computation)
   64, 63, 62, 61, 60, 59, 58, 57
   [5]
   56, 55, 54, 53,
   [4]
   52, 51, 50, 49, 48, 47, 46
   [5]

II. C.Q.
   $1 \leqslant$ BLKCOL $\leqslant 2$ and blanks when inapplicable

III. F.D.
   46-59 [C, 379]
   60-64 [not available]
   46-64 [C, 436]

TYPNON

I. Type of Nontaxable Income
   64, 63, 62, 61, 60
   [4]
   59, 58, 57, 56, 55, 54, 53, 52, 51, 50, 49, 48, 47, 46
   [4]

II. C.Q.
   Alphabetic codes   M   Military deduction
                        S   Student income
                        R   Retirement income
                        C   Combination of the above
                        N   Source not ascertained

III. F.D.
   46-59 [C, 380]
   60-64 [C, 320]
   46-64 [C, 437]

IV.   N.D.
      This variable is a key to the type of nontaxable income [NOTXIN] a tax-
      payer may have. As with NOTXIN, the taxpayer was never asked to list
      the sources of his nontaxable income so the information is available only
      if the taxpayer volunteered it.

PERC

  I.   Ratio of the Largest NOTXIN to the Total
       NOTXIN Field
       64, 63, 62, 61, 60
       [4]
       59, 58, 57, 56, 55, 54, 53, 52, 51, 50, 49, 48, 47, 46
       [5]
 II.   C.Q.
       $0 \leqslant PERC \leqslant 9$ and blank
III.   F.D.
       46-59 [not available]
       60-64 [C, 404]
       46-64 [C, 438]
IV.   N.D.
      WAIS 689-027 gives the following information concerning this variable:
      PERC size 1. —the ratio, in tenths, of the maximum NOTXIN field on the
      A card (the field whose TYPE was inserted in the TYPE field of the
      supplementary record) to the total NOTXIN, as recorded on the supple-
      mentary record. For example, if 0003456R were listed in the NOTXIN
      and TYPE columns of the supplementary record, and a 5 was present in
      the PERC field, we would know that retirement benefits (R in TYPE)
      were approximately 0.5 of the total nontaxable income, or retirement
      benefits were about 1728. PERC, however, is rounded to the nearest tenth,
      so R could actually have been, in this example, anywhere from 45 to 54
      percent of the total.
            A zero in this column has two possible meanings: (1) If NOTXIN is
      blank, a zero in PERC means nothing. (2) If NOTXIN is some nonzero
      number, it means that the number listed was the only component of the
      NOTXIN total; it was 10 tenths of the total, or 100% of it. Since only one
      column is available for recording PERC, a 0 is used to indicate "10".
            If more than one A card exists for a given ID, all the nontaxable
      income sources are added together to form NOTXIN on the supplementary
      record. If for one ID, more than one instance of a single TYPE is
      encountered, i.e., there exist 2 N fields, each field is treated as a separate
      item in the maximum calculation. All the fields with the same TYPE are
      not added together, and then a maximum found and percentage calcu-

lated. Rather, the maximum *single* field is found, the percentage of the total calculated from that figure, and the TYPE of that maximum field recorded. This may seem an unsatisfactory way of handling this situation, but it was thought that the effort needed to program around this problem was not worthwhile, since in scanning the A and L cards, no instances of this problem were found.

TERR

I. Taxpayer Error Code
    64, 63, 62, 61, 60
    [4]
    59, 58, 57, 56, 55, 54, 53, 52, 51, 50, 49, 48, 47, 46
    [5]
II. C.Q.
    $1 \leqslant \text{TERR} \leqslant 70$
III. F.D.
    46–59 [not available]
    60–64 [C, 405–406]
    46–64 [C, 439–440]
IV. N.D.
    WAIS 690-012 gives a complete outline of this particular variable. The codes are as follows:

TERR CODE	Description
1	TØTINC was computed incorrectly from income sources.
2	STNDED was incorrectly computed.
3	NTI was incorrectly computed (i.e., the computational step which arrived at NTI was wrong).
4	Gross normal tax (which unfortunately is not on the WAIS file) was incorrectly computed. This often was due to taxpayer looking at the wrong line in the tax table.
5	EXEMP allowance was greater than legally allowed.
6	TØTAX was computed incorrectly.
7	Incomplete return. This error was due primarily to microfilm errors especially on form 4. Codes 13, 14, and 15 were used whenever possible to more definitely define the missing data.
8	AUTBUS was computed or entered incorrectly by the taxpayer.

9	AGI was computed incorrectly from correct TØTINC and AUTBUS entries.
10	TØTDED was computed incorrectly from the itemized entries.
11	IBFDØN was computed incorrectly.
12	DØN was greater than 10% of IBFDØN or the taxpayer transferred the wrong amount from the donation schedule to the itemized deduction schedule.
13	Sources of income are not available either because the taxpayer did not supply them or because the microfilmers missed that page.
14	Itemized deductions entries are not available due to taxpayer or microfilmers.
15	Both 13 and 14.
16	Taxes were paid on social security benefits. In this case the S.S. payment is entered into SSREC and not in any of the usual taxable income sources. But TØTINC includes the amount of SSREC on which taxes were paid.
17	NBSINT or MED entries were computed incorrectly leading to a TØTDED error.
18	NETINC was computed incorrectly.
19	The taxpayer in 1959, -60, or -61 used the incorrect table from which to compute his tax (i.e., used NTI with the optional table or AGI with the regular table).
20	Omission in calculating TØTAX, esp. in 1961 when taxpayer had 65% grace.

When an error was machine corrected 50 was added to the taxpayer error code. (See Appendix F.)

Table E-10
Transformation Variables

Merged	Descriptor	Old	New	Size
441–442	NEWOC	–	–	2
443–450	PROPIN	–	–	8
451–458	WAGSAL	–	–	8
459–466	SELFIN	–	–	8
467–474	EARNIN	–	–	8
475–482	ERNEXP	–	–	8
6 Fields				42

I. Recoded Occupation Group
    64, 63, 62, 61, 60, 59, 58, 57, 56, 55, 54, 53, 52, 51, 50, 49, 48, 47, 46
    [3]
II. C.Q.
    $01 \leqslant \text{NEWOC} \leqslant 12$
III. F.D.
    46–59 [not available]
    60–64 [not available]
    46–64 [C, 441–442]
IV. N.D.
    The codes for this transformation are based on what the occupation is.
    NEWOC provides a more general code for occupation. The coding scheme
    is as follows:

Transformed Variables
1. NEWOC

If OCC is:	NEWOC is:	Category
1–10	1	Professional
11–17	2	Semiprofessional
18, 19 or 22	3	Managerial
20	4	Self-employed business
21	5	Self-employed farm
25	6	Clerical
26	7	Sales
27–29	8	Service
24, 30–31	9	Skilled
23, 32–34	10	Semi-unskilled
35–38	11	Not in labor force
99	12	Not ascertained

PROPIN

I. Property Income
    64, 63, 62, 61, 60, 59, 58, 57, 56, 55, 54, 53, 52, 51, 50, 49, 48, 47, 46
    [3]
II. C.Q.
    $-9999999 \leqslant \text{PROPIN} \leqslant 9999999$
III. F.D.
    46–59 [not available]
    60–64 [not available]
    46–64 [C, 443–450]

IV. N.D.
Components of this variable are as follows:

INT + DIVI + RENT + CPGAIN + TRUST = PROPINC

If any of the components are 9999999, then PROPINC will be 9999999. Fields such as RENT and CPGAIN which might be negative are checked for negatives.

WAGSAL

I. Wages and Salaries
64, 63, 62, 61, 60, 59, 58, 57, 56, 55, 54, 53, 52, 51, 50, 49, 48, 47, 46
[3]

II. C.Q.
-9999999 ≤ WAGSAL ≤ 9999999

III. F.D.
46-59 [not available]
60-64 [not available]
46-64 [C, 451-458]

IV. N.D.
Components of WAGSAL are WAGE1 + WAGE2 + OTHWGE = WAGSAL. If any of the components are 9999999 then WAGSAL will be 9999999.

SELFIN

I. Self-Employment Income
64, 63, 62, 61, 60, 59, 58, 57, 56, 55, 54, 53, 52, 51, 50, 49, 48, 47, 46
[3]

II. C.Q.
-9999999 ≤ SELFIN ≤ 9999999

III. F.D.
46-59 [not available]
60-64 [not available]
46-64 [C, 459-466]

IV. N.D.
Components of SELFIN are BUS + PSHIP = SELFINC. If either of the components are 9999999 then SELFIN = 9999999. Each of the components and the final SELFIN is checked for negatives.

EARNIN

I. Earnings
64, 63, 62, 61, 60, 59, 58, 57, 56, 55, 54, 53, 52, 51, 50, 49, 48, 47, 46

(see N.D.)
[3]
II.   C.Q.
      -9999999 ≤ EARNIN ≤ 9999999
III. F.D.
      46-59 [not available]
      60-64 [not available]
      46-64 [C, 467-474]
IV.   N.D.
      Components of EARNIN are WAGSAL + SELFIN = EARNIN. If either of
      those components is 9999999, then EARNIN = 9999999.

                                                                    ERNEXP

I.   Earnings—Expenses
      64, 63, 62, 61, 60, 59, 58, 57, 56, 55, 54, 53, 52, 51, 50, 49, 48, 47, 46
II.   -9999999 ≤ ERNEXP ≤ 9999999
III. F.D.
      46-59 [not available]
      60-64 [not available]
      46-64 [C, 475-482]
IV.   N.D.
      Components of ERNEXP are EARNINGS minus AUTBUS = ERNEXP.
      If either of the components is 9999999, then ERNEXP = 9999999.

Table E-11
Deduction Indicators (Total or Deductible 46-60 only)

Merged	Descriptor	Old	New	Size
483	MEDIND	389	—	1
484	FTXIND	390	—	1
485	DONIND	391	—	1
3 Fields				3

                                                                    MEDIND

I.   Medical Expense Indicator
      64, 63, 62, 61, 60
      [5]
      59, 58, 57, 56, 55, 54, 53, 52, 51, 50, 49, 48, 47, 46
      [4]

II. C.Q.
     T or D or blank
III. F.D.
     46–59 [C, 389]
     60–64 [not available]
     46–64 [C, 483]
IV. N.D.
     WAIS 712–016 gives the following information about this variable:

      MEDIND
           Moyer (1966b, p. 42) indicates that the amount deductible
      was recorded for the first 2/3 of the name groups and the total
      amount was recorded for the last 1/3 of the name groups. At
      some point an indicator was added to each record to show if the
      amount in the medical amount field was the total or the amount
      deducted. No clear documentation is given concerning what deter-
      mined whether a T or D was placed in the indicator field. WAIS
      645–060, a documentation of the consistency check program,
      indicates that it attempts to sum the following variables with both
      the total medical expense and the deductible medical expense:

      Wisconsin TAX PAID
      + UNION DUES
      + MEDICAL-DENTAL EXPENSES
      + TOTAL INTEREST PAID
      + BUSINESS INTEREST PAID
      + DIVIDEND DEDUCTIBLE
      + OTHER DEDUCTIONS
      + ALIMONY PAID
      + FOREST CROP LAND
      _____

      = TOTAL DEDUCTION before FEDERAL TAX and DONATION

           The documentation in 645–060 states that these fields were
      summed and then compared to the Total Deductions Before Federal
      Tax and Donation Deduction (TOTDED) with the total amount
      of medical expenses deducted or the amount deductible figure
      used in the computation. According to the documentation there
      were 3755 itemized deduction records which did not equal
      TOTDED when either interpretation of the medical expense field
      was applied.
           It appears that originally the medical expense indicator was
      machine coded as T if the amount was greater than the maximum
      allowed for that year but other than that there is no documenta-
      tion concerning how it was determined which records contained
      the total medical expenses and which contained the amount of
      medical expenses deductible.
           This algorithm appears inconsistent upon first examination of

the file because the T and D indicators are interspersed throughout on the first 2/3 of the file. However careful examination
reveals that the T indicator was used only when deductions were
itemized but no medical expenses were deducted. Whenever the
medical expense deduction was used in the first 2/3 of the file
the D was indicated. In approximately 100 records distributed
throughout the file which were checked against the source document, all but 1 had the correct indicator.

    In checking the accuracy of the indicator against the source
documents it is reasonably accurate. However, occasionally the
indicator field is blank when it should have an indicator in it.

FTXIND

I.   Federal Tax Indicator
     64, 63, 62, 61, 60
     59, 58, 57, 56, 55, 54, 53, 52, 51, 50, 49, 48, 47, 46
     [4]
II. C.Q.
     T or D or blank
III. F.D.
     46–49 [C, 390]
     60–64 [not available]
     46–64 [C, 484]
IV. N.D.
     WAIS 712-016 gives the following information about this variable:

     FTXIND
         The Federal Tax Indicator code does not follow the algorithm
     presented in Moyer (1966b) for the distribution of T and D.
     Moyer (1966b) states that the first 2/3 of the name groups contain
     the amount deductible and the last 1/3 of the name groups contain
     the total amount written. However, in examining 60 records
     interspersed throughout the file which had itemized deductions,
     the T and D indicators appear to be scattered throughout, often
     with a T for a particular ID number for one year and a D for the
     same individual for the next year.
         Of the 60 records checked for this field, 5 records showed an
     inconsistency with the source document: 1 record had the wrong
     amount punched, which was caused by an unclear microfilm copy;
     2 were errors caused by taxpayer miscalculation of the 3 percent
     NETINC which is deductible. The other 2 errors were a simple
     case of the wrong indicator being put in. The error occurs twice
     for a single individual (28000700) for 1952 and 1954. In both
     cases that indicator is D but should be T.
         In cases where there is no itemized deduction, the indicator
     is blank.

DONIND

I.   Donation Indicator
     64, 63, 62, 61, 60
     [5]
     59, 58, 57, 56, 55, 54, 53, 52, 51, 50, 49, 48, 47, 46
II. C.Q.
     T or D or blank
III. F.D.
     46-59 [C, 391]
     60-64 [not available]
     46-64 [C, 485]
IV. N.D.
     WAIS 712-016 gives the following information about this variable:

     DONIND
         Moyer (1966b) states that about 2/3 of the name groups have
     the amount actually deducted punched in this field and the last
     1/3 has the amount punched which was actually donated (total).
         In examining approximately 40 records distributed through-
     out the file it appeared that the only time a T was used as an indi-
     cator was when deductions were itemized but the amount in the
     donations field was zero. In the remainder of the cases (some of
     which were in the last 1/3 of the file) the indicator was always D
     and the amount matched with the amount deducted from the
     source document. It should be mentioned, however, that not
     many taxpayers have total donations of greater than 10 percent
     of the IBFDON field. Therefore almost all amounts are the
     amount deductible.
         In summary, even though we lack adequate documentation
     on how the indicators were computed, they seem to be reason-
     ably reliable. The most suspicious indicator seems to be FTXIND
     but even these irregularities seem to be random rather than the
     result of a programming bug on computing the indicator.

Appendix F
Detecting Inconsistencies in the
Master File

F.1 Comments on Development of the
Editing Procedure

This appendix documents the Master File inconsistency-detection program, MASTER/EDIT, and explains the role MASTER/EDIT plays within the total perspective of processing the Master File. The program located all possible errors, and then printed appropriate error messages, one record per page, which coders could then use in verification of the error. There are two important advantages to such an approach when compared with the alternative of making programmed corrections via machine whenever an error is noticed. The approach allows users to distinguish taxpayer errors from coder and keypunch errors. The former type of mistake is simply flagged and allowed to remain in the file so as not to destroy this interesting information. The latter errors are, of course, corrected. The second advantage of computer printout and coder correction stems from the fact that the Master File does not contain all amounts on the tax form. Hence, it is not always possible to pinpoint an error without referring to the tax return document. For example, on the tax returns gross normal tax (GNT) is the total amount of tax due based on the person's net taxable income (NTI). From GNT he is to subtract personal exemptions (EXEMP) to determine net normal tax (TOTAX), i.e., NTI × Rate = GNT − EXEMP = TOTAX. As GNT was not keypunched, machine error detection could only compute TOTAX based on the NTI and EXEMP entries. If the computed and keypunched TOTAX amounts were not equal, this fact could be noted in a printout, but no machine determination could be made as to whether EXEMP, TOTAX, or the taxpayer's computation of GNT was in error. That determination had to be left in the hands of the coders.

Development of the amount field checks took place in stages. Since Form 4 (short tax forms for 1962-1964) was the simplest, it was checked first.

After checks on Form 4 had been completed, a procedure was added to compute itemized deduction totals. Forms 2 and 3 (long forms for 1962 and 1963-1964 respectively) could then be processed. The program was then modified to handle the alternative tax computation schemes available on Form 1 (all returns 1959-1961). Form 1 was then checked. It would, of course, be possible to extend the program to check the first collection of MF as well as any future tax records with similar entries. Table E-2 defines form numbers used.

Throughout the development process various changes were made to the error messages. The design of the program is conducive to such dynamics and the cooperative and observant coders helped improve the efficiency of the overall operation. Additional information supplied to the coders appeared to provide more efficient data correction. Even though some data are redundant or seldom used, there were instances in which they proved invaluable. For example, even though the amounts of social security and nontaxable income received are not included in computing total income, the keypunched entries in these fields helped the coders discover keypunching and taxpayer errors in total income amounts.

F.2 Thé Editing Procedure

Table F-1 lists the tests carried out by the MASTER/EDIT program. Comments on the procedures required follow.

First, a word of caution on the limits of the editing process—in editing the demographic codes it was not always possible to insure that the entry was indeed correct. Some fields are entirely independent of other fields on the record. For example, within one record it is impossible to tell whether or not the occupation change code (OCCH) was correct since only the current tax year occupation is coded on the record. Hence, only illegal values of the code can be detected, not erroneous values. (For OCCH an *inter*-record edit could verify such codes.) Likewise, not *all* contingencies can be checked. For example, if county of residence (CNTY) and county of residence previous year (CNTYPR) are the same, address change (ADDRCH) could still legitimately be 0 (no move), 1 (change within tax district), or 2 (change within county) so ADDRCH coded as 0 when it really should be 1 could *not* be detected.

Mnemonics are used freely in the remainder of the paper. A list of field boundaries and their associated mnemonics are found in Appendix E. Although Table F-1 lists the legitimate values of demographic variables in a logical manner, the actual Boolean procedures used passed the value TRUE if the specified variable was incorrect. This allowed the procedures to be called as the second half of an IF-THEN statement. For example, the statement:

IF INCLUSIVE (ENCL,0,7) THEN WRITEINCLUSIVE (ENCL,0,7), "ENCL")

would call the WRITEINCLUSIVE procedure if the value of ENCL was NOT within the legitimate range of zero through seven.

The amount edits are somewhat more complicated. The following is a short description of the various procedures while their logical relationships are shown in the Figure F-1.

Table F-1
Editing Effected on the Master File
Completed Legitimate Code Checks

Field Name	Legitimate Values
FILED	0–3, 9
CØNS	0, 1, 9
CNTY	0–72, 96–99
CNTYPR	0–72, 96–99
ADDRCH	0–4, 7–9
NØRES	0, 1, 9
ØCCH	0–9
RETPR	0–3, 7–9
LABPR	0–7, 9
MSTAT	0–4, 9
MSCØN	0, 1
SEPINC	0–3, 9
INCRL	0–2, 9
MARR	0–3, 9
DISMAR	0–2, 9
DEP[a]	0–15
STU[a]	0–5
DEPADR	0–9
SØURWGE	0–7, 9
HEADFM	0–3, 9
AUTØEX	0–3, 9
SUPSCH	0–3
ENCL	0–7
REL	0–3
NXTYR	0–4, 8, 9
YR	49–64
TYPE	M, S, R, N, blank
CØMP	0
CØNTIN	A, L, K, Z
SDIV	0, 1, 9, blank

Each digit in SS was checked to insure that numerical amounts were entered or that the code NØ8 was entered if SS was not available.

Contingency Checks

An error was written if:[b]

(CNTY EQL 98 AND NØRES NEQ 1) ØR (NØRES EQL 1 AND CNTY NEQ 98)
(CNTY NEQ CNTYPR) AND ADDRCH NEQ 0, 1, or 2)
STU GTR DEP
(HEADFM DQL 1 ØR 2) AND DEP EQL 0
DEP EQL 0 AND DEPADR NEQ 0
MSTAT EQL 1 AND SEPINC EQL 0
(MARR GEQ 1 AND LEQ 3) AND MSTAT EQL 0
(DISMAR EQL 1 AND MSTATE NEQ 3) ØR (DISMAR EQL 2 AND MSTAT
    NEW 4)
CNTY EQL CNTYPR AND ADDRCH GEQ 3 AND ADDRCH LEQ 8
WAGE1 LESS WAGE2

Table F-1 (continued)

YR EQL 64 AND NXTYR EQL 8
SØURWG = 0 AND (WAGE1 NEQ 0 ØR WAGE2 NEQ 0 ØR ØTHWAGE NEQ 0)
SØURWG = 1 AND (WAGE1 EQL 0 ØR WAGE2 NEW 0 ØR ØTHWGE NEQ 0)
SØURWG = 2 AND (WAGE1 EQL 0 ØR WAGE2 EQL 0 ØR ØTHWGE NEW 0)
(SØURWG GEQ 3 AND LEQ 7) AND (WAGE1 EQL 0 ØR WAGE2 EQL 0 ØR
    ØTHWGE EQL 0)
NØTXIN EQL 0 AND TYPE NEQ blank
NØTXIN NEQ 0 AND TYPE NEQ M, S, R, ØR N
AGI GTR TØTINC + 200^c
NTI GTR AGI AND TYP NEQ 4
STNDED NEQ 0 AND (UNIØN, TXPD, MED, NBSINT, ØTHDED, ALMNY ØR
    CREXP NEQ 0)
TYP EQL 4 AND (UNIØN, TXPD, MED, MBSINT, ØTHDED, ALMNY ØR
    REEXP NEQ 0)
ALMNY GTR 80000
DØN GTR ((.1 TIMES IBRDØN) + 200)
STNDED NEQ 0 AND TØTDED NEQ 0
INST1 GTR TØTAX
CØNTIN = A AND (UNEMP, NØTXIN, SSREC AND ØTHDED EQL 0)
CØNTIN = L AND (ADJTI AND TØADTX = 0)
CONTIN = K AND (UNEMP, NOTXIN, SSREC, OTHDED, ADJTI, AND
    TOADTX = 0)

TYPE = M AND PERC = 0 AND NOTXIN GRY 100000
WSTXWH NEQ 0 AND TYP = 1
TYP NEQ 1 AND YR GEQ 59 AND YR LEQ 61
TYPE EQL 2 AND YR NEQ 62
TYPE EQL 3 AND YR NEQ 63 AND YR NEQ 64
TYPE EQL 4 AND (YR LSS 62 ØR YR GTR 64)
SEPINC = 0 AND INCRL NEQ 9
INCRL = 0 AND SEPINC NEQ 0
(AGE1 + AGE2 + AGE3 + AGE4) NEQ DEP^d
AUTOEX EQL 0 AND CASLS NEQ 0
AUTØEX EQL 1 AND (CASLS NEQ 0 ØR AUTBUS EQL 0)
AUTØEX EQL 2 AND CASLS EQL 0
AUTØEX EQL 3 AND (CASLS EQL 0 ØR AUTBUS EQL 0)
FILED NEQ 0 AND FILED NEQ 2 AND (if any field besides NXTYR or RETPR
    are nonblank)

---

^{a}The upper limits were arbitrary and used to verify outliers.
^{b}The following are ALGØL Operators:

EQL is equal to	GTR is greater than
NEQ is not equal to	GEQ is greater than or equal to
LSS is less than	LEQ is less than or equal to

^{c}Cents are included without decimal, therefore 200 means $2.00.
^{d}AGE1 . . . AGE4 are the 4 digits of the field called AGE.

(1) TØTALINCØMETHRUNTI (FØRMTYPE)

This is a main procedure through which all records (if they are within the year range of 1959-1964) must pass. It computes the sum of keypunched incomes from the various sources applicable on the different forms and compares

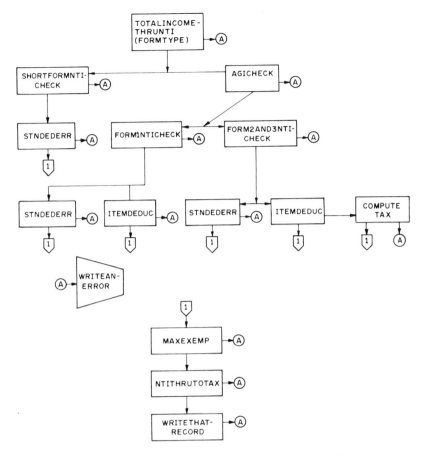

Figure F-1. Flowchart for Editing Amounts on Tax Records

this total to keypunched TØTINC.[1] It then calls the next procedure appropriate for the form type being edited—SHORTFORMNTICHECK for Form 4's and AGICHECK for all others.

(2) SHORTFORMNTICHECK

This procedure makes the computational check: TØTINC - STNDED $\stackrel{?}{=}$ NTI. If not, the procedure STNDEDERR is called. (Of course, as is true throughout the program, if an error has been found in TØTINC, and TØTINC - STNDED $\neq$ NTI, then the computed value of TØTINC would be used in the TØTINC - STNDED $\stackrel{?}{=}$ NTI test. If the latter is true, we infer that keypunched TØTINC is incorrect and computed TØTINC and keypunched STNDED are correct.)

(3) STNDEDERR

This procedure determines if the keypunched value of **STNDED** conforms to the tax law appropriate during the tax year in question.

(4) AGICHECK

This procedure makes the computation $T\emptyset TINC - AUTBUS \stackrel{?}{=} AGI$ for forms 1, 2, and 3.

(5) FORM1NTICHECK

This procedure first determines whether the taxpayer filed using the optional tax table and based his tax on **AGI** or whether he determined his tax by computing his **NTI**. In the former case a switch was set and processing continued. In the latter case it had to be determined whether the taxpayer used STNDED ($450 for those whose AGI was greater than $5000) or if he itemized. For those using STNDED, only the tests of $AGI - STNDED \stackrel{?}{=} NTI$ and AGI GEQ 500000? and $STNDED \stackrel{?}{=} 45000$ were made.[2] For all others the procedure ITEMDEDUC was called.

(6) FORM2AND3NTICHECK

This procedure, which was utilized for long forms of 1962–1964, first determined if standard or itemized deductions were used. If STNDED was used, the computation $AGI - STNDED \stackrel{?}{=} NTI$ was made and if incorrect the procedure STNDEDERR was called. For those itemizing deductions ITEMDEDUC was called.

(7) ITEMDEDUC

This procedure first summed the various itemized deduction entries and compared it with **TØTDED**. Then in Form 1 the following checks were made:

i. $AGI - T\emptyset TDED \stackrel{?}{=} NETINC$
ii. $NETINC - FSSDED \stackrel{?}{=} IBFD\emptyset N$
iii. $IBFD\emptyset N - D\emptyset N \stackrel{?}{=} NIT$

(8) MAXEXEMP

Since the program was an intrarecord test only and since the law states that a husband and wife can split their exemptions in any way desired, one could not determine if the EXEMP codes were exact. As a best alternative this procedure computed the maximum amount of exemptions allowable to a person, then compared it with the coded EXEMPT entry. If the EXEMP amount was greater than the computed maximum amount an error message was printed.

(9) NITTHRUTØTAX

This procedure takes the value of (Computed Gross Normal Tax) as determined in CØMPUTETAX and then makes the following calculation of TOTAX and compares it with the keypunched value for form 1 for 1959:

(Computed Gross Normal Tax - EXEMPT) + .25 TIMES (Computed Gross Normal tax - EXEMP) $\overset{?}{=}$ TØTAX

Form 1 for 1960-1961: Uses the same test except 0.20 is the surtax rate rather than 0.25 for forms 2, 3, and 4:

Computed Gross Normal Tax - EXEMP $\overset{?}{=}$ TØTAX

(10) CØMPUTETAX

This integer procedure computes the tax on any value of NTI for the years 1959-1964 passed to it. For taxpayers using the optional tax table in 1959-1961, a computed value of NTI based on the formula:

AGI - .09 TIMES AGI

was passed to it.

(11) WRITEANERRØR

This is the general error-writing procedure called any time an amount field error was found and printed the message. Messages for one tax record year only were allowed on each page of output.

(12) WRITETHATRECØRD

This procedure wrote the entire 480-character record onto an error file on disk if at least one error was located in the record. These files were then used in the error correction routine described below.

F.3 The Error Correction Process

The error verification process raised many questions regarding the legitimacy of various codes as well as a few other quirks of taxpayers which were not anticipated in the Master File Codebook. WAIS 689–030 was a preliminary report on coding difficulties. However, since it was written before the bulk of edits were checked, additional problems were raised. One necessitated machine correction even before editing and error verification. Some taxpayers did not complete the TØTINC entry and skipped to AGI, on Forms 1 and 3. This occurred when the taxpayer had no AUTBUS expense to deduct from TØTINC. The program (B-5500 program 1019 titled MASTER/MTAPE in WAIS 689–008) arbitrarily entered the total of AGI + AUTBUS to the TØTINC field; to show the machine correction, 50 was added to the taxpayer error, TERR, field.

This TERR field documented in Appendix E was added to the record to indicate instances in which the taxpayer made an error which caused an amount field error. The codes refer to the first instance in which an error occurred. So as not to delete information, the reported amount is retained in the field but if a user wishes to use amounts which *should* have been entered he will have to recompute the relevant information. The codes are documented in Appendix E. Besides the many taxpayer errors there were a few errors which were so straightforward that they could be machine corrected and were ignored by the coders. This step is point VIII on the flow chart in Figure F-2. Machine correction followed completion of coder verification or corrected records. The machine corrections included:

i.   If SEPINC = 0 and INCRL = 0 then
     if MSTAT = 9, move 9 to SEPINC and INCRL;
     if MSTAT = 0, 2, or 3 move 0 to SEPINC.
ii. If YR - 64 and (NXTYR - 4 or NXTYR = 8) then move 9 to NXTYR.
iii. If CNTY = 73 then move 98 to CNTY.
iv. If CNTYRP = 73 then move 98 to CNTYPR.
v.   For Form 1,
     if AUTOEX = 2 and AUTBUS ≠ 0 move 3 to AUTOEX;
     if AUTOEX = 0 and AUTBUS ≠ 0 move 1 to AUTOEX;
     if AUTOEX = 3 and AUTBUS = 0 move 2 to AUTOEX.
     For forms 2 and 3,
     if AUTBUS = 0 and CASLS = 0 move 0 to AUTOEX;

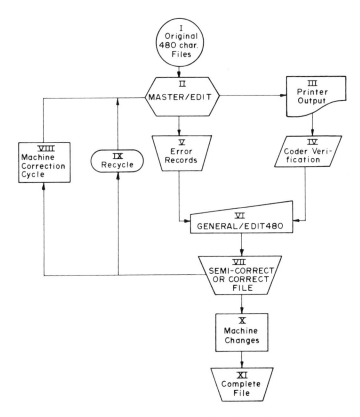

Figure F-2. Flow of Editing and Correction Operations on the Master File 1959–1964

 if AUTBUS ≠ 0 and CASLS = 0 move 1 to AUTOEX;
 if AUTBUS = 0 and CASLS ≠ 0 move 2 to AUTOEX;
 if AUTBUS ≠ 0 and CASLS ≠ 0 move 3 to AUTOEX.
 For form 4,
 if AUTBUS ≠ 0 or CASLS ≠ 0 move 0 to AUTBUS, CASLS.

vi. If SS not numberic move all nines to SS (i.e., removes the NØ8 code from Social Security Code).

vii. If NOTXIN ≠ 0 and PERC = blank, move 0 to PERC.
 If NOTXIN = 0 and PERC ≠ 0, move 0 to PERC.

Machine correction following re-editing (point X in Figure F-2) included:

i. Negative values of TØTINC were carried through, and correctly computed entries were placed into AGI (TØTINC – AUTBUS into AGI) and NTI (AGI – TØTDED or STNDED into NTI). This step was required since many taxpayers with negative TØTINC did not carry through with AGI and NTI computations.

ii.   AGI - .09 × AGI into NTI in cases in Form 1 where the taxpayer computes his tax using AGI in the optional tax tables.

iii. TØTINC into AGI in Form 4.

There were other problems which could not be resolved as easily as the above. The general approach followed the "Principle of Minimum Intervention." This means that the file should show primarily what the taxpayer did, not what he should have done. Using this rule all nontaxable income amounts, e.g., the first $1000 of military pay, on which taxes were in fact paid, would go into the appropriate taxable income field. In addition, if the taxpayer did not take all exemptions entitled him or did not use his standard deductions fully we did *not* change these entries nor code a taxpayer error since perhaps for some reason he wished to overpay his taxes.

Many other questions arose over the proper location for various sources of income reported by taxpayers. For example, we placed receipts for blood sold in OTHER (rather than in some property income field). OTHER was also the receptacle of miscellaneous sources of income which could not be considered usual labor income. For example jury duty, election duty, and retirement pensions on which taxes were paid were entered there. Also state and federal tax refunds, if the person paid a tax on them, were entered into OTHER.

Tips and remuneration for odd jobs should be located in the WAGE1, WAGE2 and OTHWAGE fields with tips combined with the wage as one source of income. Hopefully the original keypunchers followed this convention because, unless some other error was made in the field, MASTER/MFEDIT would not locate it. Army pay, even though the first $1000 is nontaxable, was included in a separate source of wages in the SOURWG field. One rule, established during the original coding, hence carried out in the edit checks, was that bonuses and commissions were entered in the OTHER field.

Sometimes households entered the separate income amounts in the correct husband-wife columns on the form but then summed all entries and placed the total income only in one of the two, usually the husband's. In these instances, TERR = 1 was placed in both records but no other changes made.

Another amount field problem which arose concerned loss carryover. It was decided that the file should indicate actual yearly income and not income as defined for tax purposes. Hence in the few instances where the problem arose, the gross amount of profit or loss before netting out loss carryover was entered.

One error which, though it did not cause major coding problems, did arise frequently on Form 1 was the entry of AGI amounts in the space on the tax form reserved for NTI. The taxpayer used the optional tax table and did not compute NTI. Keypunchers would, of course, punch the amount into the NTI field. The correction process then amounted to moving the amount from NTI to AGI.

About the only real problem in the demographic fields concerned the combinations of CNTY, CNTYPR, MØVED, and NØRES. CNTY was always coded identically to the code entered by the state tax department for revenue sharing purposes. One difficulty which was removed via machine was that the state used code 73 to indicate a nonresident whereas this is 98 in the WAIS codes. Another problem is that for some nonresidents the state still assigns in-state county codes; the code indicates the geographical origin of that income. In these cases we kept the NØRES code at 1 (nonresident) and CNTY as entered by the tax department coders. The state coders were rather erratic, however, and changed year-to-year county codes even though the taxpayer obviously did not move. We attempted to have a MØVED code indicate as closely as possible what the taxpayer *did*, not what CNTY or CNTYPR indicated, hence would code MØVED = 0 in the above case.

The verification of data entered, though tedious for the coders, seems to have worked out quite well. One reason for this and a point to be remembered in future similar steps is that the coders seemed to have a good feel for what was being done and also were interested enough to actually think while coding. To insure even closer coordination between coders each evening the supervisor should determine if any coding conventions had been set that day and, if so, Xerox copies of the updated instructions and distribute them to all coders.

The teletype (TTY) portion of the job, step VI in Figure F-2, has also proven quite satisfactory. The speed and cross checks of GENERAL/EDIT480 makes the operation probably more economical than utilizing keypunchers and some type of add-merge program.

F.4 Re-editing of the Master File

This section describes the re-editing process on the Master File using the program MASTER/REDIT. The basic program was that described above, with re-editing shown as steps IX and II in Figure F-2.

MASTER/REDIT differed from MASTER/EDIT in only a few minor ways. Most important was the check of the TERR field whenever an inconsistent amount was found. If, upon checking the TERR field, it contained a code that indicated the inconsistency was due to the taxpayer, no more amount edits were performed on that record. For example, if computed and keypunched TØTINC differed and TERR = 1, the program skipped all remaining amount edits and considered the amount fields correct.

The second change involved addition of a counter for the various types of

Table F–2
Inconsistencies Located on Re-editing

	Number of Edited Records Input to REDIT	Number of Edited Records Containing at Least One Error Subject to Further Correction	Error Rate as a Percent of Edited Records	Total Records on the File	Residual Error Rate as a Percent of all Records
Form 1	11,487	1,607	14.0%	43,390	3.7%
Form 2	3,690	601	16.3%	14,548	4.1
Form 3	10,661	1,351	12.7%	29,466	4.6
Form 4	2,343	552[a]	23.6%	9,126	6.0

[a]The relatively high error rate for Form 4 was due to an oversight. Even if TERR = 3, if NTI was found in error it was printed out. This type of error can not be corrected by scanning the tax forms. This mistake simply inflated the error rate; it did not invalidate any checks.

Table F–3
Distribution of Taxpayer Error Codes on New Master File

TERR Code	Form 1	Form 2	Form 3	Form 4	Total
1, 51	304	135	276	111	826
2, 52	76	11	12	33	132
3, 53	104	76	177	102	459
4, 54	188	54	174	149	565
5, 55	61	29	35	35	160
6, 56	275	32	59	32	398
7, 57	4	3	10	7	24
8, 58	0	2	1	0	3
9, 59	45	10	100	0	155
10, 60	126	38	132	0	296
11, 61	69	25	82	0	176
12, 62	69	44	96	0	208
13, 63	128	33	57	0	218
14, 64	40	19	20	0	79
15, 65	13	9	33	0	55
16, 66	14	3	4	3	24
17, 67	3	3	2	0	8
18, 68	92	0	0	0	92
19, 69	332	0	0	0	332
20, 70	187	0	0	0	187
Total	2130	526	1269	472	4397
Percentage of entire file with TERR ≠ 0	4.9	3.6	4.3	5.2	4.5

TERR codes. Totals were then printed on the last page of printout. (See Table F-3.)

The print file and disk input file were the only two files in the program. Hence, when an error was found, such information was printed (one record per page) but the record was not placed onto a disk file of error records.

Some demographic tests were altered slightly. The contingency checks for AGI > NTI and TØTINC > AGI were removed. Added to the printout from the check between CNTY, CNTYPR, and MOVED was additional information concerning NØRES.

Of perhaps more significance was the fact that the check for EXEMPT greater than MAXEMPTION was removed since (a) unavailable age information means that for taxpayers over 65 the program would find their EXEMP codes in error, (b) splitting of exemptions between husband and wife while dependents are coded only within the male's record implies that for many wives we would think there were errors when in fact there were none. These two problems could be easily remedied later (a) by adding birthdate or age in 1965 information and (b) by using an interrecord edit.

By removing the LINE and BADRCDS files and including the skip-out routine when TERR corresponded to the amount field error, speed of the program increased markedly. Processing 2300 records took approximately 7 minutes of processer and 12 minutes of elapsed time.

Table F-2 presents summary information on errors found in the re-edits. Distributions of TERR codes are shown in Table F-3 for each formtype.

The percentage of the total file with TERR ≠ 0 gives a good indication of the extent to which machine correction of all errors would have destroyed information concerning taxpayer behavior.

The recycling process (point IX in Figure F-2) was completed once. MASTER/REDIT found on the average, about 4 percent of the records on the files (column 6 of Table F-3) to still contain inconsistencies; however, most of these were due to overly stringent consistency tests. Substantive discrepancies would amount to a small percent of the error file; hence for the entire MF about .25 percent (or perhaps 250 records) still contain serious errors.

Notes

Chapter 1

1. Thus, as state employees, under Wisconsin statutes we were legally responsible for nondisclosure of identifiable data.
2. Further redundancy and positive assurance of identification is provided by place of birth, race, and father's name.

Chapter 2

1. From 1947–1952, the filing of a combined return was permitted for husbands and wives. A 9 percent deduction was built into the tax tables; but for 1947–1948, gross receipts were limited to $3500; and for 1949–1952, they were limited to $5000. Households would file a combined return provided the maximum income of either showed no tax liability according to the "Optional Tax Tables." Also of note for the period is that children's income was filed on a parent's return.
2. These filing requirements changed substantially in 1954 and again in 1961. In 1952, the amount of *total* receipts which required an individual to file was changed from $5000 to $4000.
   There were substantial changes during tax years after 1953. The minimum filing level for married persons was changed from $1600 to $1400 combined income for husband and wife. Single persons with gross income of $600 or more were required to file a return (the previous minimum filing requirement had been $800).
   The tax rate range changed and also some of the rules concerning exemptions. Until 1954, a married person filing the optional form had to take all exemptions allowed or claim no exemptions. But beginning in 1954, husband and wife with separate incomes could file separate returns and divide the dependents between them for maximum advantage. There was also a change in the law concerning what constituted a dependent. A head-of-family exemption was established. Members of the armed forces who previously were exempt from tax on military pay, now were required to pay tax on military pay beyond the first $1500.
   The range of deductible medical expenses also changed in 1954, from $50–$500 to $75–$1500.
3. The initial intention was to get a sampling ratio of approximately 1 percent of returns filed for 1958. When the criteria were applied to the whole state the realized sampling ratio was closer to 0.75 percent.
   The clustering resulting from the choice of name groups introduces a negligible increase in variance of AGI as the within name-group variation in AGI is almost as large as the variance between groups.

4. In addition, we have available such files as Standard and Poor's "Compu-stat" which provides additional data on other aspects of the data contained in these files. Similar ancillary files were developed for companies whose data was not already obtainable from Compustat or similar sources.
5. These operations were subsequently centralized.
6. When no diary was left, the household was asked to complete the same schedules at the time of interview.
7. Incompatibility of tape channels or character recognition systems on dif-ferent types of hardware have been an enormous problem for the research of the WAIS project.
8. Our experience, which will be reported in Chapter 6, indicates that the latter approach may be the most economical, both for the research staff and for the total use of computer records.

Chapter 3

1. The estimates are all biased downwards, as date of birth was not known for a part of the sample. Those of unknown age are likely to be older per-sons without social security numbers, but no principle for allocating such persons was available (see David, 1971; and David and Miller, 1970).
2. Schroeder and David (1970) give some relevant statistics on the interstate migration that occurred during the sample period.
3. Although an attempt was made to organize the tax returns so that family income data could be reconstructed, the effort was only partially success-ful. Family unit information is available in the archive for social security beneficiaries (see Section 4.5).
4. The law requires a "reconstruction" of the joint returns of newly married persons for years prior to marriage. Net losses were excluded from the average as the tax code already provides for some carry-over of losses. The Wisconsin definitions of personal credits and deductions were modified, wherever sufficient information was available, to conform more closely to the federal definitions (see David, et al., 1970).

Chapter 4

1. The work described in this chapter deals exclusively with the first collection of tax-record data. Substantially more birth data and SSN's were recorded in the second batch of tax records collected for 1960–1964. That informa-tion was combined with the ID File (see Chapter 8). No effort was made to retrieve ER that could be linked to individuals through SSN's obtained in the second batch of records.
2. The standard reference on the coverage of the social security laws in this period is U.S. Committee on Ways and Means, 1966.
3. The linkage that we have created parallels the linkage that is currently being attempted on a national scale, using census, Internal Revenue Ser-vice, and social security records on the same individuals (Steinberg, 1969).

4. In practice, these relationships were not always well defined. After linking tax records to wage data we discovered the 80-year-old dependent (coded as a son) of a 50-year-old (coded as the head of household). Inability to distinguish familial relationships led us to integrate all records for each individual under the adult identifier.

5. One additional complication occurred. The second collection of ER's had a different format than the first. Thus records from the second collection had to be reformatted to make them compatible with the prior ER's.

6. To reconcile the number of ER's and the number of matches on the current WAIS File, one must reduce the total accounts received by the number of multiple WAIS ID's sent to SSA. One must also reduce the file for any cases of multiple SSN's which were integrated under one WAIS ID by our staff. The number of such multiple accounts in the second data shipment is not known. There were 170 individuals with multiple accounts in the first shipment (as indicated by the difference in the record count on Wisconsin's Data and Program Library Service Unit documentation and the letter of transmittal from SSA dated March 6, 1964). If the same rate of multiple-account holding occurred in the second shipment, we can conclude that 202 ER's should be integrated with another record in the WAIS files.

7. The file includes records for social security beneficiaries without tax records and 141 individuals in name group 70, which is outside the sample name clusters. It does not include information for institutional and non-sample recipients of death benefits. These details will be explained in Section 4.5.
   These counts include no information for taxpayers and birth dates identified during the second tax record collection.

8. Double counting was possible in arriving at this total, to the extent that information on 269 persons recorded in the supplementary age data file were also recorded in the Benefit File.

9. Some persons with SSN may not be eligible for benefits on their own account and may receive benefits as a spouse. Hence not all persons in the intersection of II and III are primary beneficiaries.

10. That logical structure is reflected in the record structure used in encoding the data. The details of that system are documented in Appendix C.

11. The complete Benefit File contains 4,766 accounts and 18,918 logical records (roughly 4.0 cards per account). Out of a total of 3,217 accounts identified by the SSA as being in claims status, we have 3,208 of these claims cases in our Benefit File. Therefore, there are 1,549 individuals receiving benefits from a social security account other than their own (or 1.48 beneficiaries per account in claims status).

Chapter 5

1. Disk storage was not available to the project until 1967.

2. This concept of data descriptors is identical to the file dictionary used by the OSIRIS system (Institute for Social Research, 1973).

3. The assignment of identifiers is discussed in Appendix B.
4. Systems procedures for tape labelling can automatically convey file status and information necessary to protect the security and permanence of the data. The minimum information required and the relationship of systems-generated labels to housekeeping is discussed in Sections 7.4 and 7.5.
5. The HSF provides linkage capabilities for sequential media which would be unnecessary if the interdependent files could all reside simultaneously on direct-access media.
6. Although the process is illustrated for tape files, the flow diagram applies equally well when other storage media are used. With disk or drum storage substantial gains in efficiency are possible (see Section 6.1). Use of direct-access media reduces the costs of file handling so that segregation may be unnecessary. Records can be efficiently located through "hashing" and direct-access techniques (see Chapter 8).
7. For example, arrays can be related to data descriptors as follows:

FORTRAN: *EQUIVALENCE (A(223), AGI), . . .*
ALGOL: *DEFINE AGI = A(223), NTI = A(113), . . .*
COBOL: *03 MASTER DATA SZ 504*
     05
     .   *AGI SZ 8*
     .
     .
     05
03 MASTER–X REDEFINES MASTER-DATA
05 ELEMENT SZ 8 OCCURS 64 TIMES

8. This was the case in one income tax archive with which we are familiar.
9. The link consists of the identification number plus a count of the number of intervening records on the income-source file.
10. The individuals included the head and the women to whom he was married at some time during 1946–1964. Children were given a separate summary record because such individuals could not be consistently identified as living with the parents.

Chapter 6

1. Removable disk packs (moveable head) present the same problems as tapes of mounting and operator error.
2. If errors are extensive, old contents and data descriptors can be supplied on the original error listing.
3. The data descriptor is an acronym for a field and the data element is the content of a field. It is convenient to refer to data elements generically by the following notation "<name>". *Name* can be either English or an acronym for the field in question.
4. Message C is repeated until the sortfield definition has been typed in by the

user satisfactorily. Experience has shown that the message B is not too helpful, but this has also provided its rare moments. Out of curiosity individuals have attempted to use the program in pirate fashion and never proceeded successfully beyond this point.
Currently, the sortfield is limited to 13 characters in no more than three sets.

5.   On the first request, the address of the middle record in the file is taken as the address of the last record used.

6.   See Chapter 8 and Burroughs, 1969, pp. 12–69.

7.   We used such logic applied to our tax-return data, as described in Geffert, 1966, pp. 60–65.

Chapter 7

1.   In the case of statistical operations, the output was temporarily stored on tape for two reasons: the expense of printing output could be avoided if the run proved abortive; and multiple copies could often be more conveniently (and less expensively) produced by repeated listings than by using multiple-part paper. The latter phenomenon may be a peculiarity of the University of Wisconsin computing environment.

2.   These observations may be prejudiced by our experiences with the University of Wisconsin computer systems. However, we judge that this experience is sufficiently universal to justify discussion of a strategy for dealing with large files.

Chapter 8

1.   The order may or may not have substantive content. If the documents are identified by a name used outside the archive, the order assigned has external content. If, as is more common, the data gathering process generates an identifier that has no significance outside the archive, then the order created by the identifier has little significance. In the case of WAIS identifiers, little external significance attaches to the identifier, as it reveals only the alphabetic cluster containing the surname of the individual in question and his or her sex.

2.   Alternatively the computer must be able to use an algorithm to compute the new locations from the tags on each subset record. This is the concept of relative addressing typical of most computer algorithms for assigning the use of memory.

3.   Tagging the last record of the chain with the address of the first record eliminates this problem and creates a *ring* data structure.

4.   Beginnings of this approach are in use in several systems. The archive developed by Easthope and Hershey (1972) is stored using pointers and weights for replications of similar observations. OSIRIS III (Institute for

Social Research [1973]) permits retention of matrices of frequency counts for further manipulation.

5. The algorithm attempts to store the record at the address indicated by the remainder r. If that location is nonzero a pointer is generated to a location $r + k$, where k is a constant. This process is continued until a vacant location is found.

6. See Y.C. Yang, Data and Computation Center publication TP-7, June 1969, University of Wisconsin, p. 11, for discussion.

7. The capital letters refer to data descriptors in Appendix E.

Appendix F

1. In this test as well as in the other amount-checks below, some degree of error was allowed.
    (a) For the sum of incomes from various sources relative to the coded TØTINC an error was noted if the computed and coded amounts differed by more than $5 *and* if the percentage margin of error found as the ratio:

    (absolute difference between computed and keypunched TOTINC)
    (keypunched TØTINC)

    was greater than 1 percent. Or even if this percentage error was less than 1 percent, if the absolute error margin was greater than $200, an error was noted.
    (b) For all other computations an absolute error margin of $2 was allowed. This degree of tolerance alone decreased the error rate on forms 4 from 34 percent to 22 percent.

2. The field checks the character set and a decimal is implied between the second and third digits from the right. Hence "500000" is interpreted as 5000.00.

Bibliography

Aron, J.D. [1969] "Information Systems in Perspective." *Computing Surveys* 1: 213.

Atkinson, T.R. [1956] *The Pattern of Financial Asset Ownership: Wisconsin Individuals, 1949*. Princeton: Princeton University Press.

Bauman, R.A. [pending] "The Extent of Temporal Variation in Personal Incomes." Unpublished dissertation, University of Wisconsin.

Bauman, R., David, M.H., and Miller, R.F. [1967] "The Wisconsin Assets and Incomes Studies Archive." *Social Science Information* (December): 49–50. Also in, Ralph Bisco (Ed.), *Data Bases, Computers, and the Social Sciences*. New York: Wiley, 1969.

Berztiss, A.T. [1971] *Data Structures: Theory and Practice*. New York: Academic Press.

Bhatia, K. [1970] "Accrued Capital Gains, Personal Income and Savings in the United States, 1948–1964," *Review of Income and Wealth*, Ser. 16, No. 4 (December).

Blau, P., and Duncan, O.D. [1967] *The American Occupational Structure*. New York: Wiley.

Brown, E. [forthcoming, 1973] The effects of income variation on housing purchase and consumption. Ph.D. Dissertation, University of Wisconsin.

Burroughs Corporation Document Number 1044609 [1969] *Disk Forte User's Manual for Burroughs 500 Disk Systems*.

Burroughs Corporation Document Number 1024247 [1968] *Burroughs B5500 Information Processing Systems COBOL REFERENCE MANUAL*.

Burroughs Corporation Document Number 1028024 [1968] *Burroughs B5500 Information Processing Systems EXTENDED ALGOL REFERENCE MANUAL*.

Burroughs Corporation Document Number 1021334 [1967] *Sorting on the Burroughs B5500 Using COBOL-61 EXTENDED*.

Bussman, W.V. [1972] A model of investors' portfolio behavior. Ph.D. dissertation, University of Wisconsin.

Cook, Billy Dee [1967] "Studies of Income Tax Reporting and Compliance." Unpublished manuscript.

David, M. [1969] "Time-series Versus Cross-section Lifetime Earnings Patterns in Different Occupational Groups." *Proceedings of the American Statistical Association,* Business and Economics Section, No. 213, p. 664–674.

David, M. [1971a] "Legislation, Enforcement and the Filing of Tax Returns." *National Tax Journal* 24: 519–520.

David, M. [1971b] "Lifetime Income Variability and Income Profiles." *Proceedings of the Social Statistics Section of the American Statistical Association,* 285–292.

David, M., Groves, H., Miller, R.F., and Wiegner, E. [1970] "Optimal Choices for an Averaging System—A Simulation Analysis of the Federal Averaging Formula of 1964." *National Tax Journal* 23: 275–295. Also Social systems Research Institute Reprint Series Reprint 234.

David, M., and Miller, R.F. [1969] "A Proposal for Revision of the Capital Gains Tax Provisions of the Federal Internal Revenue Code and Critique of Treasury Proposals in Related Areas." Testimony presented to the Committee on Ways and Means, House of Representatives, U.S. Congress, March 28, 4273–4309.

David, M., and Miller, R.F. [1970] "A Naive History of Individual Incomes in Wisconsin, 1947–1959." *Journal of Income and Wealth* (March): 79–116.

David, M., and Miller, R.F. [1972] "The Lifetime Distribution of Capital Gains." In *The Economics of Federal Subsidy Programs*, Pt. 3, (July 15): 269–285.

Dodd, G.G. [1969] "Elements of Data Management Systems." *Computing Surveys* 1: 117.

Dunn, E. [1967] "The Idea of a National Data Center and the Issue of Personal Privacy." *American Statistician* 21: 21–27.

Durant, Ronald P. [1965] "An Analysis of Earnings Dynamics of Wisconsin Taxpayers, 1948–1960." Ph.D. thesis, University of Wisconsin.

Easthope, C. and Hershey, W. [1972] "A Set Theoretic Data Structure and Retrieval Language" *ACM Special Interest Group on Information Retrieval Bulletin* 7 (Winter, 1972): 45–55.

Farber, S. [1963] "Changes in Annual Wage Credits as Workers Age: A Cohort Analysis." *Proceedings of the American Statistical Association*, Social Statistics Section, p. 183–210.

Ferber, R., and Maynes, S. [1969] "Validation of a National Survey of Consumer Financial Characteristics." *Review of Economics and Statistics* 51: 436–444.

Geffert, J.A. [1966] "Computerized Error Correction Applied to Income Tax Returns." *The Tax Executive* (October): 60–65.

Gold, M. [1969] "Time-Sharing and Batch-Processing: An Experimental Comparison of Sheer Values in a Problem-Solving Situation. *Communications of the Association for Computing Machinery* 12: 249.

Goodman, L.A. [1970] "The Multivariate Analysis of Qualitative Data Interactions Among Multiple Classifications." *Journal of the American Statistical Association* 65: 226–257.

Gosden, John A. [1972] "The Making of a Management Information Data Base." *Computer Decisions* (May): 20–23.

Hanna, F.A., Pechman, J., and Groves, H. [1949] *Analysis of Wisconsin Income.* Vol. 9 of *Studies in Income and Wealth.* New York: National Bureau of Economic Research.

Harary, F., Norman, R.Z., and Cartwright, D.P. [1965] *Structural Models: An Introduction to the Theory of Directed Graphs.* New York: Wiley.

Hoffman, L.J. [1969] "Computers and Privacy: A Survey." *Computing Surveys* 1: 85.

Institute for Social Research [1973] *OSIRIS III.* Ann Arbor: Computer Services Facility, Institute for Social Research, University of Michigan.

Inter-University Consortium for Political Research [1973]. *Guide to Resources and Services of the ICPR, 1973–74.* Ann Arbor: Institute for Social Research, University of Michigan.

Katona, G. [1961] *Survey of High Income Families: A Report to the Board of Governors of the Federal Reserve System.* Ann Arbor, Michigan: Survey Research Center, Institute for Social Research, University of Michigan.

Knuth, D.E. [1968] *The Art of Computer Programming.* Reading, Mass.: Addison-Wesley.

Lansing, J., Ginsburg, G., and Braaten, K. [1961] *An Investigation of Response Error.* Urbana: Bureau of Business and Economic Research.

Lansing, J., and Morgan, J.N. [1971] *Economic Survey Methods.* Ann Arbor, Michigan: Institute for Social Research, University of Michigan.

Lassen, G.L. "Income Fluctuations About the Poverty Line." Ph.D. dissertation, University of Wisconsin (forthcoming).

Light, R.J., and Margolin, B.H. [1971] "Analysis of Variance for Categorical Data." *Journal of the American Statistical Association* 66: 534–544.

Maddala, G.S. [1971] "Use of Variance Components Models in Pooling Cross-section and Time Series Data." *Econometrica* 39: 341–358.

Miller, R.F. [1969] "Stock Portfolio Evaluation from Tax Return Data." In Ralph Bisco (Ed.) *Data Bases, Computers, and the Social Sciences.* New York: Wiley. Also Social Systems Research Institute Workshop Paper No. 6706.

Miller, R.F. [1971] "Computers and Privacy: What Price Analytic Power?" *Proceedings of the Association of Computing Machinery,* p. 706–716.

Miller, R.F., and David, M. [1971] "Simulation in a Tax Model." *Proceedings of the Association for Computing Machinery,* p. 236–244.

Miller, R., David, M., Wiegner, E., and Groves, H.M. [1969] "A Proposal for Revision of the Averaging Provisions of the Federal Internal Revenue Code." Testimony presented to the Committee on Ways and Means, House of Representatives, U.S. Congress 5 (March 3, 1939).

Minton, G.S. [1969] "Inspection and Correction Error in Data Processing." *Journal of the American Statistical Association* 64: 1256–1275.

Morgan, J.N., David, M., Cohen, W.J., and Brazer, H.E. [1962] *Income and Welfare in the United States.* New York: McGraw-Hill.

Moyer, M. [1966a] "The Validity of Income Distributions from a Multi-Year Sample of Wisconsin Income Tax Returns." Monograph 1, Wisconsin Assets and Incomes Study. Madison: University of Wisconsin, Social Systems Research Institute; also available as an unpublished Ph.D. dissertation, University of Wisconsin.

Moyer, M. [1966b] "The Processing of Data from a Multi-Year Sample of Wisconsin Tax Returns." Monograph 2, Wisconsin Assets and Incomes Study. Madison: University of Wisconsin, Social Systems Research Institute.

Murray, A.P. [1964] "Wage-withholding and State Income Taxes." *National Tax Journal* 17: 403.

Nerlove, M. [1971] "Further Evidence on the Estimation of Dynamic Economic Relations from a Time Series of Cross Sections." *Econometrica* 39: 359–382.

Orcutt, G.H., et al. [1961] *Microanalysis of Socioeconomic Systems.* New York: Harper & Row.

Pechman, J., and Okner, B. [1969] "Application of the Carter Commission Proposals to the U.S.: A Simulation Study." *National Tax Journal* 22: 2–23.

Pechman, J., and Okner, B. [1972] "Individual Income Tax Erosion by Income Class." In *The Economics of Federal Subsidy Programs,* Joint Economic Committee, U.S. Congress (92nd Congress, 2nd Session) May 8, 13–40.

Penniman, and Heller, [1959]. *State Income Tax Administration* Chicago: Public Administration Service.

Rosander, A.C. [1970] "Analysis of the Kaysen Committee Report." *American Statistician* 24: 20–24.

Schroeder, L. [1971] "A Model of Labor Mobility and Earnings Differentials." Ph.D. Thesis, University of Wisconsin.

Schroeder, L., and David, M. [1970] "Long- Versus Short-term Impacts of Mobility on Income and Earnings. *Proceedings of the American Statistical Association,* Social Statistics Section, p. 354–360.

Sonquist, J., Baker, E.L., and Morgan, J.N. [1971] *Searching for Structure.* Ann Arbor: Institute for Social Research, University of Michigan.

Steig, D.B. [1972] "File Management Systems Revisited." *Datamation* (October): 48–51.

Steinberg, J. [1969] "Some Aspects of Statistical Data Linkage for the Individual." In. Ralph Bisco (Ed.), *Data Bases, Computers and the Social Sciences.* New York: Wiley.

Swami, P.A.V.B. [1970] "Efficient Inference in a Random Coefficients Model." *Econometrica* 38: 311–324.

University of Wisconsin Computing Center B5500 User Manual. [1968]. Volume VII, Revision C, Working Draft No. 2., University of Wisconsin Computing Center.

U.S. Committee on Ways and Means [1966] *Compilation of the Social Security Laws: 1965.* (89th Congress, 1st Session, Document Number 312), U.S. Government Publications Office.

U.S. Senate Committee on Finance [1962] *Hearings on the Revenue Act of 1962.* Part 1, April 2, 1962. Washington, D.C.: Government Printing Office, p. 145–164.

Wiegner, E. [1968] "Income Averaging and Tax Policy." Ph.D. Dissertation, University of Wisconsin.

Wisconsin Taxpayer's Alliance [Serial]. *Taxes, [Year]* 335 W. Wilson St., Madison, Wis.

General Index

Data Descriptor Index

About the Authors

Martin H. David received the Ph.D. from the University of Michigan and is professor of economics at the University of Wisconsin. He was study director for the National Interview Survey and has been associated with the WAIS project since its second year of data collection. He has published widely on subjects related to capital gains, income maintenance transfers, public finance and consumer survey data.

William A. Gates received the B.A. in computer science from the University of Wisconsin and is presently with the Institute for Environmental Studies—Lake Superior Project. He has been associated with Wisconsin Assets and Income Studies and the Center for Demography and Ecology where he focused on data collection, organization, retrieval, and restructuring.

Roger F. Miller is professor of economics at the University of Wisconsin. He received the Ph.D. from the University of California, Berkeley in 1958 and, as original principal investigator, has been involved in the development of the WAIS project since 1960. He has published in the areas of theory, econometrics and statistics, and mathematical economics, as well as in computer and data oriented areas associated with WAIS.

Date Due